Instructional Techniques
in Higher Education

Instructional Techniques in Higher Education

Robert B. Kozma
The University of Michigan

Lawrence W. Belle
Rochester Institute of Technology

George W. Williams
The University of Michigan

Researcher:
Norma Pellikka

Educational Technology Publications
Englewood Cliffs, New Jersey 07632

Library of Congress Cataloging in Publication Data

Kozma, Robert B
Instructional techniques in higher education.

Bibliography: p.
Includes indexes.
1. College teaching. I. Belle, Lawrence W.,
joint author. II. Williams, George Warner, 1939-
joint author. III. Title.
LB2331.K66   378.1'2   78-18384
ISBN 0-87778-126-5

Printed in the United States of America.

Library of Congress Catalog Card Number:
78-18384.

International Standard Book Number:
0-87778-126-5.

First Printing: September, 1978.

Second Printing: December, 1979.

ACKNOWLEDGMENTS

The authors are indebted to the following for permission to reproduce copyright materials in this text:

American Educational Research Association, Washington, D.C. Excerpts from pp. 33-34, 38, 55, Jamison, D. *et al.*, "The effectiveness of alternative instructional media: A survey," *Review of Educational Research*, 1974, *44*(1), 1-67. Copyright © 1974, American Educational Research Association, Washington, D.C.

Excerpts from pp. 173-174, McKeachie, W. J. and Kulik, J.A., *"Effective college teaching,"* in F.N. Kerlinger (Ed.), *Review in Education,* Vol. 3, F.E. Peacock, 1975. Copyright © 1975, American Educational Research Association.

Excerpt from p. 12, Popham, W.J., "Higher education's commitment to instructional improvement programs," *Educational Researcher,* 1974, *3*(11), 11-13. Copyright © 1974, American Educational Research Association, Washington, D.C.

American Society for Engineering Education, Washington, D.C. Excerpts from p. 106, Lindenlaub, J.C., "Audio-tutorial instruction at Purdue University." In L.P. Grayson and J.M. Bredenbach (Eds.), *Individualized instruction in engineering education.* Copyright © 1974, American Society for Engineering Education.

National Society for the Study of Education, Chicago. Excerpts from p. 15, Berliner, D. and Gage, N.L., *The psychology of teaching methods.* Copyright © 1976, National Society for the Study of Education. Excerpts from p. 125, Olson, D.R. and Bruner, J.S., "Learning through experience and learning through media." In D. E. Olson (Ed.), *Media and symbols: The forms of expression, communications, and education.* Copyright © 1974, National Society for the Study of Education.

Oregon State University Press. Page 131, Lewis, R., "Course content in structured knowledge areas," *Improving College and University Teaching,* 1972, *20*(3), 131-133.

Prentice-Hall, Inc., Englewood Cliffs, New Jersey. Table from p. 68, Gronlund, N.E., *Constructing achievement tests.* Copyright © 1968, Prentice-Hall, Inc.

Rand McNally College Publishing Co., Chicago. Figure on p. 504, Gage, N.L. and Berliner, D.C., *Educational psychology.* Copyright © 1975, Rand McNally.

John Wiley & Sons, New York. Excerpts from pp. 147-148, 150-151, 153, 155-156, 163, 166, 168, 174, 186-187, 202, 217-218, Mann, R., *The college classroom: Conflict, change, and learning.* Copyright © 1970, John Wiley & Sons.

PREFACE

There are two series of trends in higher education which we believe have created a need for this book. One is the increase in both the variety and sophistication of the instructional methods which are available to you, the college teacher who is our intended reader. The other group of trends is the simultaneous increase in the heterogeneity of the college student population, the increase in pressure for faculty productivity, and the effective decrease in institutional budgets. Although we feel that the resources created by the first series of trends provide partial relief of the problems created by the second, information on a variety of instructional techniques is generally not available in a form that is easily used. This book is our attempt to provide you with a personal reference containing information from research and experience on techniques ranging from lecture to computer applications.

However, as a result of working with faculty members on these problems, we came to the decision that merely providing you with a list of instructional techniques was insufficient. Teachers tend to be very aware of the limitations of particular instructional approaches when applied to their own disciplines or students. For this reason, we view the selection of media not as a choice from a menu, but as a match between your own instructional situation and the best approaches to teaching. In this volume we try to provide you both with information on instructional techniques and the context within which their selection is made.

There were several concerns that we had as we toiled to make this a useful, readable book. The most difficult problem was to present information which is frequently unnecessarily technical and filled with jargon in a way that is useful and readable. To the extent that we were successful in this effort, it is due to several of our colleagues from various disciplines who were willing to take the time to review this volume. From time-to-time, however, we encountered a term or phrase for which meaning would be sacrificed if a substitution were made. Our compromise, which we hope is acceptable, was to include a glossary for the more technical terms and those common terms with special meaning.

A second concern was our use of the research literature. We had a particular purpose in mind when we decided to refer to various studies. Although we did not want to bore you with endless descriptions of research results on college teaching, we did want to indicate that our conclusions had some foundation in the research literature. On the other hand, this is not a review of research. Our intended audience is teachers, not educational researchers. We have tried to address the problems and issues that teachers are confronting. Unfortunately, educational research is currently not extensive or conclusive enough to address these problems with confidence. Yet the questions remain and need to be answered. To meet this need we tried to stretch or extrapolate findings that we could locate. With some techniques, such as the Personalized System of Instruction, the research was extensive enough to enable us to make extensions with comfort, if not confidence. With other techniques, such as gaming or role playing, we were much less comfortable. We hope that our language conveys the tenuousness of our statements. And for those conclusions which are later found to be groundless, we apologize in advance and hope that a greater number are found to be fruitful.

A third concern of ours had to do with the gender of personal pronouns. To reflect the fact that our readers and their students are both males and females, we decided to randomly alternate between the use of "he" and "she." We felt this was more readable than the use of "he or she," "he/she," or the exclusive use of plurals.

Our concern with usability also extended to the format of chapters. An understanding of our format decisions will facilitate easy access to desired information. The first section is concerned with the context of instructional decisions. After the introductory first chapter, there is a chapter on each of the aspects, or elements, of this context—the instructor, the subject matter, media, the students, evaluation, and environment. Each chapter begins with more abstract or conceptual considerations and becomes increasingly applied. Toward the end of each chapter, we present a number of constructs, techniques, or questionnaires which you can use to help you describe your classroom situation. The first section ends with a summary chapter on the implementation of the ideas presented earlier.

Section Two is composed of chapters on a variety of instructional techniques. Each of these chapters is formatted in the same way for easy reference. A chapter begins with a description of the technique followed by a consideration of its advantages and disadvantages. Then the technique is discussed in regard to its appropriate use with various types of subject matter content, students, instructors, and classroom environments. The implementation of the technique is presented in a section on "How to do it." Finally, the chapter ends with a brief bibliography of references selected for their practical usefulness. Each of these techniques is presented in an objective non-judgmental way, but is supplemented with an enthusiastic testimonial from a selected teacher. This format is based on an approach to analyzing media that can be applied to any instructional strategy—those currently used but not covered in this book and those yet to be developed.

You should not take the chapters in Section Two as a complete list of the options available to you. Although we tried to be comprehensive, several interesting and promising techniques were finally dropped because of the lack of enough literature to write a chapter.

Finally, there are a great many people whose help we would like to gratefully acknowledge. Norma Pellikka was our researcher and did an excellent job in collecting references and writing the vignettes describing the innovative uses of techniques by faculty from all over the country. Dorothy Black Crow and Louisa Tarullo spent many hours reviewing and editing the manuscript. The Fund for the Improvement of Postsecondary Education provided us with grant support for a project that preceded this effort. We would also like to acknowledge the inspiration of our colleagues at the Center for Research on Learning and Teaching, Bill Mc-Keachie, Stan Ericksen, Jim Kulik, Don Brown, Karl Zinn, and Jan Lawrence. Many faculty members and friends reviewed and commented on portions of the manuscript. They are: Syd Bernard, Shirley Cooper, Scott Folger, Jerry Gaff, Fred Goodman, Andy Modigliani, Joel Samoff, Beverly Smith, and Russ Stambaugh. We are also deeply indebted to the people who typed the various versions of this volume: Leslie Czechowski, Anita Ernst, and Jane Marshall. To the extent that this book is useful it is due in large part to the assistance of all of these people. We must take responsibility for errors of omission or commission. We would also like to make special acknowledgment to special people who gave us the support and time needed to write this book: Marnie Adams; Sean and Traci Kozma; and Pat, Sarah, Jason, and Rachel Williams.

Robert B. Kozma
Lawrence W. Belle
George W. Williams

TABLE OF CONTENTS

Instructional Techniques
in Higher Education

SECTION ONE

The Instructional System

Chapter 1

COLLEGE TEACHING: AN OVERVIEW

A Faculty Perspective

Teaching is just one of many duties of a college professor. A faculty member must divide his time among research, publication, keeping up with the field, counseling students, serving on committees, and other activities. The large majority of professors find the time needed to perform each of these tasks competently. But at some point in almost every professor's career, teaching becomes paramount. For very personal reasons a faculty member is caught by the desire to become an outstanding teacher and to be recognized as such by students and colleagues. Teaching is approached with fresh or renewed interest; the faculty member wants to make good performance even better.

The motivations for this concern are diverse, and with the joys of teaching also come problems. For example, a young assistant professor of English, in her first position, is assigned to teach Elizabethan literature. Having recently mastered her specialty, she is anxious to share her enthusiasm with her students. However, while she is interested in teaching the subtleties of the sonnet form, her students are still struggling with the composition of a paragraph.

On the other hand, a full professor of physics has distinguished himself in his field; now, ten years from retirement, he seeks a new challenge. He asks to teach the introductory physics course, viewing it as a way to reestablish relationships with younger students. But students have changed, and he finds that age differences are compounded by differences in social class and educational background.

Another example is an associate professor of sociology, for years considered a good teacher by his students, who has been asked by the provost to head a center for instructional improvement. Although his teaching concerns formerly centered on his own particular course, he must now approach teaching from a broader perspective, dealing with different disciplines and issues.

The motivations for a renewed interest in teaching are not always intrinsic. Sometimes change is the result of external pressure, and is accompanied by anxiety and dread. For example, an instructor adopts a student rating system, only to find his own opinion of his teaching ability differs greatly from that of his students. Another professor is put in charge of coordinating and training departmental teaching assistants and has to consider once again the first steps toward developing a good teaching style.

Aside from making a major commitment to teaching, for one reason or another, there are the day-to-day questions that confront professors as they plan their lessons and reflect on their teaching. Typical of the myriad issues are: How do I help my poorest students? How do I challenge my brightest students? Do I tell students the answer or let them discover it? How do I conduct a simulation game so that it doesn't degenerate into a play period? How do I construct a test that measures something more than rote memorization? Should I use a film for this lesson? Is programmed instruction better than lecture? Is the Keller Plan really as good as it is reported to be?

Whether an instructor is reorienting her teaching values or selecting a medium for a lesson, she is likely to encounter problems and issues. These issues are the result of a variety of changes occurring in higher education: the increasing heterogeneity of student attitudes, abilities, and backgrounds; the exponential growth of knowledge; the contracting job market; the increased complexity of instructional technology; and teachers' own re-evaluations of their role in the classroom.

A teacher confronting the problems created by these changes will find that there are no simple answers. The response to the question, "What is the best thing to do?" will be, "Best for what and for whom?"

Research on College Teaching

One resource used by teachers wrestling with these problems is the advice from their colleagues in education and psychology. A growing phenomenon on campuses around the country is the establishment of centers of instructional improvement. Frequently staffed by psychologists and educational researchers, one of the functions of these centers is to translate research on teaching into recommendations useful for the faculty. Those instructors who come hoping to find answers to the problems cited above often leave less than impressed with the resulting counsel. As W. James Popham (1974), perennial critic of current educational practices, has noted:

> For too many years we found professors of education peddling vapid platitudes such as 'meet learners where they are' and 'teach students, not subject matter.' Having encountered such educationist pap, what clear-thinking professor would not be revulsed? (p. 12)

It is not from ill intentions that educators have nothing definitive to say about college teaching; rather, it is the dismal state of research findings on the topic. A long history of research on college teaching has been conducted in an attempt to provide answers for some of the pressing problems facing higher education. Unfortunately, it is filled with "no significant differences" and inconsistent results. In the search for guidelines, a number of paths have been explored only to end in blind alleys. Although these approaches have not yet produced the answers hoped for by their proponents, the questions are getting better. Educational research is moving from simple questions with no answers, to complex questions with tentative answers. Educational researchers now know which questions to ask, some things that do not work, and some things that do in special situations. Although these complex questions are harder to answer, educational researchers are beginning to acknowledge something many professors already know: each instructional situation is unique and complex.

In Search of the One Best Way

The early approach to research on teaching did not acknowledge this uniqueness or complexity. Researchers tried to identify the "one best way" to teach all things to all students. The approach tended to focus on the "things" of teaching—the techniques and the media. It rested on the premise that learning is essentially the same for all students and that the only thing that need be done to improve instruction is to find that technique or method which maximizes learning. Since the objective of the approach was to find the *one* way, implications for instruction were simple. Recommendations would amount to "use television" or "programmed instruction is best," depending on who was giving the advice. Many instructors remained unimpressed by these oversimplified positions.

The research which accompanied this approach to instructional improvement was essentially comparative. A typical study would hypothesize that some recently developed instructional method or technology would result in more learning than the old method (i.e., lecture). Each new method or technology that was developed would foster a surge of such experiments. More than two decades of this research has left teachers with no panaceas.

Jamison, Suppes, and Wells (1974) examined the research on the effectiveness of traditional instruction (TI), instructional television (ITV), programmed instruction (PI), instructional radio (IR), and computer-assisted instruction (CAI). The studies compared each of the new technologies to either traditional instruction or to another technology. Consistent significant differences were not found. A sample of summary statements are:

> These evaluations indicate that IR (supplemented with appropriate printed material) can be used to teach most subjects as effectively as a live classroom instructor or ITV. (pp. 33-34)

> ... it is reasonable to conclude that PI is generally as effective as TI ... (p. 41)

> ITV can teach all grade levels and subject matters about as effectively as TI ... (p. 38)

The authors conclude their review by saying that:

> Students learn effectively from all these media, and relatively
> few studies indicate a significant difference in one medium over
> another or of one variant of a medium over another. (p. 55)

Wilbert McKeachie of the University of Michigan continues 25
years of research on college teaching with a recent series of reviews
(1974a, 1974b; McKeachie and Kulik, 1975). The tone of these
articles is suggested by the title of one of them, "The Decline and
Fall of the Laws of Learning." In these articles, McKeachie reviews
research on a variety of instructional technologies including the
Keller Plan, programmed learning, computer-assisted instruction,
simulation and games, as well as instructional strategies such as
feedback, reinforcement, and questioning. Each section is summarized by such inconclusive statements as:

> Thus it appears that CAI has no special magic that will solve our
> instructional problems. (1974b, p. 173)

> Despite the increasing popularity of simulation and educational
> games, little evidence on their instructional effectiveness has
> emerged. (1974b, p. 174)

> Knowledge of results is not necessary for learning. (1974b, p.
> 186)

One is left to conclude after reading McKeachie's work that,
with the possible exception of the Keller Plan, no one medium has
been demonstrated to be better than any other when the outcome
measured is performance on a final exam. As for instructional
strategies, "... what we psychologists look to be verities are principles that hold only under limited conditions." (1974b, p. 186)

In a review of the psychology of teaching methods, David Berliner and N. L. Gage (1976) concur: "We should expect any teaching method to be about as 'good' as any other when the criterion
is student achievement or knowledge or understanding, and the
content coverage of the methods is similar." (p. 15)

Reviews such as those cited above leave the "one best way"
approach to instructional improvement virtually indefensible.
Limiting the instructional question to "appropriate media" ignores
the uniqueness of the learner, the structure of the discipline,

and the style of the teacher. An approach which seeks to find a technique that will work for every student and every teacher in every situation—or even most students, teachers, and situations— disregards the complexity of learning and is doomed to failure.

Accounting for Individual Differences

Whereas the "one best way" approach dealt only with the methods or treatments of instruction, recent instructional research includes a second and very important element—the student. By acknowledging the relevance of learner characteristics, or aptitudes, to instruction this research begins to describe the complexity of the learning situation. Not only does it include two elements (the instructional treatment and the student), it presumes that these elements interact in a way that affects learning. It presumes that learning results from a certain mix between students and teaching methods.

This "mix" implies that one method may be good for students with certain characteristics, whereas a different method would be better for the rest of the learners. A differential effect such as this is termed an *interaction*, thus giving this research approach its name: aptitude-treatment interaction (ATI).

An example of the way characteristics of the student can interact with the instructional situation is demonstrated by George Domino (1971). Using a personality test, Domino identified two types of students. One group, those scoring high on measures of Achievement-via-Conformance, described themselves as capable, efficient, organized, responsible, and sincere. Students scoring high on Achievement-via-Independence described themselves as mature, foresighted, demanding, and self-reliant. Domino also arranged for two types of instruction. One class was taught in a highly structured manner: material was presented solely through lectures; emphasis was placed on factual knowledge; attendance was required; and the lectures paralleled the textbook. The other type of instruction encouraged independence by placing emphasis on ideas rather than facts, and upon active participation by students. Domino found that neither of these teaching styles was consistently better than the other for all students. Rather, he found that final exam scores and teacher ratings were higher for the Achievement-via-Independence students when they were taught in the unstructured class, while these scores were higher for the Achievement-via-Conformance students when they were taught with the structured style.

Had Domino ignored the student traits of Achievement-via-Conformance and Independence, his study would have come out with no differences between structured and student-centered styles and would have been thrown into a pile of studies which have no implications for college teachers. Including these traits in the study changes the picture dramatically. Such results emphasize the difference between the aptitude-treatment interaction approach and the less sensitive "one best way" approach.

The ATI approach has several implications for teachers. The general heuristic is: adjust instruction to the characteristics of the learner. One method would be to give the same kind of instruction to different students but in different amounts. This is particularly appropriate for a student whose aptitude is susceptible to change or improvement, for example, low previous achievement. Such students could be given supplementary reading assignments covering the topics in which they are deficient.

Other characteristics, such as ability or personality, are not as easy to alter. In these cases the instructor may provide different kinds of instruction to compensate for student weaknesses or to capitalize on strengths. A student who has trouble visualizing abstract concepts may be shown an animated film depicting the interaction of chemical molecules. The student who performs best with less structure may be given an independent study or a laboratory project.

However, if this approach is to be useful, substantial research must be done to provide guidelines. The research must indicate which of the plethora of student traits are important and how each should be accommodated. Unfortunately, systematic aptitude-treatment interaction research has been conducted only recently. The amount done so far has left researchers with few concrete results but a great deal of optimism.

David C. Berliner and Leonard S. Cahen (1973) conducted a review of fifty-five ATI studies. They found an increase in the number of confirmed interactions over earlier reviews in this area.

The more recent studies have been arranged specifically to test interactions based on meaningful theoretical positions. A more recent and comprehensive review by Lee Cronbach and Richard Snow (1977) examined hundreds of ATI studies and found many interactions between various instructional methods and student attributes.

Although results in this area are encouraging, they can leave an instructor less than satisfied. The very nature of this research approach prohibits generalizations; instead it produces results which are useful given particular content, student, and environmental factors. This approach acknowledges the uniqueness and complexity of the instructional situation, but it does not provide the instructor with a paradigm for instruction, a way to conceptualize and analyze the class situation. This book presents a conceptual framework for solving instructional problems, intended to correspond to the intuitive notions of teachers and the preliminary findings of researchers.

The Instructional System

Although a great deal of research is still needed, educational thinking is clearly moving from simple to complex, and from static to dynamic. Thoughts of the one best way have been abandoned. A large number of variables in the instructional environment influence learning. It also seems that these variables interact in a complex way. They are interdependent; the alteration of one affects the others.

This orientation toward instruction corresponds to the intuitive notions of many instructors about their classroom situations. Each discipline is unique, with its own complexities and nuances. History cannot be taught in the same way as physics. Each class of students is also unique, each learner with his own peculiarities and idiosyncracies. To teach them all the same way would be a travesty.

The complex, unique, and interdependent nature of the instructional situation may best be represented as a system. A system, simply defined, is a collection of interrelated parts or elements which can be conceptually separated from its surroundings (Banathy, 1968). The interrelationship of its parts is determined by the purpose or function of the system as a whole, and the nature and contributory function of each of the elements.

The identification of the elements of the instructional system is a simple matter—one needs only to look around. On examining a college classroom, five distinct elements are apparent. The most obvious of these are the teacher and the learner. Upon closer examination the less visible elements of the system become apparent. Attention is given to a certain body of knowledge, presented via some form of media. Eventually some kind of evaluation will take place. All of this activity occurs within the social and physical environment of the classroom, or other learning situation, and the macro-environment of the college and the society at large.

Each element can be distinguished from the others by its function. If the function of the whole system is to bring about learning (broadly defined) in the students, the function of each element can be delineated: the teacher is the manager of the system, the arranger of the conditions of learning, and, by merit of her subject matter expertise, the selector of the course content. To draw on communication theory (Berlo, 1960), she is the *source* of the instructional message; she selects the message and the medium by which it is sent. The subject matter is the *message* to be communicated, whether knowledge or values. The *medium* is the means of communication; its function is to facilitate the transmission of the subject matter to the learner. The student is the *receiver* of the message. The function of the *evaluation* (of both teacher and student) is to indicate the effectiveness of the process—(did the message get through?). Finally, the *environment* supports the system: the value and purpose of the system are derived from the larger environment. A functional arrangement of the elements of the instructional system can be seen in Figure 1.1.

The precise interaction of these elements will vary from situation to situation. The professor of art history teaching German Expressionism to 150 first year students in an introductory course relates to and communicates with her students very differently from a professor of psychology discussing behavior modification with his graduate students, or the professor of chemical engineering critiquing a student's proposal for a chemical plant. Decisions

Figure 1.1. The Instructional System.

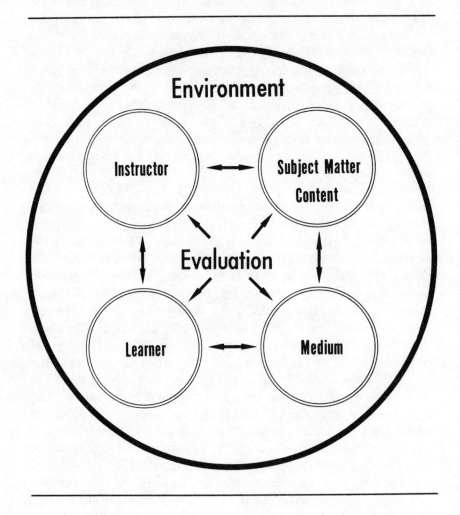

about instructional methods, media, and evaluation are based on the peculiarities of each situation.

But unique as each situation is, there is bound to be some commonality. The professor of art history may share her regard for accurate observation and critical analysis with the professor of psychology. Behavior modification may be seen as similar to the design of a chemical plant in that both involve the application of techniques to solve problems. And some of the freshpeople in art history may resemble the chemical engineering student in their preference for working in unstructured situations.

To perceive the implications of an instructional situation, the instructor must recognize both how it is unique and how it is similar to other situations. This enables him to make appropriate generalizations from previous experience and the research literature. The remaining chapters in Section One will provide instructors with constructs and instruments useful for examining and assessing each of the elements in their instructional situations. These chapters will also examine the ways in which the instructor, the content, the medium, the learner, the evaluation, and the environment interact. With this knowledge, instructors will be able to orchestrate a better mix of elements in their classrooms. Section Two presents techniques and methods of teaching. In describing the appropriate uses of various methods, the chapters in Section Two will frequently refer to the paradigm and constructs of Section One.

Chapter 2

THE INSTRUCTOR

All too often discussions about systematically designed instruction are limited to the process of planning a lesson. Stress is placed on specifying objectives in precise terms, assessing students' entering capabilities, selecting appropriate media, and revising the instruction based on classroom trials. Frequently this sequence of events is diagramed with boxes and arrows, giving a mechanistic tone to the whole process. It is forgotten that education is, above all else, an interpersonal phenomenon. The interaction between the teacher and the student, even when mediated by an overhead projector, is the essence of instruction. And although the student is cast as the principal character in the instructional drama, the professor most certainly is the producer and director. The failure to regard each faculty member as a person, with a particular teaching style and an idiosyncratic set of values, characteristics, and behaviors, is a serious oversight.

Instruction at the college level is very much what the faculty member makes it. While the nature of the subject matter, the preparation and motivation of the students, the expectations of peers and administrators, and the institutional climate all play a part, it is clearly the instructor who decides what will be taught and by what means. Yet most faculty members think of themselves primarily as chemists or historians rather than as teachers. Consequently, it is sometimes difficult for them to be reflective about teaching and what it means to be a college teacher. Without some knowledge of potential styles of teaching, and of the charac-

17

teristics and behaviors associated with effective teaching, the instructor is less likely to develop the most suitable instructional design for himself and his own purposes.

Who Are College Faculty Members?

Until recently, professional academicians received relatively little attention from social science researchers—themselves professional academicians. This situation has changed dramatically. Ladd and Lipsett's book, *The Divided Academy* (1975), reports faculty attitudes on a variety of issues ranging from preferred automobiles to unionization. And although differences may be more important than averages, norms are enlightening.

Among the findings to emerge from the rapidly growing field of faculty sociology (Blackburn, 1971, 1974; Eckert and Williams, 1972; Freedman and Sanford, 1973), of which the Ladd-Lipsett work is only the most current and widely publicized, are the following:

- College faculty members are typically married, white middle class males with children. The average age is forty plus, and this average is increasing. (The efforts of women and minorities to obtain representation in the academic work force proportionate to that which they hold in the national work force, not to mention salaries, promotion, and tenure comparable to white male faculty, are unlikely to succeed because of the "stationary state" expected in higher education for the remainder of the century [Carnegie Commission, 1973].)
- They are a certain kind of people: intelligent, responsible, and academically ambitious. They believe that self-improvement requires hard work, are willing to sublimate immediate desires for long term goals, and tend to prefer solitary intellectual activities. They find it difficult not to equate humanity and intelligence with these qualities.
- Faculty members like working with students, congenial colleagues, the freedom to do their own work on their own terms, and autonomy. Faculty members dislike poor students, committees, low pay, and poor facilities.
- Most academicians chose to specialize in a discipline before

they chose to teach. Teaching, for many, is a somewhat inadvertent outcome.

- Intensively trained to do published research in their field, typically most faculty members do not publish.
- Until recently all but nine percent of those who remained in college teaching could count on reaching the highest rank, professor, by age sixty. This advancement rate is unequaled in any other career.
- Vocational satisfaction is higher for faculty members than for any other occupational group. Yet even if tenured, academicians show an exceptional degree of nervousness and insecurity about their positions. Freedman and Sanford (1973) discovered a widespread sense of vulnerability and threat among the faculty members they interviewed, even before the steady-state in higher education.

Robert Blackburn's essay and comprehensive bibliography, "The Meaning of Work in Academia" (1974), summarizes much of what is presently known about academic attitudes and values. Studies done at a variety of institutions clearly establish that faculty members devote 55 to 60 hours a week to teaching, research, and service—more hours per week to their work than any other professional group. Their complaints are not so much about the amount of time required for their work, but that they do not have enough time for all they want to accomplish. They tend to like contemplative recreation—hiking and gardening—rather than competitive sports. They are likely to be thinking about their specialty or preparing to teach class even when they are not at "work."

College professors are more likely to associate with each other than with nonacademic members of the community in which they live. In this sense, they resemble army officers more than doctors, lawyers, or dentists.

Professors are stereotyped as liberal, even radical. In fact, they are quite diverse politically; regarding academic change and innovation, they are generally conservative. They strongly prefer influence and status to defined positions of power, and are prone to intense interpersonal conflict in their competition for recognition.

Blackburn has very aptly described the core of the academic occupation: "What a professor does is not a job; what a professor does is to lead a distinctive way of life within a particular community of professional people—a college or university faculty." (1974, p. 77)

Adult Development and College Faculty Members

Research on adult development has shown that different periods in an adult's life are characterized by different issues, goals, and crises. These periods have impact on the college professor's life in very particular ways. Again, these are subjective norms with which many faculty members will not agree.

The work of Levinson *et al.* (1974) and Gould (1972) has been applied to college faculty by Hodgkinson (1974). The young Ph.D. enters her first college teaching position during a period which Levinson refers to as *getting into the adult world*. She has just completed a stage during which she has gained independence from her family, a process begun during undergraduate school. She is beginning to develop a new world view and to make provisional commitments to adult roles and responsibilities. This stage in adult development is characterized by the formation of the "dream," a vision of the future that provides her with direction and meaning. The dream can be that of becoming a famous scholar, a great writer, or a wielder of power and influence.

A young scholar approaches thirty in a state of transition. She asks, "What is life all about now that I am doing what I am supposed to?" This questioning results in either a reaffirmation of her original career goals and directions, or a shift, possibly out of academia.

The thirties are a time of *settling down*. Major concerns for most adults during this period are "establishing order" and "making it"; this period is a time of working toward the realization of the dream. For the college faculty member, making the dream come true means deciphering the "real" requirements for tenure and obtaining it. The thirties culminate with concern about *becoming one's own person*, a search for independence from those in authority and control.

The early forties are another transitional period. There is a need for reaffirmation, often associated with a symbolic key event, such as a promotion. The dream may also be scaled down: the realization comes that one will never be a full professor at Harvard.

By the late forties, the college teacher is at the stage of *restabilization and flowering*. During this time, most adults become resigned to the finite nature of time and come to accept their lives as set. Investment in personal relationships increases. Faculty members renew their self-confidence, increase their institutional loyalty, and define productivity by personal rather than external criteria.

Passage through these stages may influence the relative importance a faculty member assigns to teaching. Some young instructors may approach teaching with enthusiasm, since it is central to their vision of a great professor. Others may slight teaching in their eagerness to establish their reputations as renowned scholars. Senior professors may discover increased enthusiasm for teaching, viewing it as a challenge and a form of personal renewal.

Faculty Members as Teachers

The most important finding to emerge from faculty sociology is that the majority of college professors like teaching and think it is important. Several studies (Bayer, 1973; Gaff and Wilson, 1971; Eckert and Williams, 1972) examined faculty attitudes toward students and teaching. Most college faculty members consider teaching to be a major source of satisfaction.

More guardedly, Kenneth Eble (1972) concluded from his personal visits to many campuses, classrooms, and faculty lounges:

> I have also observed that faculty members respect teaching and are somewhat interested in it, but comparatively few incline toward developing teaching as an art or themselves primarily as teachers ... (p. 24)

> The most accurate term I can find for the common faculty attitude is *respect*. It is not *enthusiasm*, though enthusiasm can be aroused among faculty members once discussions get going about the particulars of teaching. It is not *hostility*. Although many faculty members get impatient with teaching and many find ways of reducing the burden, few are hostile about it. (p. 25)

Generally, faculty members show some interest in improving their teaching skills, but rightly or wrongly, most already view them-

selves as effective teachers. Cross (1977) indicated that 94 percent
of the faculty members in her study rated themselves as above
average teachers.

While there is little conscious sharing of instructional theory or
method among faculty members, most define their instructional
goals as covering course content and introducing the concepts and
methods of the field. Most faculty members are considerably less
concerned about students' general intellectual and human development. Good teaching is thought to be an amalgam of an instructor's knowledge, current research, attractive personality, and ability to motivate students.

The typical faculty member's professional training and career
prospects do not support teaching. As Sanford (1971) has pointed
out, chemists, sociologists, literary critics, and historians have, as
professionals within their respective fields, undergone similar training. As content experts they share a body of specialized knowledge, concepts, language, and methods with others in their field.
As teachers of undergraduates, however, they do not similarly
share a common training or fund of educational knowledge,
theory, and method. It has been difficult for faculty members to
develop a coherent image of themselves as engaged in the common
work of promoting learning. Until recently, there has been a con-
spiracy of silence about teaching and learning in academic culture.

In addition, Light (1974), Light and Marsden (1972), Hoyt
(1974), and McKeachie and Lin (1975) have shown that the
distribution of tenure, promotion, and other major rewards within
colleges and universities have not been regularly used to distinguish
between effective and ineffective teaching. While it is not yet common practice to reward faculty members who engage in instructional development, the rapidly growing faculty and instructional
development programs reported by Gaff (1975) and Centra (1976)
are leading to heightened awareness of effective teaching and instructional alternatives. Colleges and universities may yet systematically reward those who vigorously engage in the role of undergraduate teacher.

Teaching Style

Although they may not be able to define the differences

precisely, most faculty members and students are aware that instructors are distinguished by various teaching styles. Each teacher appears to have a pattern of instructional behaviors which is consistent over time and provides a certain flavor to his or her classes. This teaching style is related to the faculty member's content orientation, intellectual style, professional training, adult development, and core values.

Some participant observers of classroom culture have developed typologies for describing teaching styles. Joseph Adelson's (1962) powerful division of teachers into shamans, priests, and mystic healers is both parsimonious and amusing. In *The University Teacher as Artist*, Joseph Axelrod (1973) presents a more useful taxonomy which offers sketches of teachers typified by their respective content-, instructor-, intellect-, and person-centered styles.

The *content-centered* instructor teaches what she knows. Characterized by a deference to her discipline, she is concerned about covering the material in a systematic way. Her primary interest is in teaching the facts and principles of the field. Students in turn are expected to display their mastery of the material by accurately restating and applying it.

The *instructor-centered* prototype teaches what she is. She offers herself as a model of the educated or professional person. She sees herself as representing a certain intellectual or artistic process, which students are invited to emulate. She is overtly involved in role modeling, an important, if sometimes unacknowledged dimension of most college teaching.

The *intellect-centered* instructor trains minds. For her, knowledge is a *process,* not a product. The focuses of teaching and learning should not be the products of rational inquiry but rational inquiry itself: the how and why of knowledge rather than the what. She emphasizes intellect-rational development and the rigorous use of reason, language, and problem-solving skills.

Finally, the *person-centered* instructor teaches students as people. She does not believe that intellectual development can be separated from other aspects of the students' emotional and personal development, and to attempt to do so is harmful. She believes that the whole range of a student's growth and development should be dealt with in the teaching and learning processes.

The Axelrod typology lists as discrete categories characteristics found in all instructors to a greater or lesser degree. Like all such constructs, these are not descriptions of reality but schemes for organizing observations and experience. Models such as these can help an instructor to identify the dominant characteristics of his or her unique teaching style.

These categories should not be used to judge teachers, for Axelrod makes no claim of special instructional effectiveness for any of the teaching styles. Rather, each style has its own implications for treatment of course content and the relationship of teacher to student. For example, the content-centered instructor might choose programmed instruction, as described in Chapter 20, with its methodical insistence on learning the subject matter, while the person-centered instructor might prefer role playing or simulation as described in Chapters 16 and 17.

Axelrod's impressionistic typology can be contrasted with a taxonomy of teaching style based on Herman Witkin's (1976) study of cognitive styles. Cognitive styles are characteristic and consistent modes of processing information, constructing relationships, and solving problems. When given a problem to solve, people are likely to differ in the way they perceive the problem, conceptualize it, and formulate its solution.

Witkin makes a distinction between what he calls field-dependent and field-independent styles. The scheme is based on perceptual tests, which require the subject to separate a figure from its background (for example, identifying an object embedded in a complex field). People differ in the amount of time they need to perform these tasks; specific sets of characteristics are associated with the length of time required for identification.

Field-dependent people—those whose perception is strongly dominated by the prevailing field—are also strongly influenced by context in social situations. Those with field-dependent styles are more attentive to the human content of the environment. Their attitudes, beliefs, feelings, and self-perceptions are more easily influenced by the people around them, especially authority figures, than are those of field-independent people. They spend more time looking at faces during conversations; they excel in attention to and memory of the social content of verbal messages; and they have more highly developed social skills than people with field-independent styles. Field-independent people, on the other hand, are more independent of their surrounding context and tend to operate on a more abstract and analytical level.

These categories have implications for college teachers. People who teach tend to be more field-dependent, as do managers, counselors, and sales people. In contrast, field-independent people select occupations which are more analytical, such as engineering, mathematics, and the sciences. Within the teaching profession, those that are relatively field-dependent will teach in the social sciences and humanities, while those that are field-independent will specialize in the physical sciences or more analytical subspecialties in the social sciences, such as experimental psychology.

Furthermore, field-dependent instructors show a preference for discussion in their classes and are more inclined toward democratic instructional arrangements. In contrast, more field-independent teachers prefer lecture and discovery methods and are more directive with their students.

Witkin cites some interesting studies which examine the effects of matching and mismatching teachers and students by their respective cognitive styles. Students who shared a teacher's style described the instructor in positive terms. The feelings of the matched teachers were mutual. However, the students and teachers who were matched field-dependents tended to interact with each other more in class than those who were matched field-independents.

Furthermore, mismatched students and teachers used negative terms in describing each other, a finding which has obvious implications for grading and student ratings. It is as yet unclear whether a field-independent instructor *may* be more effective in teaching an analytical subject like mathematics to field-dependent students, even though they may not like each other much. An example of the potential benefit of this mismatch is among the findings reviewed by Witkin *et al.* (1977), that field-independent teachers prefer to give corrective feedback, and field-dependent learners perform better when given such feedback.

Teaching Behaviors

What are instructor characteristics and behaviors that most effectively foster student learning? College faculty members and students, both in impressionistic reports and controlled studies, generally agree on the characteristics and behaviors that typify good teachers. Published statements by teachers on teaching range from the classicist Gilbert Highet's work (1950, 1976) to Martin Duberman's fictional dialogue in *Black Mountain* (1972), involving himself, the artist Albers, and several other faculty members at that experimental college. Like Kenneth Eble (1976), these teachers focus on common factors: generosity with knowledge and time; energy and enthusiasm for teaching and for students; variety in presentation, pace, and materials; good speaking and listening abilities; relation of learning to life with relevant examples and illustrations; and intellectual and personal honesty and fairness.

In analyzing statements on teaching written by twenty-three Canadian college and university professors nominated as outstanding teachers, Sheffield (1974) found certain common characteristics. Virtually all the respondents emphasized the involvement of students in their own learning. Most professors were student-oriented; with only two or three exceptions, their attitudes toward students were positive. Enthusiastic about their courses, they liked to teach. Collectively, these master teachers believed in stressing general ideas rather than details, using feedback to and from students, and appropriately challenging students.

Most, but not all, of the characteristics and behaviors identified in these impressionistic writings correspond to those which students, in empirical studies, perceive as contributing to an instructor's effectiveness. Hildebrand, Wilson, and Dienst (1971) asked three hundred and thirty-eight students at the University of California-Davis Campus to identify the characteristics that distinguished the "best" from the "worst" instructors. Some expected characteristics and behaviors proved to be non-discriminating: good preparation, friendliness toward students, emphasis on conceptual understanding, and the use of examinations requiring synthesis. Of these, Hildebrand (1973) says, "As in bathing and washing dishes, doing these things well is not a distinction, but their neglect is noticed." (p. 44)

The ninety-one items by which students identified the instructors considered to be most effective were subjected to a factor analysis, resulting in five clusters:

- *Analytics and Synthesis*: The instructor's command of her subject, or "scholarship"—not the scholarship of the specialist, but the scholarship through which the instructor teaches analytic and conceptual understanding of ideas, their implications, and their origins.
- *Organization and Clarity*: The instructor's ability to make herself clearly understood, characterized by well-chosen examples, logical progression of ideas, appropriate placement of emphasis, and timely use of summaries.
- *Instructor-Group Interaction*: The instructor's ability to develop group participation, interaction, and rapport within the class, including also effective use of demonstrations, questioning, discussions, and assignments.
- *Instructor-Individual Interaction*: The instructor's ability to respond to students as individuals, whether during office hours or after class.
- *Dynamism and Enthusiasm*: The instructor's flair for awakening student interest and stimulating involvement and response.

Thus, a pattern of agreement emerges in faculty and student descriptions of effective instructors. The general headings of *teaching skill, rapport, organization, enthusiasm*, and *challenge* subsume many of the positive characteristics that show up most in the descriptions of effective instructors.

However, there is no clear evidence that students of instructors with these characteristics and behaviors learn more. While some studies (Frey, Lenard, and Beatty, 1975; Gessner, 1973) have found significant positive correlations between student perception of an instructor's effectiveness and the amount students learned, other studies (Rodin and Rodin, 1972; Turner and Thompson, 1974; Greenwood, Hazelton, Smith, and Ware, 1976) have either shown no correlations or a negative relationship. Kulik and McKeachie (1975) conclude their review of the research: "Perhaps the most impressive thing about studies relating class achievement to class ratings of instructors is the inconsistency of results." (p. 235)

The work of Tom and Cushman (1975), nevertheless, does suggest that there are some specific and identifiable instructor behaviors that may yield more effective instruction. Instead of dealing with rather global characteristics, such as organization, enthusiasm, and rapport, they identified specific instructor behaviors, for example, providing students with practice, using illustrative examples, and emphasizing learning objectives. They also examined the relationship between these behaviors and student perceptions of achievement in seven types of learning, such as gaining factual knowledge, improving logical thinking, and developing creative abilities.

These researchers collected data from 402 instructors and 12,792 students at ten colleges. They obtained statistically significant correlations between twenty-eight discrete teacher behaviors and students' perceptions of their own achievement on the seven general teaching objectives. While the teacher behavior items in Tom and Cushman's list are not novel, they have tied certain patterns of behavior to student achievement. Of the teaching behaviors studied, regardless of objective, the most important item was providing students with practice. All other behaviors were effective only for a particular set of instructional outcomes. The relationship between behaviors and objectives is shown in Table 2.1.

Distinguishing the good teacher from the bad is as difficult as demonstrating that video is consistently better than lecture. The problem again is the "one-best-way" fallacy. Just as student learning style, the structure of the subject matter, or the interpersonal classroom environment might suggest discussion for one situation and lecture for another, so the characteristics of a "good teacher" are dependent on the nature of the particular instructional situation. The best instructor to teach factual knowledge in engineering may well be a content-centered, field-independent teacher who gives step-by-step instructions and well-organized lectures. On the other hand, the best instructor to influence attitudes in the humanities may be a person-centered, field-dependent teacher who uses a variety of teaching techniques and initiates conversation with students before and after class.

Table 2.1

Correlation of Specific Instructor Behaviors with
Student Achievement on Instructional Objectives
(Tom and Cushman, 1975)

INSTRUCTOR PROVIDED:	OBJECTIVES*						
	Item 1	Item 2	Item 3	Item 4	Item 5	Item 6	Item 7
1. Practice (Experience) in Recalling Factual Knowledge (Terminology, Classifications, Methods, Trends).	x	x	x	x			
2. Practice (Experience) in Recalling Fundamental Principles, Concepts, or Theories.		x				x	x
3. Practice (Experience) in Logical Thinking, Problem-Solving, and Decision-Making.			x			x	x
4. Practice (Experience) in Developing Specific Psychomotor (Manipulative, Manual) Skills.				x			
5. Practice (Experience) in Developing Skills in Organizing Ideas and Presenting Them.			x			x	x
6. Opportunities to Be Creative (Imaginative, Inventive, Original).			x			x	x
INSTRUCTOR:							
7. Pointed Out What Was Important to Learn in Each Class Session.	x	x			x		
8. Gave Step-By-Step Instructions When Needed by Students.	x	x			x		

Table 2.1 (Continued)

INSTRUCTOR:	OBJECTIVES*						
	Item 1	Item 2	Item 3	Item 4	Item 5	Item 6	Item 7
9. Stated the Objectives of the Course.		x			x		
10. Promoted Teacher-Student Discussion (As Opposed to Mere Response to Questions).						x	x
11. Displayed Concern That Students Learn.		x			x		
12. Encouraged Silent Students to Participate.						x	x
13. Initiated Conversation with Students Before and After Class.					x	x	
14. Addressed Students by Name.						x	
15. Made Positive Statements About the Subject Matter of the Course.	x	x			x		
16. Spoke with Expressiveness and Variety in Tone of Voice.					x		
17. Indicated When a New Topic Was Being Introduced.		x					
18. Used a Variety of Teaching Techniques.					x	x	
19. Used a Variety of Teaching Materials.				x	x		
20. Used Understandable Vocabulary.					x		
21. Related Course Material to Real-Life Situations.					x		
22. Used Example to Help Make a Point.		x			x		

Table 2.1 (Continued)

INSTRUCTOR:	OBJECTIVES*						
	Item 1	Item 2	Item 3	Item 4	Item 5	Item 6	Item 7
23. Summarized Material Presented in Each Class Session.		x					
24. Presented Well-Organized Lectures.	x	x					
25. Praised Students During Class.						x	x
26. Provided Answers Along with Objective-Type Homework Assignments.			x				
27. Provided Relevant Information in Response to Student Questions.	x	x			x		
28. Made Written Comments on Student Papers.							x

*The objectives were:

Item 1—Gaining Factual Knowledge (Terminology, Classifications, Methods, Trends).

Item 2—Learning Fundamental Principles.

Item 3—Improving Logical Thinking, Problem-Solving, and Decision-Making Abilities.

Item 4—Developing Specific Psychomotor (Manipulative, Manual Skills).

Item 5—Developing a Favorable Attitude Toward the Subject Matter.

Item 6—Developing Creative (Imaginative, Inventive, Original) Skills.

Item 7—Developing Skills in Organizing Ideas and Presenting Them in Written Form.

Chapter 3

THE SUBJECT MATTER

Although professors frequently refer to what they teach as "content" or "subject matter," they are using the terms in a rather specific sense. Course "content" usually connotes the facts, concepts, and principles of the instructor's discipline, be it history or chemical engineering.

Content, as the term is used in this chapter, has a much broader significance. The content is the total message delivered to the student by the college experience. It is the goals and outcomes of the teaching-learning process, both intended and actual. It is the skills, the capabilities, the attitudes, and the characteristics which students take away from the classroom. These potential changes range from the trivial to the profound. Although they include the fundamental ideas of the discipline, they also reflect the basic goals and values of the instructor, the college, and the whole process of higher education. These new perspectives are *learned* as much as any of Newton's Laws.

Teachers are often not aware of content in this broader sense, because they reflect more on the structure of their disciplines than on the goals of higher education. These goals are frequently diverse, personal, and unarticulated. But if it can be assumed that college students acquire more than the facts and principles of their selected specialty, then it is fitting that those additional results be considered part of the content of the learning system.

This chapter will begin with an examination of content in its broadest sense and conclude with a discussion of the implications of the smallest curricular unit, the instructional objective.

Content as the Goals of Higher Education

The goals of higher education probably differ from school to school, from discipline to discipline, and from teacher to teacher. However, they can be clustered into three principal groups; intellectual development, personal development, and career development.

Intellectual development. The primary goal of a liberal education is the development of the intellect. With its philosophical locus in the humanities, it seeks to accomplish this goal by introducing students to the dialogue among great thinkers. It presents the cultural and intellectual heritage of Western man: the great thoughts and eternal truths represented in the books of Plato, Aristotle, and Virgil. Tastes and sensitivities are refined which will allow students to share in this tradition. The function of a liberal education is not to impart skills but to enlighten, disturb, and inspire. It demands the sober consideration of the difficult and enduring human questions as they have found expression in philosophy, literature, history, and politics.

Since the historical roots of liberal education are in the leisure class, it is common to find a disdain for the vocational among its proponents. They contend that it is not specialized knowledge which is needed to confront the major problems of the modern world, "... but an active, methodical intelligence which, being grounded in a discipline of thinking, is able to think also about unfamiliar matters." (Bowra, 1964, p. 188) The capabilities acquired in a liberal education are more general abilities of reasoning and articulation.

Such mental acuity is obtained through arduous study of the most rigorous and demanding subjects. Traditionally this course included Latin and classical Greek, and the Medieval Trivium (grammar, rhetoric, logic) and Quadrivium (arithmetic, geometry, astronomy, and music). More recently this program has expanded to include the study of the natural and social sciences in the general education curriculum.

The goals of a liberal education are frequently met by curricular arrangements which reflect the broad issues addressed by this educational approach. Interdisciplinary courses and freshman seminars allow students to probe in-depth questions which span a number of fields.

Personal development. Late adolescence is viewed by psychologists as a time of identity crisis. On the threshold of adulthood, students are confronted by the "real world." They must decide who they are. They must choose a career, a life-style, a set of values, and a self-image. During this emotionally intense period, the student's focus is on ideology. The existence of choice leads the student to question the deepest assumptions of the culture and his own upbringing.

College serves a special function during this transitional period. It provides a protected environment, removed from parental control but not devoid of adult guidance. It allows the student to make provisional commitments to value systems and styles of thought. It fosters emotional and personal development. The result is an increase in personal integration, autonomy, flexibility, and open-mindedness.

This growth is maximized if students are given the freedom to make their own decisions about their education. By taking responsibility for their education, students have a stake in what is learned. They see the reason for it, and self-reliance is thereby encouraged.

By providing choices about what is learned and how it is learned, the instructor recognizes not only differences in personal goals, but differences in students' rates of learning, life situations, and learning styles. Independent study and peer teaching are frequently used as strategies to accomplish the goal of personal growth. Contract learning (see Chapter 23), where student and instructor jointly decide on what is to be learned, instructional resources needed, and how learning will be demonstrated, also encourages independence and self-determination.

Career development. Aside from law and medicine, which have traditionally held central positions in the university, a concern for the practical arts has come late in the history of higher education. Impetus came in 1862 with the passage of the Morrill Act, which established land grants for agricultural and mechanical colleges.

Initially rejected by established colleges as nonacademic, professional programs ranging from urban planning to broadcasting now flourish in most major universities. It is now the case that the majority of students entering college do so for career-related reasons (American Council on Education, 1971).

This shift has had a profound effect on the goals and functions of higher education. The goals of career development are to provide students with the special skills and technical knowledge needed to get a job. The function of a university under this goal is threefold: First, it must sort undergraduates into two groups— those acceptable for employment and graduate professional training, and those not. Secondly, it must make the more discriminating decision of ranking students along scales of excellence in achievement and aptitude (this has become increasingly important as competition grows for limited positions). And, finally, the college must include in its curriculum skills and knowledge which are prerequisite for employment or admission into graduate school.

The shift in emphasis has even affected the non-professional general curriculum. Majors in natural and social sciences increase at the expense of history and the humanities, as students view a B.A. as a pre-professional degree rather than an end in itself.

The methods and emphasis of instruction are affected also. Internships, field work (as described in Chapter 23), and even cooperative arrangements with local businesses and agencies reflect the applied orientation of career development. Preparatory classroom instruction requires the mastery of factual knowledge, the application of rules and procedures, and the acquisition of fine motor skills in the operation of equipment and machinery.

Career development, personal development, and development of the intellect can be seen as three distinct sets of goals and values in higher education. Each has distinctly different implications for the function of the college and the process of instruction. But because these goals are so broadly stated, their implications are not always apparent; it remains for the instructor to interpret their meaning and apply it in the classroom. Phrases dedicating a college to "the preparation of the student for the world of work," or to "the cultivation of the intellect through a solid foundation in literature and science," are of little use to an instructor planning a course syllabus, much less a single lesson. Although such ideological statements give a general orientation, a more precise analysis of educational goals is needed.

Content as the Structure of the Discipline

An instructor's discipline usually provides the precision needed to analyze the goals of education. With rare exceptions, knowledge presented in colleges is packaged in courses under headings like chemistry, history, or geology. This is due in part to the fact that these courses are taught by people who call themselves chemists, historians, and geologists, and who spend a great deal of their time studying and adding to knowledge which is compartmentalized under these and other such terms.

Although some view these divisions as a clerical expediency that most directly serves the academic priesthood, others build a good case for disciplinary structure as a basis for the structure of the college curriculum. Specifically, Phillip Phenix, of Teachers College, Columbia University, argues:

> The most impressive claim the disciplines have upon the education is that they are the outcome of learning that has actually been successful. A discipline is a field of inquiry in which learning has been achieved in an unusually productive way. Most human efforts at understanding fail. A very few succeed, and these fruitful ways of thought are conserved and developed in the disciplines. Every discipline is simply a pattern of investigation that has proved to be a fertile field for the growth of understanding. (1964, p. 36)

As important as disciplines are, they are sometimes perceived by students as merely a collection of miscellaneous facts and details. Oxford's Jerome Bruner (1960) contends that it is the *structure* of the discipline that should provide the content of the curriculum, not chemical properties, historical events, and geological formations.

The term "structure" refers to the parts of an object and their relationship. Each discipline is composed of a number of fundamental ideas or concepts: force in physics, bonding in chemistry, motives in psychology, and group in sociology. These basic concepts within a discipline are interrelated, so that it is impossible to talk about force without talking about other fundamental ideas, such as energy and work, or mass and acceleration. Although the structure formed by these interconnected ideas is sometimes expressed mathematically, this is not so with most disciplines. Sociologists can competently explain, and sometimes predict, the behavior of groups and their members in terms of affiliation, roles, authority, norms, and conformity without the need of mathematical equations. It is the structure created by the fundamental ideas and their interrelation which gives each discipline and its scholars a unique way of describing and analyzing phenomena.

Bruner (1960) makes four claims for basing the curriculum on the fundamental structure of a discipline:

(1) Understanding fundamental ideas makes a subject more comprehensible. Specific phenomena become instances of the more general case rather than unrelated occurrences, and thereby are more easily learned.

(2) Understanding the structure of a subject facilitates memory. Without an anchoring structure, that which is learned is soon forgotten. The structure of a subject provides a shorthand for memory. What is remembered is not the distances traversed by falling bodies in different gravitational fields at different times, but the formula $s = 1/2gt^2$. Thus, memory loss is not total loss. What remains allows for the reconstruction of details.

(3) The understanding of fundamental principles and ideas provides for transfer of training. The student can apply what is learned to previously unencountered situations.

(4) Emphasis on the structure of a discipline closes the gap between elementary knowledge and advanced knowledge. What is learned in the introductory course differs only in detail or degree of complexity from that which is learned in a graduate course or a current journal article.

It is the teacher's task to describe the structure of her discipline, or some subset germane to the course, and to communicate it to the students. Describing this structure, however, is not a trivial task. It takes a scholar of the discipline, one who has studied it diligently and is on its cutting edge—thus the lengthy training required to teach a college course. The specific structure of a discipline may not be apparent even to those intimately involved with its study. That which is fundamental may be shrouded by volumes of detail and data. Bruner (1960) and others (Schwab, 1964; King and Brownell, 1966) identify a number of sources of information that an instructor can use to define the structure of her discipline.

One source of information on structure is the nature of inquiry within the discipline, beginning with the *object* of investigation. Psychology, sociology, and political science all study the behavior of humans, while physics and astronomy study the behavior of physical bodies. The domain and range of the structure are implied by the questions asked when conducting disciplined inquiry. Thus, somewhat different structures evolve for each of the disciplines. The concepts, principles, and ideas represented by the discipline's major schools of thought are another component of its structure.

It is also important to analyze the *process* of investigation within the discipline. What are the methods or modes of inquiry? What are the canons of evidence and the criteria of proof required of one who wishes to contribute new knowledge to the field?

Another important source of information on disciplinary structure is the scholars themselves. What are the competencies and habits of these practitioners of the discipline? What is their specialized language, and what modes of communication do they use? What are the attitudes and values required to become a member of the community?

These features of the discipline as well as the questions raised by Ralph Lewis (1972) in Table 3.1 can aid instructors who are interested in basing their course curriculum on the structure of knowledge within their discipline. Application of these analyses will result in a set of interconnected ideas which would compose the content of the course.

Table 3.1

*Useful Questions for Constructing the Structure of a Discipline
(Source: Lewis, 1972)*

I.   *Questions to be put to courses in areas of fundamental knowledge, such as physics, chemistry, geology, biology, psychology, sociology, economics, political science, and linguistics:*

(1)   What are the names of the laws and theories, or their equivalents, that give structure to the knowledge covered in the course?

(2)   What are the postulates, theorems, and other propositions that are central to each of the theories?

(3)   What are the headings of the classes of facts interrelated by each of the laws and theories?

(4)   What are the references to the key works in which these laws and theories were first stated in the form taught in the course?

(5)   What are the major limitations of each of the laws and theories?

(6)   What are the key references that discuss and explain these limitations?

(7)   What knowledge is presented in the course that does not fall within the limits of applicability of the laws or theories enumerated?

(8)   What method or methods have been used to organize this knowledge?

II.   *Questions to be put to applied courses such as agriculture, medicine, business, education, agricultural economics, forestry, communications, geography, horticulture, marketing, microbiology, public health, resource development, and social work:*

(1)   Upon what body or bodies of fundamental knowledge does this course draw?

(2)   What are the names of the laws and theories, or their equivalents, in the fundamental knowledge that give organization to the knowledge being applied?

(3)   What are the postulates, theorems, and other propositions that are central to each of the theories?

(4)   Cite examples of how the laws and theories in the fundamental knowledge have been fruitfully applied.

(Continued on next page)

Table 3.1 (Continued)

(5) What practical forms of organization in the course take precedence over the organization that stems from the structure of the fundamental body of knowledge?

(6) In what ways does the practical form of presentation increase the pedagogical efficiency as compared to a presentation based upon the structure of the fundamental body of knowledge?

(7) What classes of facts in the course fall outside the limits of applicability of the laws and theories in the fundamental body or bodies of knowledge upon which the course is dependent?

The Psychological Structure of Knowledge

Some psychologists like to make a distinction between the logical structure and the psychological structure of knowledge. While the structure of knowledge based on the disciplines is organized around the manner in which existing knowledge was discovered or acquired, or around the way it is divided into fields or sub-fields, the psychological structure of knowledge is based on how it is learned.

This approach focuses on the learner and the capabilities that the learner is to acquire, rather than on a certain body of knowledge, such as chemistry or English. When learning occurs, the individual accomplishes something that she was not previously able to do—whether writing a sonnet or performing an experiment. Thus content is described in terms of capabilities. Content is thus not a set of fundamental ideas, such as bond, or group, or force, but the learner's application and use of these ideas as represented by such behaviors as "to solve," or "to explain," or "to critique."

The psychological structure of knowledge is a description of the dependent and independent relationships among these competencies. The implications of such a structure for learning and instruction are direct. The structure determines the order of instruction, by indicating when the sequence can be random or optional and when sequencing must be carefully planned so as to build from simple skills to more complex ones.

The construction of a psychological structure is described by the leading proponents of this approach, Robert Gagne (1970) and

Leslie Briggs (1968), both of Florida State University. An instructor begins the construction of a *learning hierarchy* (the term used by Gagne and Briggs) by stating one of the desired outcomes of instruction in terms of the learner's capability. Next, the question is asked, "What would an individual have to know how to do in order to achieve successful performance of this class of tasks, given only the direction to perform it?" The answer to this question would be one or more steps, or sub-skills, required to perform the skill. The process is continued by repeating the analysis with the generated skills, and so on with subsequent capabilities until a hierarchical structure of subordinate skills is constructed. One could, of course, continue this process indefinitely, but in practice the instructor stops when he arrives at a level of skills that he knows, or at least can assume, the learners already possess.

An example of a hierarchy derived by this process is presented in Figure 3.1. As is illustrated, the titration of a solution to determine its normality (an objective taken from an introductory chemistry course) is based on three prerequisite skills. Each of these skills is in turn dependent on other capabilities. These skills and their interrelations form a learning hierarchy. Although this particular hierarchy has not been verified, it is capable of verification. This is done by checking to see that anyone who is able to perform one of the higher order skills is also able to perform each of the skills assumed to be subordinate to it.

Upon examination of a learning hierarchy, the sequence of instruction becomes obvious. Instruction for any of the two or more skills which may be on the same horizontal level could be presented in optional chronological order. However, instruction for all of the subordinate skills should be presented before the instruction for a higher-level skill. For example, the skills in boxes 16, 17, and 18 in Figure 3.1 can be taught in any order, but all of them must be learned before the student can titrate a solution to determine its normality.

Although the distinction exists between a logical and a psychological structuring of knowledge, it should be clear that these two schemes are not necessarily incompatible. The psychological structure should reflect the structure of the discipline. The capabilities embedded in the psychological structure should correspond to the

Figure 3.1. An Example of a Learning Hierarchy.

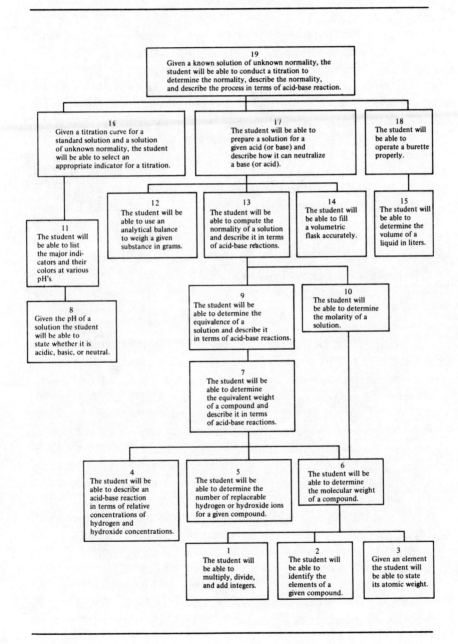

fundamental ideas and principles of the discipline. The difference is likely to be in the orientation and arrangements of the structures rather than their content. Psychological structures are likely to be more problem oriented, with their emphasis on the capabilities of the learner. These capabilities will be arranged in a way that facilitates learning rather than one that corresponds to the way the discipline divides itself along sub-disciplines. In fact the structure, at its lower levels, may drift into other disciplines, much as an analysis of physics would betray its tie with mathematics, or sociology with psychology. In these ways the two approaches are different.

Content as the Objectives of Instruction

In the 1930's, Ralph Tyler, then of the University of Chicago, proposed the practice of specifying the content of instruction in terms of observable student change. Debated, refined, and promoted, the use of instructional objectives has currently become widespread. As Tyler (1949) defines them, objectives are statements of changes that take place in students. They are the particular skills, capabilities, and attitudes that students acquire as a result of taking a course.

Specifying the outcomes of learning in this way avoids a major difficulty in higher education: identifying that which is important to learn. Within any discipline, knowledge has accumulated to the extent that no one could possibly learn everything. It has been said that Francis Bacon was that last person to consider all of man's knowledge as his domain. Since then students have had to content themselves with some rather limited subset of that domain. Thus, identifying that which is important to learn becomes critical. Although a commonly expressed goal of higher education is to bring students to the point of making their own decisions about what is important, they are sometimes not in a position to judge. In practice their performance on exams or essays is frequently measured by what the *teacher* thinks is important. The student's task then becomes to decipher what the teacher thinks most important to learn. In many classes, principles are obscured by details, and concepts are camouflaged by facts. The resulting behavior degenerates to a mental version of hide-and-seek.

The use of instructional objectives avoids this situation. Objectives are statements by the instructor to the student of what is important to learn. They are study guidelines for students who can in turn accept, reject, or modify them.

A method for constructing instructional objectives was popularized by Robert Mager (1962). According to Mager, an objective must:

(1) specify a behavior or capability related to some aspect of the subject matter;

(2) state the behavior in terms of what the student can do (rather than what the professor will cover);

(3) state the circumstances under which the behavior will be performed; and

(4) indicate the criterion used to assess the performances.

Good instructional objectives clearly communicate to students what they must be able to do after the completion of a unit of work. Mager describes a good objective as "one that succeeds in communicating your intent; the best statement is the one that excludes the greatest number of possible alternatives to your goal." He provides two lists of words that demonstrate how to eliminate misinterpretations and be specific:

Words Open to Many Interpretations	*Words Open to Fewer Interpretations*
to know	to write
to understand	to recite
to really understand	to identify
to appreciate	to differentiate
to fully appreciate	to solve
to grasp the significance of	to construct
to enjoy	to list
to believe	to compare
to have faith in	to contrast

Critics of this practice raise some important concerns. The use of objectives oversimplifies curricular outcomes. Lists of objectives are permeated with simple statements of trivial consequences.

Content regresses to that which can be easily specified. Long-term or personal outcomes are slighted because they cannot be easily measured within the course of the semester. Pervasive concepts such as motivation, entropy, and equilibrium which have a broad range of application tend to be lost because they cannot be treated in one sitting. Attitudes and values are de-emphasized because they cannot be observed.

Popham (1971) counters these arguments. He concedes that many objectives written to date are trivial. But, he contends, the specification of outcomes allows for their evaluation. Petty objectives can thus be eliminated. Goals stated more generally elude this scrutiny. Attitudes, values, and other internal states, Popham points out, are not worth much if they are not manifested in more observable behavior. More sophisticated subjective judgments and instruments which go beyond multiple-choice exams are being developed to tap the more affective objectives.

The use of taxonomies of instructional objectives. Several attempts have been made to organize or classify instructional objectives. The most widely cited was constructed by a committee of educators headed by Benjamin Bloom of the University of Chicago (1956).

Bloom's taxonomy grew out of an attempt to resolve the ambiguity of objectives such as, "The student will understand the Cubist style." This statement might mean that the student could recall the characteristics of the style, give an example of a Cubist painting, or paint a picture in the Cubist style. The taxonomy made distinctions among various types of behavior based on the competency component of the objectives. The taxonomy was intended to be purely descriptive so that every type of goal could be represented, without placing value on one category over another. Bloom began with the cognitive domain; subsequent authors have extended this work to affective and psychomotor areas.

The cognitive domain, those objectives dealing with "knowing," is divided into six categories. These include *knowledge* (recall of facts, principles, etc.), *comprehension* (ability to restate knowledge in new words), *application* (the ability to use abstractions in particular and concrete situations), *analysis* (the ability to break down material into its component parts and to detect relationships among the parts), *synthesis* (the ability to produce wholes from parts, such as the production of a plan of operation), and *evaluation* (the ability to judge the value of something). The taxonomy is hierarchical, with each category building on the previous one and running from simple to complex, and from concrete to abstract behavior.

Application of Bloom's categories to the objective cited above results in a more precise specification of objectives. Instead of "The student will understand the Cubist style," the instructor can specify one or more of the objectives:

- *Knowledge:* Give three distinguishing characteristics of the Cubist style of painting.
- *Comprehension:* Given a set of paintings, identify those which are painted in the Cubist style.
- *Application:* Given a painting from any period, show how it differs from a painting of the Cubist school.
- *Analysis:* Examine various paintings of the Cubist style and derive the distinguishing characteristics of the style.
- *Synthesis:* Paint a still life arrangement in the Cubist style.
- *Evaluation:* Using knowledge of the Cubist style, evaluate a painting from this school.

Eight years after Bloom's monograph, the work on taxonomies continued on the "feeling" objectives of the affective domain (Krathwohl *et al.*, 1964). The problems of meaning seemed to be more severe for objectives within this domain. An objective like "The student will appreciate art," could mean that she pays attention to it when it is around, she seeks it out, she experiences an emotional thrill from it, or she can evaluate and critique it. The affective domain is divided into five categories based on intensity of response, and running from attention to internalization, and from simplicity to complexity of value systems. The divisions include *receiving* (attention to and awareness of feelings and values), *responding* (behaviorally and emotionally), *valuing* (acceptance and commitment to values), *organization* (the construction of a value system), and *characterization* (the development of a philosophy of life).

Krathwohl gives many examples of affective objectives, some of which are:

- *Receiving:* Develops some consciousness of color, form, arrangement, and design in objects and structures around him in descriptive or symbolic representations of people, things, and situations. Attends to values and judgments expressed during class.
- *Responding:* Responds emotionally to a work of art or musical composition. Enjoys participation in varied types of human relationship and in group undertakings.
- *Valuing:* Deliberately examines a variety of viewpoints on controversial issues with a view to forming opinions about them. Actively participates in arranging for the showing of contemporary artistic efforts.
- *Organization:* Forms judgments as to how the respect for human dignity can be related to the directions in which American society will move in the next decade.
- *Characterization:* Develops a consistent philosophy of life.

Elizabeth Simpson (1971) continued the tradition by analyzing the "doing" objectives of the psychomotor domain. The taxonomy is divided into seven categories, representing continuums running from awareness to response, from simple behaviors to complex and from trial through precision to innovation. Psychomotor objectives are either *perception* (sensory stimulation and cue selection), *set* (mental, physical, and emotional preparation), *guided response* (imitation, and trial and error), *mechanism* (habituation), *complex overt response* (automatic performance), *adaptation,* and *origination* (which deal with creating new behaviors).

Instructors have found several benefits in the use of these taxonomies. They can aid in assuring the comprehensiveness of a curriculum. To be comprehensive, course objectives should not just be facts, but applications and evaluations. Objectives should not just be cognitive, but affective and psychomotor. And although disciplines are distributed differently along these categories, the taxonomies can serve as checklists to assure completeness.

The classification of objectives can also facilitate instruction. As was illustrated in Chapter 2, facts are learned and taught differently from applications, and cognitive skills differently from psychomotor skills. The acquisition of factual knowledge is enhanced by using step-by-step instructions and well-organized lectures, while the development of psychomotor skills is aided by the provision of practice and the use of a variety of teaching materials. Thus, identification of objectives according to categories can aid the instructor in making decisions about media, strategies, and evaluations.

Chapter 4

MEDIA

Learning occurs every day without the aid of a slide projector, or even a teacher. But in the classroom, learning and teaching are frequently associated with such techniques as lecture, discussion and, on occasion, devices such as instructional television. Robert Gagne (1969) of Florida State, broadly defined instructional media to be those components of the learning situation which stimulate the learner—in other words, communicate with him. And although the teacher is the principal source of stimulation for the student, tools ranging from books to computer terminals can be used as well.

The difference between learning in the natural setting and class-room learning is that in the classroom, experience is mediated. The use of media is based on a set of assumptions about knowledge and how it relates to experience. David Olson and Jerome Bruner (1974) cite these assumptions: "... that the effects of experience can be considered as knowledge, that knowledge is conscious, and that knowledge can be translated into words. Symmetrically, words can be translated into knowledge; hence, one can learn, that is, one can acquire knowledge, from being told." (p. 125) Given this perspective, in a very real sense the first instructional innovation was the teacher. By mediating between direct experience and knowledge, the teacher facilitates learning.

There are a number of ways an instructor can accomplish this goal. One means is by contriving direct experiences through which students can discover knowledge. There are an infinite number of phenomena that the student could experience; and the whole of human history has been an attempt to understand their significance. There is a certain efficiency in the instructor's using his knowledge to select from the infinite those experiences (i.e., demonstrations, field placements, etc.) which would foster student insight.

The instructor can also mediate between direct experience and learning by providing a model of experience. People frequently learn by observing the experiences of others. By providing a model, either of herself or of someone else, the instructor can show the students how to operate a piece of equipment, how to react in a social situation, or even how to conduct scientific inquiry or develop a logical argument. Through imitation, despite errors and false starts, the student will ultimately learn more quickly than if left to his own experience.

Another technique of mediation is the use of symbolically coded information: information transmitted through the spoken or written word, film, diagram, and so on. This type of symbolically represented experience is commonly associated with formal schooling. Although it is common to think of media as being the machines of the classroom, lectures, books, and role plays are also media. The term, as used in this chapter, is meant to include any form of communication that the teacher uses, either directly or indirectly, to transmit knowledge and affect to the students.

The Form of Media

To use media effectively, it is necessary to understand it in more detail—to know what it is and how it affects the message that it is to communicate. By understanding the nature and operation of media, an instructor has a basis for selecting the appropriate medium with which to deliver a particular content message to a particular student audience.

One of the simplest ways to describe media is in terms of the reciprocity of flow in the communication. Ronald Havelock (1969) makes a distinction between one-way and two-way media. One-way, or presentational, media such as lectures, films, televised instruction, books, and demonstrations are characterized by a flow of information from the instructor to the student without reciprocity. When these media are employed, the student has little or no opportunity to influence the instructor or to change the message. The student cannot enter into a dynamic relationship with the teacher or the content, since the medium does not require—in fact inhibits—an active response. The student can accept the message or ignore it; sometimes it can be turned off. But the student cannot alter the message other than to distort it with her own biases and preconceptions. Nevertheless, when used appropriately, these one-way processes have some distinct advantages. There is probably no more efficient way to transmit large quantities of information to large numbers of people in the shortest possible time. Such presentations can be highly motivational and stimulating in some situations.

Two-way, or interactive, media such as discussions, games, tutoring, and role plays are reciprocal. Although they are not as efficient as presentational media in transmitting information, they do allow the student to play an active part in learning. The student can affect the pace, repetition, and content of the message. The teacher, in turn, receives information from students on their understanding and acceptance of the course content. This information can be used by the teacher to refine the instruction.

To these two categories can be added a third class of media—self-instructional media, which include programmed instruction, personalized instruction, audio-tutorial instruction, and contract learning. While similar to two-way media in being interactive, these types of media tend to be more structured. Self-instructional media involve regular student responses of a particular kind. These may range from the highly specific responses in programmed learning, to the more general projects and reports in contract learning. These methods allow a student to proceed with learning at his own pace and with his own interests, independent of immediate instructional supervision. They do, however, require a great deal of planning on the part of the instructor, who must create materials and arrange for other supporting resources.

This simple breakdown of media into three groups calls attention to certain common attributes, but it does not address the more complex features which distinguish the various forms of media within each group. The commonly used means of dis-

tinguishing between and categorizing media is based on supportive hardware such as computer terminals, motion picture projectors, and television monitors. Thus, we have computer-assisted
instruction, audio-visual instruction, and instructional television.
This is part of the reason why it is not typical to consider a small
group discussion as a medium—it has no hardware. Although terms
like lecture and programmed instruction are useful in general conversation (indeed, they are used as chapter headings in the second
section of this book), they give no indication of how these forms
of communication are used by students, or how they function in
learning. The inefficacy of a media taxonomy based on common
terms is most apparent when comparing two forms, like television
and motion pictures—is there any difference between these media
as they are viewed by students?

Donald Tosti and J.R. Ball (1969) attempt to describe media in
a way that corresponds to its impact on students. According to
these authors, media vary in the way they perform three functions
critical to learning: present a stimulus, require a response, and
manage the immediate instructional environment. The way each
medium performs these functions will determine the instructional
task for which it is appropriate.

The stimulus is information which is presented to the student; it
may vary in the way it is encoded and in the duration of its
presentation. Film, for example, is a pictorial medium of brief
duration, while charts have symbolic and persistent stimuli. Stimuli may also be verbal, as in lectures, books, or discussions, or
"environmental," as in models or demonstrations.

Media may also differ in the nature and frequency of the
responses they request from students. While programmed instruction requires a frequent written response, discussion requires a
less frequent vocal response, and lecture requires a covert
response.

Finally, media may differ in the way in which they are used to
manage the instruction. With the use of branching, programmed
instruction and computer-assisted instruction can vary the information presented to each student based on her previous skills and
her successful understanding of the content presented. Some
media increase a student's access or control of instruction, and sys-

tems like the Personalized System of Instruction and Audio-Tutorial Instruction provide frequent encouragement to maintain the student's motivation for learning.

The selection of an instructional mode should be based on the stimulus, response, and management demands of the task and the students. Thus, verbal information could be presented by audio tape, discussion, or lecture. If repetitive information is needed, an audio tape would be preferable; if verbal response is required, discussion would be more effective than lecture.

According to the perspective described by Tosti and Ball, although television and motion pictures differ greatly in hardware, they affect the learner similarly. They are both transient, pictorial presentations, requiring covert responses and providing little instructional management. However, for reasons of finance, equipment availability, or other logistical reasons, a teacher might pick one over the other even though they provide equivalent results in most learning situations.

Media selection. Media are selected by matching the characteristics of the medium to the demands of the instructional situation —the characteristics of the instructor, the content, the student, and the environment. Section One of this book aids the instructor in describing the characteristics of the instructional situation. The second section describes the characteristics of each medium. This chapter attempts to summarize and conceptualize instructional media characteristics.

Table 4.1 lists seventeen media categories (most of which are included in Section Two of this book) and identifies their characteristics by using a taxonomy adapted from the Tosti and Ball (1969) article. Definitions of the more technical terms are in the glossary. Each medium is rated on the way it is typically used in the classroom. It is important to note, however, that these media are more or less flexible and can be adapted to a certain extent to fit the instructor's needs. So, for example, although lecture is limited to a covert response as it is typically used, an instructor can elicit an overt selective response by asking for a show of hands on some question. Similarly, although slides are transient as typically shown in a group, they are persistent when viewed by an individual student at his convenience. Also, several media can be com-

Table 4.1

Media Categories

Stimulus Encode	Environmental (i.e., "life-like")	Pictorial	motion, full	motion, simulated	Symbolic	Verbal	Kinesthetic (sense of movement)
Lecture	L,T					T	
Books, Print					P	P	
Film, Video	TE	TE	TE			TE	
Pictures, Slides, etc.		P	LP	✓			
Audio						TE	
Models	P	P					
Figures, Charts, Graphs					P		
Demonstrations	T		T				✓
Discussion						T	
Role Play	T					T	
Simulation, Games	T				T	T	
PSI							✓
A-T		✓	✓	✓			✓
PI						P	✓
CAI						T	✓
Laboratory						T	✓
Contract, Experiential						T	✓

A check (✓) means the characteristic is applicable to the medium. Any other letter means the characteristic is applicable with the following qualifications:

L   limited applicability or use

T   transient, pertaining to stimuli which are available for a relatively short period of time

TE   transient but stored in an enduring form

P   persistent, stimuli which are available as long as they are needed

S   seldom required

F   frequently required

Table 4.1 (Continued)

Response		Lecture	Books, Print	Film, Video	Pictures, Slides, etc.	Audio	Models	Figures, Charts, Graphs	Demonstrations	Discussion	Role Play	Simulation, Games	PSI	A-T	PI	CAI	Laboratory	Contract, Experiential
Covert		S	F	S	S	S	S	S										
Overt	selective (choice)										S	S	F					
	vocal									F	F	F		F				
	constructed												F	F	F	F	S	
	written												F	F	F	F	F	F
	motor													S			F	F
Affective		✓	✓	✓	✓	✓			S	✓	✓	✓					✓	✓
Feedback										L	L	L	✓	✓	✓	✓	L	L

A check (✓) means the characteristic is applicable to the medium.
Any other letter means the characteristic is applicable with the following qualifications:

L limited applicability or use	TE transient but stored in an enduring form	S seldom required
T transient, pertaining to stimuli which are available for a relatively short period of time	P persistent, stimuli which are available as long as they are needed	F frequently required

Table 4.1 (Continued)

Technique	Management: Adjust presentation to learner's need	content of presentation	medium of presentation	strategies	Student control of pace: access to presentation	content presented	strategies	Reiteration until mastery	Motivation
Lecture									
Books, Print		√	√			L			
Film, Video			L			L			
Pictures, Slides, etc.			L			L			
Audio			L			L			
Models			L			L			
Figures, Charts, Graphs			L			L			
Demonstrations									
Discussion	L		L		L	L	L		L
Role Play	L	L	L		L	L	L		L
Simulation, Games	L	L	L		L	L	L		L
PSI	√	L	L	√	√	√	L	√	√
A-T	L	L	L	L	√	√	L	√	√
PI	√				√	√		L	√
CAI	√		√	√	L	L	√	√	√
Laboratory			L	L	L	L	L	L	L
Contract, Experiential	√		√	√	√	√	√	√	√

A check (√) means the characteristic is applicable to the medium.
Any other letter means the characteristic is applicable with the following qualifications:

L   limited applicability or use

T   transient, pertaining to stimuli which are available for a relatively short period of time

TE   transient but stored in an enduring form

P   persistent, stimuli which are available as long as they are needed

S   seldom required

F   frequently required

bined to increase impact and reduce limitations. Common combinations include slides with audio tapes, readings with discussions, and lectures with demonstrations.

It should also be noted that the rating categories used in Table 4.1 actually represent a continuum. Although discussion is rated as requiring a frequent response (F), it is not required as frequently as with programmed instruction, but more frequently than with contract learning. Similarly, information presented through an A-T learning center may be more accessible to the student than with personalized instruction, but less accessible than with a book.

It can be seen from Table 4.1 that every characteristic applies to more than one medium, but each medium has a particular pattern of characteristics. The instructor may find that some situations require a particular set of characteristics, thus identifying one medium or a combination of media. However, in many situations, only one or two characteristics will be pertinent, thus leaving the instructor to choose from among several media the one which would be the least expensive and most convenient to implement.

From time to time, a professor may encounter a highly constrained problem where characteristics of the instructional situation will conflict with regard to their demands on media, or where a particular medium is indicated but not available. As an example of the first situation, an abstract concept might be most efficiently presented via lecture, but some subset of students requires a visualization of the abstraction. An example of the latter is the presentation of a process which involves motion, but motion picture or video equipment are not available. These problems may be solved by combining other media to suit the needs of the situation, as in the first case by combining lecture and animated film. If not, the "next best thing" may be chosen: a medium which meets most of the requirements but which conforms to the constraints of the situation. If motion needs to be depicted it can be simulated by showing a rapidly changed sequence of slides; if slides are not available, the process can be described verbally and augmented by a symbolic illustration on the chalk board.

In summary, any media decision will require instructor selection of the medium which is most effective for the instructional requirements, but which is the cheapest and/or easiest to use.

The Functions of Media

The obvious physical characteristics and capabilities of a medium can often overshadow other attributes. The spectacular electronic effects of color video have an inherent appeal for many instructors. However, the subtler nature of media may be more critical for learning.

In addition to form, media also have functions. They are the strategies used to design and present the instructional message, whether via lecture, video, or programmed instruction. For example, the strategy of "gaining attention" can be used with each of these media, although operationalized differently for each.

Although psychologists and educators have not had a great deal of success in establishing reliable propositions pertaining to instruction, a number of commonly accepted principles can be used as guidelines. Robert Gagne (1970) identifies nine events of instruction which correspond to the way students process information:

1. *Gain and control attention.* There are many things that compete with the instructor for the learner's attention. If the teacher is not successful in maintaining the student's attention, the instructional message will not get through. Several techniques are available to cue students to that which is important. Pointing and other gestures can direct visual attention, as can arrows, circles, and color schemes on charts or graphics. Italics, underlining, and bold type are effective in print. And phrases such as "listen carefully," or "most importantly" can be used in verbal messages.

2. *Inform the learner of expected outcomes.* The learner is told about the kind of performance to be expected of her after completing the instruction. This is commonly done by explicitly stating the instructional objective as described in Chapter 3. It can also be done by showing an example of the kind of problem that the student will be able to solve, or by posing the objective in the form of a dilemma which the student or the instructor will solve. Thus, an instructor could begin an archeology lecture on the Incan empire by showing slides of the abandoned city of Machu Picchu

and asking questions such as, "What were the systems of commerce, government, and communication needed to support such a civilization? How could such a great empire be toppled by a handful of Spaniards? How can we find answers to these questions?" Such an introduction could organize students' thinking and guide their study.

3. *Stimulate recall of relevant prerequisites.* As discussed in Chapter 3, the acquisition of most capabilities taught in college is dependent on first knowing some simpler set of prerequisite skills. It might be necessary for the instructor to remind students of previously acquired skills and knowledge which are relevant to the new learning. During an engineering lab it may be useful to remind the students to recall the principle of the conservation of energy while they are constructing their calorimeters. Although they have known this law since high school, it might be necessary to make it clear that this knowledge is relevant to the experiment. If a simple reminder does not work, it may be necessary to take some students aside and reteach the principle.

4. *Present the stimulus.* The medium must present the information or situation to which the learner has to respond. The nature of the stimulus situation is frequently used to select the medium, for the problem should look as much as possible like the situations the student will encounter in real life. The stimuli in an Art History course are the works of art, or their representation in slides or pictures. In philosophy they are the great questions, and in physics they are the problems to be solved.

5. *Offer guidance.* The instructor, or the medium, should guide and direct the learner's thinking or actions until the essential performance is achieved. This can be done by showing or telling the learner the skill or the knowledge, by prompting, or by providing clues or partial answers which can lead to the complete answer. The instructor can provide rules and/or examples from which the student can learn. Also, the instructor can guide discovery by leading the learner through a logical series of questions which should result in the correct answer.

6. *Provide feedback.* The instructor should require the student to display his new skill, asking questions, and providing problems that would indicate the extent to which the material is under-

stood. The student should then be informed of the correctness of his newly attained knowledge. Feedback from the instructor should indicate not only whether the response was correct or incorrect, but why an answer was right or wrong. Learning results not only from successful trials, but from errors which are corrected.

7. *Appraise performance.* By providing frequent opportunities for the learner to verify the achievement of the new skill, the instructor strengthens what has been learned and maintains the student's motivation to continue. Practice problems or self-check tests similar to the ones she will be required to pass can be helpful.

8. *Make provisions for transferability.* Typically the teacher would not be excited by a student's answer which was limited to the situations and examples covered in the text or the lecture. Usually the teacher would like to see evidence that the student can apply his new knowledge to unique situations, or can use it to learn even more. Transferability can be facilitated by providing a variety of real-life situations representing the entire range of applications of the new knowledge. By stretching the student's use of the knowledge, the instructor will insure that it will not be limited to a narrow range of uses.

9. *Insure retention.* The negative slope on the curve of retention is common knowledge to all professors. Learning is only half the battle; remembering is the other half. This problem is compounded by the fact that each new message decreases the chance that the old ones will be remembered. Memory can be aided in several ways. A repetition of the instruction in later lectures or review units is a common strategy. Periodic practice is another. But perhaps the most effective way to insure retention is to create an association between what is being taught and some previously learned, highly meaningful idea. Anchoring the laws of physics and chemistry to common experiences such as the motion of automobiles and the unplugging of drains are two such examples.

Each of these nine events can be used with any medium. To the extent that each is included, instruction will be more effective. However, it may not be easy to do this in some cases. Lectures and television, and other one-way media, do not lend themselves easily to events such as "provide feedback" and "appraise performance." But even the use of rhetorical questions during instruction using these media can result in covert responses; subsequently providing answers can lead to self-correction and reinforcement. Every parent of preschool youngsters is familiar with the phenomenon of children talking to the television set during *Sesame Street.*

Although these instructional guidelines are appropriate for all learning situations, they are applied differently for different types of learning. Both the selection of media and the application of instructional events are dependent on characteristics of the other elements in the system.

Content, media selection, and design. The task required by a particular instructional objective gives one clue useful in media selection and design. If an instructor is trying to teach students to critique an essay or poem, she can use written or verbal media; a lecture or a text would suffice. In guiding the learner, the instructor should offer examples of critiques. Feedback should be detailed and frequent, for these refined judgments are vague, requiring the student to build a sense of what is good and bad by seeing many examples and making many corrected attempts at critique.

Teaching titration, on the other hand, is quite visual and would require a film, demonstration, or videotape. Since it is a psychomotor task, it is also kinesthetic. During the *guidance* stage, it may be necessary to "take the learner by the hand" in order to build a kinesthetic sense or "feel" for the task. Repetition is also important. For example, to teach the skill of titration, the instructor could provide a demonstration, then give the student time to practice with water while reviewing the demonstration on videotape.

Although the ability to critique an essay can be taught through verbal or written media, a lecture on the critique of art must be supplemented with visuals. Some objects of study have more prominent visual aspects than others.

The identification or classification of species of insects is also quite visual. The guidance phase of this type of task would involve displaying examples of different insects of the same species, and highlighting those attributes which distinguish them from other species. Feedback should refer to the classification rules and the attributes of the sample. Transferability to unique examples requires practice with a wide variety of insects.

The visual nature of the object under study is a rather obvious rule to use in the selection of media. However, it is somewhat less obvious that more abstract phenomena may require visualization. The computation of wave-length given the frequency has no apparent visual aspect. But because of the abstract nature of the subject matter, a graphic or an animated film might do much to increase understanding of the relationship between these two concepts.

The learner, media selection, and design. The grouping of learners into those who are primarily visual and those who are primarily auditory has a certain intuitive appeal. Unfortunately, this position has not received much support from research, even though its implications for media selection are attractive. What appears more likely to be the case is that students can be divided by their need for structure in the learning situation. Aspects of the student's motivational set and learning style have implications for the way media are managed. Some students seem to need more direct guidance and more frequent feedback than others.

An example of this difference is the application of Herman Witkin's (1976) concepts of field-dependent and field-independent cognitive styles to the selection of media. (See Chapters 2 and 5 for a more detailed discussion of Witkin's ideas.) Briefly described, a field-dependent person is more global in his approach to problems, and is dependent on the context of the problem for its solution. Field-dependent people prefer the guidance and support of others in arriving at solutions to problems; Keller's (1968) Personalized System of Instruction would seem ideal for this type of student. The highly structured yet interpersonal features of this approach would meet the need for guidance and human interaction preferred by field-dependent students. Field-independent students are more analytical and prefer to work alone. Programmed instruction, or even independent study, might be more effective with this group of students.

These and other characteristics of the learner discussed in the next chapter, as well as features of the subject matter, are important to the selection of media and the design of instruction.

Returning to the communication paradigm of this chapter, the instructor can be compared to an orator. Much as a public speaker shapes her message to fit the audience and the topic of the speech, so too does the effective teacher match the medium to the characteristics of the instructional goal and the student audience.

Chapter 5

THE STUDENT

Whether lecturing to a large class or discussing with a seminar, the instructor is trying to teach and motivate a wide range of individuals; yet she often treats them as if they were a single entity, a "class." As Stanford Ericksen (1974) describes the situation, "The individual student brings with him distinctive resources for transforming what he studies into knowledge with personal meaning." (p. 2) "The student, not the class, is the de facto unit of instruction." (p. 3) Paralleling in certain ways the chapter on the instructor, this chapter offers some guidance toward understanding the diversity of students' needs, expectations, interests and, most importantly, students' learning styles. Understanding these differences will allow the instructor to design objectives, methods, evaluations, and other activities that take into account the variety of individual learners.

This chapter briefly summarizes some of the central findings to emerge from the substantial body of research on the college learner. It offers a choice of perspectives—socio-economic, emotional, developmental, and cognitive—for focusing on the learner, as well as a choice of simple questionnaires by which any instructor can gain specific information about the individuals in a course. Whether reading this chapter as an overview of student characteristics or as a guide to understanding a specific class, the teacher should derive a basis for selecting alternative ways of teaching, that will be appropriate for the specific needs of each individual learner or cluster of learners.

Who Goes to College?

The demographic work of Astin (1965), and the social psychological work of Feldman and Newcomb (1969), Chickering (1969), Heath (1968), and Katz *et al.* (1968), give a clear impression of the traditional student in the 1960's:

- White, male, 18-24 years old.
- He is intelligent, with both verbal and math SAT's in the mid-500's, from the upper third of his high school class, and intends to go to graduate school.
- He is from an urban, upper middle income family. His father is also college educated, and tends to be a professional or an executive.
- He is going through a number of psycho-emotional dilemmas, including separation anxiety as a result of leaving home, and insecurity and self-doubt as a result of being confronted by new challenges, roles, and people.
- He is primarily concerned with forming social and intimate relationships with peers, secondarily concerned with academic learning, and highly ambivalent about relationships with professors.

By the time scholars had evolved an accurate picture of the college student, a national decision was made to support mass higher education. With the reduction of geographical, financial, and academic entrance barriers, a host of new students enrolled in some form of postsecondary education. In the official prose of the Carnegie Commission on Higher Education (1972), "The student community is now highly diverse in ability, in achievement, in ethnic and political orientation, in age, and in academic and occupational interest—and is becoming more so." (p. 23)

Traditional students still predominate in the classrooms of private institutions, especially the most prestigious. However, a rapidly expanded system of public institutions, notably the community colleges, has been increasingly populated by new students.

The typical new student is the first member of a blue-collar family to go on to college, a member of a minority group, a female, and an adult. Though these demographic dimensions have some relevance, Patricia Cross (1971), the best known researcher and advocate of the new student, argues that race, age, sex, and socio-economic background do not define the new student. Rather, the most universal and distinguishing characteristic for the majority of new students is that they come from the lower third of their high school graduating classes. On conventional tests of academic ability, they do not do well.

When compared with traditional students, new students typically test lower on measures of previous academic accomplishment, aptitude, and fundamental skills like communication and calculation. They generally have poor study skills and related techniques. Generally, the new student has not learned to perform according to the norms of the established educational system and not infrequently has difficulty adjusting to the folkways of higher education.

Without apology, Cross has attempted to identify some of the personality traits which distinguish the new student from the traditional. New students spend more of their leisure time with other people and rate getting along with and getting to know others as even more important than do traditional students. Their motivation for education tends to be highly extrinsic: high grades, better jobs, higher salaries. New students often choose jobs working with other people, and their career choices are strongly sex-stereotyped. Their attitudes and values tend to be more authoritarian, traditional, and compliant than those of traditional students.

As subsets of the new student population, women, minorities, and adults are significant. Generalizations about the characteristics of these groups are less easily or safely made than those that can be reported for the new student population as a whole.

Data on college-bound women show that on virtually all measures of academic success, preparation, and aptitude, they are similar or superior to their male counterparts. The only exception is on measures of scientific and mathematical aptitude. They have superior study skills and devote more effort to academic achievement. On measures of academic ability, academic accomplishment, interest, and motivation, women constitute an impressive group of new students. Traditionally, women's problems in higher education have involved truncated aspirations, lower self-esteem, and the realities of overt and implicit sexual discrimination. With the recent theoretical expansion of the female role, many women are faced with conflicts between their current status and new possibilities.

Though still far short of a just representation, students from racial minorities have been entering higher education at a significantly accelerating rate. Their desire to gain entrance grows even more rapidly. While the aspiration for admission and a college degree is very high among minority students, it is not matched by preparation, aptitude, or achievement. For historical, socio-economic, and political reasons, the typical new minority student does not come to college from an environment which effectively fosters academic skills, aptitudes, and perhaps most notably, traditional communication skills. Thus, they often do not do well or test well in college. Until such time as the fundamental injustices that have produced this lack of preparation are set right, the instructor will be challenged to devise effective non-traditional teaching-learning strategies for this group of new students.

A major effect of the new student's different background is the creation of a distance between the student and the instructor. Students have trouble identifying with their professor and viewing him as a social and scholastic model. The professor has trouble adjusting his instruction to students with lower academic preparation and achievement. He prefers to use the familiar methods of his own education, suited for the most academically elite student.

College teachers are by and large the most successful of traditional students, upwardly mobile, high-achieving, verbal, and academically motivated. If their very motivation, experience, and success stand in the way of their teaching typical traditional students, as it can, how much greater are their "handicaps" when it comes to creating appropriate conditions of learning for the new students? These handicaps can be minimized if the instructor can adjust to the changes that have occurred in the student population.

Student Development

It is important for the instructor to know that she encounters her students during a very volatile period in their lives. From ages 18-24, many changes occur in student attitudes, values, and life-styles. If the instructor is prepared for these changes and adjusts for them in her instruction, the passage may be more tranquil and the student can spend more time studying effectively.

Most young adults of the ages 18-24 are in a period that Levinson *et al.* (1974) refer to as provisional adulthood. The student begins to cut ties with home and starts to form her own identity as an adult. This period is marked by a number of psychological, moral, and intellectual transitions. The following is a summary of the work of Loevinger (Loevinger and Wessler, 1970), Kohlberg (1973), and Piaget (1970), which can be applied to this general age group. College-age students are essentially moving from conformity to consciousness. It is a movement from identification with authority figures to identification with peers. It is a change from cognitive simplicity, with clear distinctions between right and wrong and standard rules for everyone at all times, to cognitive complexity, in which rules have exceptions or limited applications. Motives and consequences become more important than rules, and guilt is evoked by hurting others rather than by breaking rules. The student becomes more independent, measuring achievement by inner criteria rather than external standards. Intellectually, she moves from a concentration on concrete ideas to abstract ideas of complex relations. Although these changes are common among students of this age range, some students make the passage more quickly and less painfully than others.

The impact of these changes on learning and the instructional situation are described by Chickering (1976). First of all, the motive for education develops from an attempt to impress others and gain social acceptance, to the desire to achieve competence. Early in this transition students view knowledge as coming from external authority, but later view it as the result of personal inquiry. They move from a reliance on the teacher for direction, to more independent forms of instruction. They also move from a reliance on their teacher as the judge of the quality of their work, to the standards of their peers, the system, and themselves.

Why Do Students Go to College?

A professor may ask himself this question upon confrontation with a student over a course grade or lecture. Conflicts between instructors and students may arise from their divergent perspectives on the purpose of higher education.

Virtually all studies concur on the reasons students continue schooling after high school. The majority of students who go to college report that they do so in the hope of securing vocational or professional training, gaining opportunities for developing themselves and their interests, and earning a higher lifetime income—in that order. These statistical findings emphasize that despite what the college catalogue says about intellectual and cultural growth, the overwhelming majority of students are in college to secure vocational preparation, broadly develop their interests and personalities, and ultimately make more money.

A survey of undergraduate student attitudes and values, conducted by the American Council on Education (1971) provides a broad profile of the reasons students are engaged in undergraduate education. The survey data show that well over half the entering students consider the chief benefit of college to be a potential increase in their earning power. In recent years, with a decrease in perceived employment opportunities and with an increase in the new student population, a growing proportion of students see vocational preparation as of primary importance.

Academic learning is secondary to personal relationships for most students, and for many, its importance is only instrumental. For these students the importance of course work lies in its connection with career plans. Some have vague hopes that college is a place where they can find themselves. Perhaps for the majority of students, attending college is something that is expected of them. Whenever, by plan or chance, academic learning corresponds to students' genuine interests, they do engage in it for purposes of intellectual growth.

Unfortunately, Katz *et al.* (1968) and others have found that the current academic, intellectual program of college has a strong intrinsic interest for no more than a quarter of the students. What about the education of the other 75 percent?

For many students, grades are the central reality of academic life. They are in a sense the coin of the realm: grades determine continuation of a scholarship, access to further study, social opportunities, and many other privileges. They are closely re-

Figure 5.1. What Is Important?

	In School			Home			Free Time		
	very	some-what	not very	very	some-what	not very	very	some-what	not very
Gaining respect from other people because of the importance and significance of what I do.									
Doing something that I know I can do.									
Being able to plan or organize neatly.									
Getting other people to do what I want them to do.									
Doing something that allows me to find new solutions, make new things, be innovative or creative.									
Doing something that allows me to acquire new information, use insight and judgment.									
Establishing or strengthening meaningful relationships, working closely with other people.									
Doing what I want to do, my own way, and making my own decisions.									
Doing something that adds beauty to the world.									
Having the freedom to be the kind of person I want to be.									

Figure 5.1. (Continued)

	In School			Home			Free Time		
	very	some-what	not very	very	some-what	not very	very	some-what	not very
Working with printed materials in terms of evaluating or interpreting information.									
Using my energy and talents to be outstanding.									
Providing emotional and/or physical help to other people.									
Assuring myself of good income.									
Working under the direction and guidance of another person.									
Doing a variety of things which are new and different.									
Challenging my will-power to persist until the job was done.									
Using my hands.									
Meeting or working with people.									

lated to a student's image with peers and parents and thus to the student's self-esteem.

"Like a Calvinistic deity, [the grade point average down to the decimal point] allows for no transgressions; every slip is forever included in the cumulative record." (Katz, 1968, p. 25) Some see grades as a stimulus to achievement and as a guide for study. Others regard them as inhibiting. But for almost all students they are an inescapable reality.

Getting a job, making friends, finding themselves, getting good grades—these are the things that students are frequently concerned with. The fact that they have little to do with the content of a particular course can create a gap between the student and the professor. One way to bridge this gap is for the instructor to show a concern about the students' interests. A good way of finding out what is important to students is to ask them. The short questionnaire in Figure 5.1, or any similar instrument, can be used to tap governing attitudes, dispositions, and goals that the students bring to a course. The results will enable the instructor to check and sort out some of the general propositions made in this section of the chapter. Based on the results for a specific group of students, the instructor will be in a better position to act on a range of known student needs. The information can be used in selecting appropriate instructional objectives and strategies.

Students as Learners

The foregoing section sketches the attitudes and values of an increasingly diverse undergraduate student population in very broad strokes and is, necessarily, only background for the central concern of this chapter—student differences that affect learning.

Social scientists studying undergraduate learners have devised a rich array of typologies describing student characteristics which affect learning. One classic set of categories divides students into academic, non-conformist, collegiate, and vocational (Clark and Trow, 1966). Flowing directly from the glory days of student activists is the typology devised by Jeff Koon (1971) at Berkeley. It includes types such as "the-socially-alienated-materialist," "the-emerging-woman," and "the-emotionally-dissonant-intellectual." The abundance of such typologies can be overwhelming. What is needed is a taxonomy which identifies "differences which make a difference," to borrow from William James.

Ability, Previous Achievement, and Personality

Student characteristics frequently found to make a difference in achievement or in the differential effectiveness of instructional treatments are ability, previous achievement, and personality. Each of these traits has implications for instructional decisions and will be referred to frequently in the chapters in Section Two of this book.

Although the nature of "ability" has been debated for decades by psychologists, consensus has still not been achieved. The risk of oversimplification or overgeneralization is great, but the implications for instruction must be given attention.

Students who score low on measures of ability (such as the Scholastic Aptitude Test) can be considered deficient in abstract reasoning, information processing skills (such as attending, perceiving, and remembering), and analytical skills. Among students, differences in general ability typically account for much of the variation in achievement; high ability students score higher regardless of instructional method used. Despite expectations to the contrary, techniques which accommodate student differences, such as programmed instruction or the Personalized System of Instruction, have not neutralized this effect.

Certain strategies, while not eliminating or inverting differences, do close the gap. William Allen's (1975) review of research in this area supports this position; among his conclusions are:

- low ability students benefit more from active participation and response;
- low ability students may benefit more from corrective feedback;
- low ability students may benefit more from attention-directing procedures;
- low ability students may benefit more from advanced organization of content and the outlining or structuring of the instructional presentation.

Since these strategies benefit the higher ability student as well, Allen advises their use. On the other hand, high ability students learn well from complex, perceptually rich presentations, which are not pre-structured, and which proceed rapidly. These situations inhibit learning for low ability students and should be used with caution.

Previous achievement correlates highly with ability. When gross achievement measures such as grade point average are used, the above recommendations are applicable to the results. However, Gagne (1970) approaches the analysis of previous achievement from a more precise perspective. He contends, as described in Chapter 3, that for any given cognitive skill there are a number of other prerequisite skills. Gagne contends that, "...the superordinate capability will be more readily learned (on the average, throughout a group of students) if the subordinate capabilities have been previously acquired and are readily available for recall." (p. 239) It follows then, that an instructor can facilitate learning for those students who lack previous achievement of specific skills by providing them with some remedial assistance via programmed instruction (see Chapter 20) or some other method.

A review by Tobias (1976) found that students who scored low on tests of previous achievement (pretests) benefited especially from various forms of instructional support or assistance. Whereas students with prior familiarity of the subject matter can learn effectively with little instructional assistance, students with little familiarity of the topic learn better if provided with instructional objectives, carefully organized material, and feedback.

Personality differences among students also seem to influence instructional effectiveness. Using personality tests, traits such as Anxiety, Achievement-via-Independence, Achievement-via-Conformance, Need-to-Achieve, Need-for-Affiliation, and other personality variables have been examined by educational researchers. These characteristics have been related to instructional treatments, such as emphasis on structure, or to deductive versus inductive presentation, as well as to various instructional media.

An example of the importance of these personality traits is demonstrated in a study by Dowaliby and Schumer (1973) which contrasts teacher-centered versus student-centered teaching in a college psychology course. In the teacher-centered section, information was presented via lecture and demonstration; the teacher responded to student questions and discouraged student dialogue. Discussion was emphasized in the student-centered section, and student interaction was encouraged. Dowaliby and Schumer measured anxiety and found that the more anxious students did better on an examination in the teacher-centered section; less anxious students achieved more with student-centered instruction. Domino (1974) found this same pattern in a college English course. A review by Tobias (1977) concluded that students high in anxiety achieve more with those instructional methods that are highly structured and organized.

The role played by most personality variables does not seem to be as pervasive as that of general ability. Therefore, the implications for instruction will be considered in specific chapters in Section Two and reference to the glossary can be made for the interpretation of specific terms. Other student characteristics, such as affective styles or learning styles, seem to have broader implications.

Affective Styles

Richard Mann *et al.* (1970) have carefully observed what goes on inside the classroom from an emotional and affective point of view. Mann suggests that knowledge of this hidden dimension is worth having because it is bound to affect teaching and learning. The student with endless questions about assignments, exam dates, and grades is really involved in more than information gathering; the student who argues every point, or the one who never questions or disagrees with anything is not without an underlying emotional charge.

The instructor's conscious effort to develop some awareness of and sensitivity to the emotional dimensions of learning can positively support the goal of student learning. Mann's study of discussion sections led him to distinguish eight different styles of student behavior. Like any categorization, it lacks, by design, an account of the complexity of individual existences, but is nevertheless a useful heuristic.

- *The Compliant Students*
  [These students fit] perhaps better than any other the picture of the typical 'good student' in the traditional

classroom. Its members ... seemed quite contented with their classes, their teachers, and themselves. They were consistently task-oriented, only rarely experiencing any of the kinds of emotions that might interfere with the pursuit of that task. (p. 147) They work because their parents expect them to ... [and] because the teacher will grade them... They tended to do the work they were supposed to do in the course, no more and no less, and they achieved at about the level one would expect given ability. (p. 148) [A] kind of class that may upset them is one in which the teacher has, in their opinion, relinquished too much control. (p. 150) The main concern of this group seems to be understanding the material. (p. 151)

- *The Anxious Dependent Students*
  ...this is a large cluster, and one which forms an important part of every teacher's experience with his students. Its members are somewhat angry on the inside, but mostly frightened on the outside, very dependent on the teacher for knowledge and support, and very anxious about being evaluated. Their anxiety keeps most of them from doing anything we might call work in the classroom... (p. 153) One of the most pervasive issues in this group is the members' feeling of intellectual incompetence. (p. 155) This feeling of incompetence, together in many cases with consistent external pressures, especially from parents, combine to make these students tremendously concerned about grades. (p. 156)

- *The Discouraged Workers*
  The members of this cluster tend to say often that they are dissatisfied with themselves... When things go wrong for these people, they tend to blame themselves and not turn much hostility on other people. (p. 163)

- *The Independents*
  They are significantly older than the other students... An important subgroup of them is also especially intelligent...

They generally seem quite confident of themselves and are not often threatened by the teacher, the work, or the other students. They remain relatively independent while other students are confused or anxious or angry, looking at the material relatively objectively and working with it in creative ways. (p. 166) While they tend to favor collegial relationships with the teacher, where teacher and student work together on intellectual tasks, they also want to keep teacher and student roles clearly distinct. (p. 168)

- *The Heroes*
  [For these students], all of whom are males [this may have changed since 1970], classwork is inextricably tied to rebellion. Both are manifestations of a deep involvement with the teacher and the course work ... involvement has for them certain implications which tend to lead them not only to very productive and creative work, but also, in the same class, to extreme hostility and resentment... The feelings of superiority that are an important part of the identity of these students are accompanied by expressions of contempt for ordinary or common people represented by most of their classmates. (p. 174)

- *The Snipers*
  ... the noninvolvement of this cluster seems to be related to a low level of self-esteem and general pessimism about the possibility of fruitful relationships with authority figures. The combination of low investment and high rebellion leads to a kind of sniping at the teacher from a distance. (pp. 186-187) There are many understandable reasons why this group could make teachers angry. They can be very hostile, but they rarely move toward the teacher, and they are elusive when the teacher wants to confront them directly on an issue. (p. 198)

- *The Attention Seekers*
  [These students] tend to have a predominantly social rather than intellectual orientation. They are very con-

cerned with their relationship with the teacher and other class members, especially in the sense of wanting to please them. One way in which they do this is by trying to seem attractive by frequent talking, showing off, bragging, and joking ... their interest in people and their need to be accepted by people tends to overshadow their interest in the more cognitive aspects of work and inhibits their intellectual development. (p. 202)

- *The Silent Students*
  [These students] are characterized less by what they do in the classroom than by what they do not do. They do not participate verbally. (p. 217) The predominant quality, whether male or female, is their tremendous sense of helplessness and vulnerability in relation to the teacher. (p. 218)

As this taxonomy makes evident, the college teacher works not only in an area of relatively complex content but in a rich and perhaps somewhat frightening affective terrain as well. Short of becoming a clinical psychologist, how can an instructor cope with these student emotions?

In defining some general types of student behavior and suggesting the very broad guidelines for teacher behavior that follow, specific responses cannot and should not be prescribed. It would be a mistake to say, for instance, that since "attention seekers" expect to be nurtured, the teacher should always take that role. It would be pointless to advise that accessibility and authenticity are uniformly appropriate and possible. Rather than match teacher response to student affect one-to-one, the instructor could subscribe to a policy which is flexible enough to meet each student's needs.

Research from a variety of sources (Chickering and Blackburn, undated) shows that there are four basic qualities that virtually all students believe enhance a faculty member's relationship to students. The first is accessibility. Accessibility is not a matter of saying, "Call me any time, day or night." Rather, it is creating a climate in which the student feels that talking with the instructor is a legitimate, normal, important, and necessary part of teaching and learning. One way the instructor can give this impression is by asking for student responses and pausing long enough to let them know she is serious.

Accessibility is enhanced by a second quality, authenticity. To be authentic a faculty member need not agree with the student or reveal her innermost private thoughts. But the instructor must be willing to discuss matters of belief, personal concern, and principle. A third quality is knowledge of the students. An instructor should be familiar with the major concerns of her students—issues of identity, career development, and interpersonal relations as well as more abstract and intellectual concerns. She should know something of the social, cultural, economic, and spiritual backgrounds from which the students come.

Finally, the ability to talk with and listen to students is very important. Many faculty members convinced of their own good taste, standards, and knowledge, find it all too satisfying to give sage advice and to fluently express their own well-structured ideas. But after a day of listening to authoritative statements, most students are not interested in another lecture masquerading as a conversation. They want an accessible and authentic person who has some knowledge of who they are, and who is willing to listen. These qualities are not genetic nor the result of advanced training; they can be cultivated by virtually any faculty member. By following these guidelines, an instructor can foster comfortable student-teacher relationships which can accommodate differences in student disposition.

Learning Styles

Psychology since its inception has been engaged in investigating human learning. Educational psychology has attempted to relate general learning research and theory to the student. Behaviorist, Gestalt, and cognitive theories are currently the most widely discussed. However, because learning theories are relatively abstract and attempt to explain the general process of learning, they have little practical significance for the individual teacher offering a particular course to individual students. Fortunately, current research on learning styles offers greater prospects for instructional utility and application. It takes no special insight to realize that people see and make sense of the world—including formal instruction—in different ways. They give their attention to different aspects of the environment, learn at different rates, approach problems with different methods, construct relationships in distinctive patterns, and process information in different but personally consistent ways.

Those currently engaged in controlled research on learning styles hope that when the learning style and other characteristics of the individual student are identified and specifically matched with appropriate types of instruction, learning will be better or greater or both. Unfortunately, as has already been discussed in Chapter 1, the detailed and occasionally promising experiments being conducted in this area have yet to produce consistently significant findings, verifiable theory, or much guidance for instructional practice.

For now, the work on cognitive styles of Herman Witkin (1976) and his colleagues at the Educational Testing Service offers the college instructor the greatest general utility for understanding and responding to individual learners. The field-dependent/independent styles described in Chapter 2 were applied to students by Witkin's co-worker Johnathan Warren (1974). Warren identified two learning styles, *student-centered* and *instructor-centered,* which correspond to field-dependent and field-independent cognitive styles.

Student-centered. About half of the students studied who indicated a preference felt that they did their most effective learning in loosely organized classes, relatively unconstrained by texts and formal assignments. They favored seminars over lectures and preferred classes that connected with their own interests.

Instructor-centered. The other half felt they learned most in classes organized around explicit requirements and assignments. They preferred regular instructor contact in large lectures over occasional seminars, and they favored formal course content and an organized plan of instruction.

Those students who prefer student-centered learning want academic self-determination. They want to control the nature and content of their learning experience, in contrast to the instructor-centered student, who wants clear and specific directions.

Paradoxically, in virtually every other respect, those favoring the student-centered style appear much more dependent on the institution and want substantial individual help and attention from instructors. The students favoring the instructor-centered style of learning appear quite content to manage every aspect of their campus life and out-of-class learning on their own, as long as they are told exactly what is expected of them.

This preference in learning styles is linked to a student's choice of majors. Twice as many students in the social sciences, fine arts, and humanities preferred student-centered learning; the same was true for students undecided about their majors. The reverse was the case for students in business, health services, technologies, and physical sciences: two-thirds preferred instructor-centered learning. All courses and classes are likely to contain students whose learning will be best accomplished in one or the other of these quite different ways.

Students favoring one or the other of these two styles of learning can be compared to explorers and hikers. The student-centered learner is like the explorer who sets out for a general destination, choosing his own trail and taking along as a guide someone who knows the territory. The instructor-centered learner, like the hiker, strikes out for a specific destination, following a well-marked trail but willing to go it alone. It seems clear that a single instructional approach is unlikely to be best for both explorers and hikers.

Warren concludes his report with the following suggestions:

> A class of student-centered students might be presented with a number of options for carrying out the work of a course. The options might include small-group projects, independent study, weekly or biweekly class meetings with the instructor, field experiences or individual off-campus projects, or any activity that could be carried out individually or in small groups and would serve the purposes of the course. With respect to content, these students might be offered the usual instructor-organized sequence of topics covering the broad area of the course or a variety of specific topics to be probed in depth. The current trend toward problem-oriented curricula is consistent with this approach.

These students simply would require a range of topics from which to choose.

There is a danger with this approach, however, and it is often overlooked because of the apparent desire of these students for autonomy. They may be left too much on their own and may not get the extensive help they want—and probably need.

The instructor-centered students will probably be better served than the student-centered ones by traditional methods of instruction. They respond favorably to well-organized, carefully structured lectures and course plans. The danger in teaching these students is that their tendency not to complain and their willingness to do whatever the instructor suggests may hide confusion or misunderstanding. Serious student misperceptions may not be revealed until the end of the course, too late for correction. (Warren, 1974, p. 4)

Differing learning styles can be identified and used to guide the instructor in devising a mix of student-centered and instructor-centered learning alternatives. Complex means for assessing these two preferences or styles are not necessary. Although Warren's (1974, p. 2) complete 200 item questionnaire is available from the Educational Testing Service, the items that were the most useful in discriminating between student-centered and instructor-centered learners were these:

	Definitely No	No	?	Yes	Definitely Yes
I would like more classes without texts or assignments, organized around informal discussions.	—	—	—	—	—
I would like more small, informal seminars, even if they meet less often with the instructor.	—	—	—	—	—
The faculty should stay with topics that have caught the class's interest even if they don't cover the planned amount in the course.	—	—	—	—	—

Student-centered learners will answer "yes" or "definitely yes" to all three of these. Instructor-centered students will respond negatively. Most of the students will split on these questions in some way.

A somewhat more elaborate system for identifying learning styles is the Grasha-Reichman *Student Learning Styles Questionnaire*. In contrast to the two basic styles identified by Warren, Grasha and Reichman (Grasha, 1972; Reichman and Grasha, 1974) have developed a taxonomy of six learning styles—Independent, Dependent, Collaborative, Competitive, Participant, and Avoidant—with a definition for each:

Student Learning Styles:

- *Competitive*. This response style is exhibited by students who learn material in order to perform better than others in the class. They feel they must compete with other students in the class for the rewards of the classroom, such as grades or teachers' attention. They view the classroom as a win-lose situation, where they must always win.

- *Collaborative*. This style is typical of students who feel they can learn the most by sharing ideas and talents. They cooperate with teachers and peers and like to work with others. They see the classroom as a place for social interaction as well as content learning.

- *Avoidance*. This response style is typical of students who are not interested in learning course content in the traditional classroom. They do not participate with students and teachers in the classroom. They are uninterested or overwhelmed by what goes on in classes.

- *Participant*. This style is characteristic of students who want to learn course content and like to go to class. They take responsibility for getting the most out of class and participate with others when told to do so. They feel that they should take part in as much of the class related activity as possible and little that is not part of the course outline.

- *Dependent*. This style is characteristic of students who show little intellectual curiosity and who learn only what is required. They see teacher and peers as sources of structure and support. They look to authority figures for guidelines and want to be told what to do.

- *Independent*. This response style is characteristic of students who like to think for themselves. They prefer work on their own but will listen to the ideas of others in the classroom. They learn the content they feel is important and are confident in their learning abilities.

A copy of the Grasha-Reichman Questionnaire is included at the end of this chapter. Any use of this instrument other than for the personal use of an instructor with his or her class should be done in consultation with Anthony Grasha at the Faculty Resource Center, the University of Cincinnati. Since the instrument is still being validated, Dr. Grasha would appreciate a copy of any data gathered with the questionnaire. In testing and validating these six styles, Grasha and Reichman (Grasha, 1975) identified the typical learning activities preferred by each of the six types.

- *Competitive*. To be a group leader in discussion or when working on projects...To ask questions in class...To be singled out for doing a particularly good job on a class related activity. No real preference for any one classroom method over another (e.g., lectures, seminars, etc.) as long as the method has more of a teacher-centered focus than a student-centered focus.

- *Collaborative*. Lectures with class discussion in small groups...Small seminars...Student-designed and taught courses and classes...Doing group rather than individual projects...Peer-determined grades...Talking about course issues outside of class with other students...Instructor group interaction.

- *Avoidance.* Generally turned off by classroom activities... Preferences include no tests...self-evaluation for grading ...no required readings or assignments...blanket grades where everyone gets a passing grade...does not like enthusiastic teachers...does not prefer well-organized lectures...does not like instructor individual interactions.

- *Participant.* Lectures with discussion...opportunities to discuss material...likes both objective and essay type tests...class reading assignments...likes enthusiastic presentations of material...prefers teachers who can analyze and synthesize material well.

- *Dependent.* Teacher outlines or notes on the board...clear deadlines for assignments...teacher-centered classroom methods.

- *Independent.* Independent study...self-paced instruction... problems which give the student an opportunity to think for himself...projects which the student can design...prefers a student-centered classroom setting over a teacher-centered one.

Since knowledge about learning styles is tentative and incomplete at this stage, the instructor should remain flexible and experimental in using the concepts and the instruments included here. Perhaps the most effective and efficient use of data obtained from questionnaires such as these is not in prescribing specific learning activities for individual students, but rather for planning a mix of methods and alternatives which accommodate groups of students. They could also be used as a basis for discussing learning styles and preferences with students.

From such data-based discussions, the teacher can develop a varied range of instructional strategies that meet the needs of most, if not all, of the individual students. The individual student can use the questionnaire results and discussion to gain greater insight into his own learning style and make more informed choices about which of the available instructional alternatives will best facilitate his learning.

Student Learning Styles Questionnaire:
Specific Class Form

The following questionnaire has been designed to help you clarify your attitudes and feelings toward this course and to identify your preferred learning style(s). Your answers to each specific question will remain in your hands and will not be made available to either your instructor or the other members of this class. Remember, formulate your answers with regard to this class and this class only.

Write your answers on the enclosed questionnaire. To the left of each question number, write the number that best explains how you feel about the statement as follows:

Mark *1* if you *strongly disagree* with the statement.
Mark *2* if you *moderately disagree* with the statement.
Mark *3* if you are *undecided.*
Mark *4* if you *moderately agree* with the statement.
Mark *5* if you *strongly agree* with the statement.

1. Most of what I know about material relating to this course, I learned on my own.
2. I have a difficult time paying attention during class sessions.
3. I find the ideas of the other students relatively useful for helping me to understand the course material.
4. I think that if the teacher lets the students in this class do whatever they want, he would not be doing his job well.
5. I like other students in this class to know when I have done a good job.
6. I try to participate as much as I can in all aspects of this course.
7. I study what is important to me and not necessarily what the instructor says is important.
8. I feel that I have to attend this class rather than feeling that I want to attend.

9. I think an important part of this class is to learn to get along with other people.
10. I accept the structure the teacher sets for this course.
11. To get ahead in this class, I think sometimes you have to step on the toes of the other students.
12. I do not have trouble paying attention in this class.
13. I think I can determine what the important content issues are in this course.
14. If I do not understand the course material, I just forget about it.
15. For this course, I think students can learn more by sharing their ideas than by keeping their ideas to themselves.
16. I think this teacher should clearly state what he expects from students.
17. I think students have to be aggressive to do well in this course.
18. I get more out of going to this class than spending that time at home.
19. I feel that my ideas about the content are often as good as those in the textbook.
20. I try to spend as little time as possible on this course outside of class.
21. For this course, I like to study for tests with other students.
22. I like the tests for this course to be taken right out of the book.
23. I feel that I must compete with the other students in class to get a grade.
24. I attend this class because I want to learn something.
25. I am confident in my abilities to learn the important material.
26. This course does not really interest me.
27. I think students in this class should be encouraged to work together.
28. I feel that facts presented in the textbook and lectures are correct.
29. I like this teacher to notice me.
30. I feel that the activities we have in class are generally interesting.
31. I like to think things through for myself before the teacher lectures on the course material.

32. I seldom get excited about material covered in this course.
33. I prefer not to work alone on the assignments.
34. Before working on a class project, I try to get the approval of the instructor.
35. To do well in this course, I have to compete with the other students for the teacher's attention.
36. I do my assignments before reading other things that interest me.
37. I do not like a lot of structure in this class.
38. I have given up trying to learn anything from going to this class.
39. I like to hear what other students think about the issues raised in class.
40. I think the teacher is the best judge of what is important to know.
41. During class discussions, I feel that I have to compete with the other students to get my ideas across.
42. I think this class is very worthwhile.
43. I work by myself on class related projects (e.g., studying for exams, preparing term papers).
44. I feel that activities in class are generally boring.
45. I prefer to work in groups rather than alone on class projects.
46. I try my best to do the assignments for this class the way the professor says they should be done.
47. I like to see if I can get the answers to problems or questions before anybody else in class does.
48. I am eager to learn about areas covered in class.
49. I do assignments for this course my own way without checking with the other students about how they are going to do them.
50. I do not feel that I miss anything if I cut this class.
51. I like to talk to other students outside of class about the ideas and issues raised in class.
52. I tend not to think or work on problems or issues related to this course unless they were first covered in the text or lectures.
53. I think a student in this course is hurting himself if he shares his notes and ideas with other students before an exam.
54. I feel that I can really learn something in this course.

55. I feel that too much assigned work keeps students from developing their own ideas.
56. I am in this course only to fulfill a requirement.
57. I try to get to know other students in this class on a personal level.
58. I think too much discussion in this class prevents the teacher from covering enough required material.
59. I like to know that I have done better than the other students in this class.
60. I do my assignments for this course whether I think they are interesting or not.
61. My ideas about content issues are often as good as those of this instructor.
62. For this course I sit where the teacher is unlikely to notice me.
63. I feel that students and the teacher should develop the kind of relationship in this course where a student can tell the teacher if he feels the course is not going well.
64. I feel that I can learn what is important in this course by doing what the professor says.
65. I think students taking this course should be graded according to how well they do in class.
66. I try to do the best that I can in this course.
67. I do not like the teacher to tell me what I have to learn.
68. I study just hard enough to get by in this course.
69. I like this course when students are encouraged to discuss course material.
70. I seldom try to learn material related to this course when it is not covered in the text or lectures.
71. I like to know how well the other students in this course are doing on exams.
72. I feel that I can get something out of going to this class.
73. I like this course when students are allowed to pursue topics that interest them.
74. I prefer that this teacher never calls on me.
75. I think learning in this course should be a cooperative effort between the teacher and students.
76. I think the teacher should emphasize the content that I must learn.

77. I only help other students with material for this course when I feel it will not hurt me.
78. In this class I sit where I can be sure to hear the professor and see what he writes.
79. If a topic raised in this class interests me, I will go out on my own to find out more about it.
80. I think one of the most important things about this course is how easy it is for me to get a good grade.
81. I try to help the other students when they have a hard time understanding the course material.
82. I enjoy this course when class sessions are highly organized.
83. I do not like this instructor to deviate from his lectures.
84. I work on the reading assignments for this course until I feel I understand the material.
85. I have my own ideas about how this course should be run.
86. I feel that this course is not relevant to what I want to do when I graduate.
87. I feel a responsibility to help the other students in this class learn course material.
88. I try my best to write in my notes everything this teacher says.
89. I try to do assignments better than the other students.
90. I do my assignments as soon as possible after the assignments are made.

Score Sheet:
Student Learning Styles Questionnaire:
Specific Class Form

Instructions:
The numbers below represent the numbers of the statements in the questionnaire. To the right of each number place the number (1 to 5) that you assigned it on the questionnaire. Add the numbers in each column. The relative totals will indicate your preferred learning style(s).

Independent	*Avoidant*	*Collaborative*
1 . . .	2 . . .	3 . . .
7 . . .	8 . . .	9 . . .
13 . . .	14 . . .	15 . . .
19 . . .	20 . . .	21 . . .
25 . . .	26 . . .	27 . . .
31 . . .	32 . . .	33 . . .
37 . . .	38 . . .	39 . . .
43 . . .	44 . . .	45 . . .
49 . . .	50 . . .	51 . . .
55 . . .	56 . . .	57 . . .
61 . . .	62 . . .	63 . . .
67 . . .	68 . . .	69 . . .
73 . . .	74 . . .	75 . . .
79 . . .	80 . . .	81 . . .
85 . . .	86 . . .	87 . . .
Total . . .	Total . . .	Total . . .

Dependent	*Competitive*	*Participant*
4 . . .	5 . . .	6 . . .
10 . . .	11 . . .	12 . . .
16 . . .	17 . . .	18 . . .
22 . . .	23 . . .	24 . . .
28 . . .	29 . . .	30 . . .
34 . . .	35 . . .	36 . . .
40 . . .	41 . . .	42 . . .
46 . . .	47 . . .	48 . . .
52 . . .	53 . . .	54 . . .
58 . . .	59 . . .	60 . . .

64 . . .	65 . . .	66 . . .
70 . . .	71 . . .	72 . . .
76 . . .	77 . . .	78 . . .
82 . . .	83 . . .	84 . . .
88 . . .	89 . . .	90 . . .
Total . . .	Total . . .	Total . . .

Chapter 6

EVALUATION

Ask faculty members what they dislike most about teaching, and grading examinations will most likely be at the top of the list. Although evaluation is most commonly thought of as grading tests, it encompasses much more than mid-terms and finals and is important for reasons other than grading. Evaluation can be viewed as the process of collecting relevant data for decision-making (Cooley and Lohnes, 1976). Since it is one of the elements of the instructional system almost totally within the control of the individual instructor, it can be creatively used to improve instruction.

A definition of evaluation which focuses on the collection of data for decision-making is broad enough to include an assessment of student learning for the purpose of assigning grades or for the purpose of prescribing remedial instruction. One might collect data on student reactions to a guest lecturer, a film, or a game to determine whether educational objectives were met. A department might wish to evaluate a curricular innovation such as an inter-disciplinary course or an experimental section of a traditional course to decide whether it should remain in the curriculum. A department may wish to collect student evaluations of faculty to be used in tenure and promotion decisions. On a broader scale, administrators might evaluate programs to determine funding priorities. Educators may wish to evaluate the impact of the college experience on personality development or may want to assess the variables which influence the selection of a major or a

97

specific college. All of these activities are classified as evaluation, since they involve collecting data for the purpose of making decisions.

The individual instructor has many opportunities for evaluation other than examinations. She might wish to measure students' familiarity with a subject before planning class time. She may wish to evaluate students' skills in mathematics prior to teaching a unit which depends on these skills. A lecture, film, or reading might be evaluated to determine whether it contributes to the unit being studied. An instructor may wish to evaluate student perceptions of the relevance of course content to their professional goals. She may choose to interview students before allowing them to enroll in an advanced course. A paper, an oral report, or some other evidence of learning might be required upon completion of a study which a student has undertaken. In a field placement situation, the instructor might choose to observe students or to rely on the observations of others in assessing student performance and effects of the experience on student development.

Evaluation, then, is a tool which connects all the elements in the instructional system. It provides the instructor and the student with information about student achievement of the content and the effectiveness of the instructional media or strategies. This information can lead to adjustments in the course objectives, the media, or the evaluation process itself. The precise information to be collected depends on the decision to be made. The data collection method is a function of the information required, the individuals involved, and the environmental constraints present in the system.

For an instructional system which is aimed at facilitating student learning, it is useful to identify three broad types of evaluation. *Diagnostic evaluation* is concerned with the assessment of prerequisite skills, the prior level of knowledge of a subject, the relevant student characteristics, and the underlying cause of student learning difficulties. *Formative evaluation* is concerned with providing feedback to the student and instructor on student learning that is in progress. *Summative evaluation* provides data on the final results of .instruction and is most often used to grade or rank students with respect to performance (Bloom *et al.*, 1971).

These three types of evaluation are used as a framework to discuss an instructor's opportunities for employing evaluation techniques at critical points in the instructional process.

Diagnosis

The pretest is a diagnostic instrument extremely important in instructional design. While in some courses it may be safe to assume that students know nothing of the subject matter, in many courses this is not the case. In a first year composition class, for example, it is not uncommon to find students who have already mastered the writing techniques taught in the course side-by-side with students who barely meet minimal high school standards. In sociology and psychology, students may have gross misconceptions concerning the content of the course. In fine arts, students will range from those filling elective requirements to those with professional interests.

A common technique in pretesting students is to give students a form of the final examination at the beginning of the semester. This practice alerts students to the manner in which they will be tested during the course; more importantly, it provides data from which an instructor can organize classes. Students may fall roughly into two groups—those with no knowledge of the course material and those whose understanding is not sufficient to waive the course requirement. Such distributions present challenges to the instructor. If one pitches instruction at the lower group, the higher group may become bored and their valuable time is wasted. However, challenging the higher group may confuse the lower group or put them so far behind that they never catch up with the rest of the class. To complicate matters, within each group is a wide range of capabilities best accommodated by individualizing instruction. Pretest data may suggest less drastic ways of accommodating differences. If the class does divide into two or more distinct groups, it might be desirable to form subgroups each with different objectives. The data may indicate that there are only one or two specific skills which separate the "highs" from the "lows." In this case remedial instruction may be all that is necessary to bring the groups to the same level.

An instructor may wish to assess the learning preferences of students (see Chapter 5) and their specific interests in taking the course. Content, technique, and assignments can then be tailored to individuals and to the group. Some groups will prefer lecture to discussion. Others will prefer small group work. Still others will prefer independent study. To the extent that it is possible, without sacrificing course objectives, an instructor should accommodate the interests and preferences of students.

Diagnostic evaluation need not be limited to the beginning of the course. If at any time an instructor feels that some problem is interfering with student learning, a specific instrument could be devised and administered to diagnose the problem.

It is important that diagnostic evaluation be presented as an important source of information for students. Students should not be graded or penalized for performance on diagnostic instruments. To maintain credibility, results of the evaluation should be shared with individual students and, when appropriate, with the group. The rationale for decisions based on such an evaluation should be made clear to the students.

Formative Evaluation

Formative evaluation is a process specifically designed to improve learning and teaching in progress. The instructor who uses this technique is committed to providing students with relevant feedback and to giving them the opportunity to demonstrate further learning. Formative evaluation differs from summative evaluation not so much in the objectives being evaluated as in timing and purpose. Summative evaluation, by definition, occurs too late to be useful for improving student performance. Formative evaluation, on the other hand, is conducted at points in the instructional design where decisions are to be made concerning student progress toward educational goals. A mid-term examination, which is usually a summative evaluation of the first half of a course, can be used as formative evaluation. If the instructor uses the results to reorganize the last half of the course, to assign remedial units to those not demonstrating proficiency, or to assess competence on objectives which will be evaluated later, the mid-term also serves as formative evaluation.

While formative evaluations tend to differ from summative evaluations more in purpose than in form, they *do* tend to be more specific and comprehensive in their assessment of student performance. Whenever an evaluation is conducted, the instructor must specify the objectives to be evaluated. Yet often the objectives for a course are so extensive that it is impossible to evaluate them all in any one instance. The instructor then samples the objectives, assuming, in the case of a test, that student performance on the sample of items would reflect performance on a complete pool of items covering all of the course objectives. Normally, formative evaluations do not employ this technique. They are administered frequently and in manageable units. All objectives are evaluated. Thus, the student receives valuable feedback on course material; the impact is not lost by studying the "wrong" material for the exam or failing to "psych-out" the instructor.

The most important aspects of a formative evaluation are the nature of the feedback given to the students and the mechanisms which are provided to help them improve their performance. In order to be of the most help, the feedback should be prompt and specific. The student should be told what strengths and deficiencies were observed and what steps to take to improve performance. Formative evaluations should not be graded.

While the primary intent of formative evaluation is to benefit students, the benefit for instructors is equally important. The instructor can adjust the pace of instruction, review a topic, or provide additional examples based on student responses. She can evaluate the effectiveness of a new technique or medium or collect information needed to make revisions in the instructional presentation.

Because instructional changes need to be specific, formative data should also be specific. A statement such as "Please indicate the sections that were unclear and why you found them so," gives specific information suggestive of changes. But a question like "Was the unit clear?" leaves the instructor at a loss if the answer is "No."

Finally, an instructor can use formative assessments of instruction to determine how the attitudes of students are affected by any teaching activity. A short instructor-designed questionnaire which assesses students' enjoyment of the course, their motivation to study, relevance of the content to their interests, or any other area of instructor concern can be of great assistance in designing learning activities. Students should be allowed to remain anonymous and should not be penalized in any way for stating their candid opinions. Unfortunately, this type of information is usually obtained on student rating forms at the end of the course—too late to be of benefit to this group of students.

Summative Evaluation
The primary reasons for conducting a summative evaluation at the end of a course are to provide feedback to students on their attainment of the course goals and to assign grades for the course work completed.

As a feedback mechanism, summative evaluation, like formative evaluation, should be specific and comprehensive. Students should be left with a clear picture of which objectives were met and which were not. A summary score on a test or a grade on a paper is not a very efficient way to communicate this information, since so much data is lost in any report of totals or averages. A useful device for feedback activity is a profile sheet. Each student can be provided with a document which both specifies objectives and indicates level of proficiency. A profile sheet for a student taking a course in Biology might contain the information shown in Figure 6.1.

Grading. Summative evaluation, the most common form of evaluation in higher education, is generally used to assign grades to students. Two general patterns of grading are used. One is an absolute standard referred to as criterion-referenced grading. Sometimes this method is associated with a pass/fail or pass/no credit course, where a "pass" is given to the students who demonstrate a pre-specified level of performance. *Descriptive grading* can also be used. With this practice, instructors make written comments and ratings on the students' work (Warren, 1971). For instructors who are stuck with the traditional grading scheme of "A," "B," etc., a certain level of performance (a specific number of units completed, or a certain number of points scored) would be attached to each grade. In courses for which fine discriminations are difficult, some instructors will use a "C" to represent the minimum output

Figure 6.1. Sample Student Profile Sheet.

Objective	Not Attempted	Incomplete	Demonstrated Mastery
1. Recognize characteristics of the major groups of plants.			X

2. Describe structural features of the following:
    a. Bacteria
    b. Blue-green algae
    c. Viruses
		
		X
			
			X
			
			X

3. Identify chemical elements found in living organisms.			X
4. Draw and label structures of amoeba and paramecium.	X		
5. Differentiate between protostomes and deuterostomes.			X
6. Interpret biological data presented in graphs, tables, and basic statistics.			X
7. Develop experimental hypotheses from a knowledge of general problems in biology.	X		
8. Design an experiment to test an hypothesis concerning a problem of interest to biologists.		X	

or quality of work which is needed to justify giving credit for the course. Beyond that, an evaluative judgment is made on the quality of the work to determine whether an "A" or a "B" should be given. *Multidimensional grading* is the use of letter grades accompanied by written statements of the general objectives and criteria of the department or instructor.

The second pattern is called norm-referenced or relative grading; it involves ranking students on the basis of their performance as compared with other students in the class. This latter approach has been criticized because students tend to compete against each other for grades. It is also criticized because it is arbitrary and fails to take individual characteristics into account.

The central problem is not so much how grades are assigned but that too much emphasis is placed on grades which are uninformative. Grades are not comparable. A grade in educational psychology cannot be compared to a grade in anthropology. Also, the reliability of grades can be questioned. The same work evaluated by different professors will be assigned different grades; indeed, the same work evaluated by the same instructor at different times may be assigned different grades. And finally, grades have been shown to be poor predictors of "success" and at best are only moderate predictors of grades in subsequent semesters (Hoyt, 1966).

The evidence of "grade inflation" warrants a careful evaluation of grading in general. It is likely that instructors can do little to change the basic system, for it has withstood many formidable attacks. An individual instructor *can* make sure that the grades assigned in his course have meaning in relation to the course objectives and that the students clearly understand the basis for assigning the grades. Grading is an administrative responsibility which should neither be taken lightly nor confused with more substantive reasons for conducting educational evaluations.

Student ratings. A second form of summative evaluation common in higher education is the use of student ratings of instruction. Like grades, these ratings are frequently initiated on the administrative level. And like grades, the meaning of student ratings is frequently ambiguous.

It is unclear what a high overall rating of a teacher signifies. Reviews by Kulik and McKeachie (1975) and Wittrock and Lumsdaine (1977) agree that student ratings typically measure non-task personal characteristics of teachers. They seldom correlate with teacher knowledge, ability, research productivity, or scholarly traits. Ratings are more likely to correlate with enthusiasm or communication ability. Studies differ in their findings on the connection between student ratings of teaching effectiveness and student achievement.

Based on these conclusions, Wittrock and Lumsdaine (1977) recommend that ratings are appropriate as personal indicators of attitudes toward an instructor. They suggest that ratings not be used by administrators to employ, promote, demote, or dismiss teachers. However, the use of student ratings for these decisions along with other measures of teacher performance such as visitations and peer evaluation is probably better than ignoring teaching altogether. Although each of these measures has deficiencies, they are adequate in combination.

Probably the best application of ratings is not summative but formative. Instructors can use student ratings to improve their instruction, but Kulik and McKeachie (1975) cite several studies which indicate that this practice has not been effective so far. They also identify some probable reasons. These studies typically measure the impact of mid-course feedback on end-of-semester ratings, thus leaving too little time for the instructor to make adjustments. Secondly, the instructor may not know how to interpret and apply the results of student ratings. And, finally, the information furnished by the ratings may be too global to be practically useful.

James A. Kulik (1976) at the University of Michigan Center for Research on Learning and Teaching has refined an idea first proposed by Wilbert McKeachie and implemented at Purdue University. Kulik's system, known as the Instructor-Designed Questionnaire, allows the instructor to tailor a rating form to supply feedback pertinent to his class. In addition to five general core items included on all questionnaires listed in Table 6.1, the instructor may select up to 25 items from a pool of almost 150 available questions. There is even a provision for the instructor to write-in several items. This allows the instructor to obtain very precise feedback on issues of special interest. Open-ended questions may

---

*Table 6.1. Core Items of University of Michigan
Instructor-Designed Questionnaire System.*

Overall, this is an excellent course.

Overall, the instructor is an excellent teacher.

The instructor motivates me to do my best work.

I feel that I am performing up to my potential in this course.

I had a strong desire to take this course.

---

also be included to highlight the statistical picture. Instead of
being limited to global items typical of most questionnaires, the
instructor can seek the extent of student agreement with
statements such as:

- The instructor makes good use of example and illustration.
- Written assignments are relevant to what is presented in
  class.
- Laboratory reports are graded fairly.
- Films are a valuable part of this course.

Another problem with ratings is that students tend to be very
generous in their judgments; the average teacher will receive above
average ratings. This makes it difficult for the instructor to interpret the results. Some computer-based systems will provide instructors with their standing relative to other professors.

If these norms are not available, there are several ways to
handle the situation. Kulik (1976) suggests that teachers pay attention to items for which a third or more students give unfavor-
able ratings. If the teacher considers an item important, he should
expect the great majority of students to respond favorably. A
second suggestion is to use personal norms. A teacher can compare
the rating results on the same items for similar courses they have

taught in previous years. Instructors can chart their progress over time and learn about factors which influence their ratings positively and negatively.

Choosing and Constructing Tests

Instructional Objectives and Evaluation Instruments

The first step in any type of evaluation is a careful examination of course objectives, since instruments must be selected or constructed which are appropriate for the objectives. It is important that the questions be matched to the nature of the task. So, for example, if the instructor were testing the application of the concept of "geometric isomerism" in chemistry the following item would *not* be appropriate:

1. Two molecules are geometric isomers if they:
   a. are mirror images of one another.
   b. contain elements from the same series.
   c. have the same composition and bonding but a different arrangement of the elements.
   d. share the same chemical properties but differ in their composition.

This item merely tests the recall of the definition of the term and does not test the student's application of the concept. A better item for the task would be:

2. Which of the following pairs of molecules are geometric isomers? (Multiple-choice examples given.)

It is helpful to classify each objective when writing test items (see Chapter 3), for evaluation will depend largely on whether the objectives involve cognitive, affective, or psychomotor objectives. A paper-and-pencil test may be appropriate for a cognitive objective while observation may be preferable for a psychomotor objective. A questionnaire or interview might best measure affective objectives.

For cognitive objectives the evaluation instrument will also depend on whether convergent or divergent thinking is involved. In convergent thinking the answer to a problem or question can be known in advance, since it is fixed by the subject matter or question or both. Cognitive tasks which are classified as knowledge, comprehension, application, and analysis in Bloom's Taxonomy (1956) are examples of convergent thinking objectives. In divergent thinking the answer to a problem or question cannot be known in advance, and each person may be expected to produce a unique response. Synthesis, evaluation, and problem-solving objectives are types of objectives requiring divergent thinking (see Table 6.2, Summary Comparison of Objective and Essay Tests).

Convergent thinking can be efficiently evaluated using one of a variety of objective instruments, such as multiple-choice test items, true/false items, matching items, and short answer objective questions. Divergent thinking is best evaluated through essay examinations, projects, papers, and simulations.

A comparison of essay and objective test instruments serves to delineate the difference between these two modes of evaluation. A basic trade-off in the use of these instruments is that objective tests are difficult to write but easy to score; essay examinations, papers and projects, interviews, and observations may be easier to develop but require much more thoughtful evaluation.

Test Construction and Scoring

When paper-and-pencil tests are appropriate to evaluate learning, a number of well-defined guidelines have been formulated for constructing and scoring test items.

Essay tests. Efforts to overcome the scoring difficulties of essay tests have resulted in identifying two types of essay examinations. In *restricted response questions*, strict limits are placed on the nature of the answer to be given. The boundaries of the subject matter to be considered, the form of the answer (list, define, outline, etc.) and other restraints, such as length of response, are specified. *Extended response questions* give the student almost unlimited freedom to determine the nature and scope of the response. While some structure is permitted, the amount will vary from item to item and the stress will always be on providing as much freedom as the situation allows.

The following general guidelines apply to using essay examinations:

    1. Score anonymously. Do not allow your impression of the student to influence your evaluation of the response.

Table 6.2. Summary Comparison of Objective and Essay Tests.*

	Objective Test	**Essay Test**
Taxonomy Outcomes Measured	Good for measuring outcomes at the knowledge, comprehension, application, and analysis levels of the Taxonomy. Inadequate for synthesis and evaluation outcomes.	Inefficient for knowledge outcomes. Good for comprehension, application, and analysis outcomes. Best type for synthesis and evaluation outcomes.
Sampling of Content	The use of a large number of items results in broad coverage, which makes representative sampling of content feasible.	The use of a relatively small number of items results in limited coverage, which makes representative sampling of content infeasible.
Preparation of Items	Preparation of good items is difficult and time consuming.	Preparation of good items is difficult, but easier than objective type.
Scoring	Objective, simple, and highly reliable.	Subjective, difficult, and less reliable.
Factors Distorting Students' Scores	Students' achievement scores are apt to be distorted by reading ability and guessing.	Students' achievement scores are apt to be distorted by writing ability and bluffing.
Probable Effect on Learning	Encourages students to remember, interpret, and analyze the ideas of others.	Encourages students to organize, integrate, and express their own ideas.

*Source: Gronlund, N.E. *Constructing Achievement Tests.* Englewood Cliffs, N.J.: Prentice-Hall, 1968, p. 68.

2. Evaluate all of the responses to one question before proceeding to the next question.
3. Construct a model response and assign points based on the model or develop a set of criteria for rating responses in advance.
4. Decide how you will judge factors not directly related to the learning you are testing (such as writing mechanics) and be consistent in this judgment.
5. Use essay questions to evaluate only complex learning outcomes.
6. Formulate questions which present a clear, definite task to the student.
7. Provide ample time for answering; give suggested time limits for each question to aid students in pacing themselves.

Objective tests. Unless there are compelling reasons to use true/false, matching, or short answer test items, multiple-choice items are preferred. Considerable research has been done on the most effective format for multiple-choice items. In general, the format should in no way interfere with the evaluation of the learning that the item is designed to test.

A multiple-choice item is composed of the stem, which presents a problem or situation, followed by several alternatives, which provide possible solutions to the problem. The alternatives include the correct answer and several plausible wrong answers, called distractors or foils.

The following rules apply to formulating multiple-choice test items:

1. Design each item to measure an important learning outcome. Do not fall into the trap of testing obscure learnings or irrelevant details. Be sure to test for higher level cognitive goals such as concept learning, rule using, and problem-solving, even though these items may be more difficult to write.
2. Present a single, clearly formulated problem in the stem of the item. After reading the stem, the student should know exactly what is required to respond to the item. Often the student who knows the correct response should

be able to answer a question or complete a statement without reference to the choices.

3. State the stem of the item in simple, clear language.

4. Put as much wording as possible in the stem of the item. Avoid repeating phrases in the alternatives which can be included in the stem.

5. State the stem of the item in positive form whenever possible. Negative wording should only be used when the negative is an important component of the learning.

6. Emphasize negative wording by underlining or capital letters whenever it is used in the stem of an item. It can otherwise be easily overlooked by the student.

7. Make certain that the intended answer is the only correct answer or clearly the best answer.

8. Make all alternatives grammatically consistent with the stem of the item and parallel in form.

9. Avoid verbal clues which might enable students to select the correct answer or to eliminate an incorrect answer.

10. Make the distractors plausible and attractive to the uninformed. Normally the most common errors or confusions make the best distractors.

11. Vary the relative length of the correct answer to eliminate length as a clue. The correct answer and the distractors should be approximately the same length.

12. Avoid use of the alternative "all of the above," and use "none of the above" with extreme caution. These phrases do not promote the careful weighing of each of the alternatives since only one contradiction eliminates the phrase as a possible correct response.

13. Vary the position of the correct answer in a random manner.

14. Control the difficulty of the item either by varying the problem in the stem or by changing the alternatives. One way to overcome the fact that partial credit cannot be given in multiple-choice tests is to include a number of items of varying levels of difficulty for each learning objective.

15. Make certain that each item is independent of the other items in the test.

16. Use an item format which lists alternatives on separate lines, under one another, to make them easy to read and compare.

Of the objective test item types, only the short answer type requires the student to supply, rather than select, the answer. Its make-up is similar to a well-stated multiple-choice item, without the alternatives. It consists of a question or incomplete statement to which the student responds by providing the appropriate words, numbers, or symbols. Since it is difficult to write items which elicit only one response, short answer items are reserved for situations in which recall of information or computational skills are required.

The following rules apply to constructing short answer test items:

1. State the item so that only a single, brief answer is possible. This is the major difficulty in writing short answer items. For example, the item:

   a. What are the incorrect responses in a multiple-choice item called?

   is constructed to elicit the response, "distractors," but equally defensible responses might be "foils," "incorrect alternatives," etc. If the question is not specific enough, be prepared to give credit for other likely responses.

2. Start with a direct question when writing an item. Use incomplete statements only when they are clearly better alternatives. Normally, direct questions will increase the probability that students will respond with the single best answer.

3. The student should only have to supply key words which relate to the main point of the statement or question. Students should not be expected to supply "the" or "an."

4. Place the blanks at the end of the statement.

5. Avoid extraneous clues to the answer. The length of the blank or the articles "a" or "an" may provide clues to correct responses.

6. For numerical answers, indicate the degree of precision

expected and the units in which responses are to be expressed.

Scoring objective tests can be done by hand. However, machine scoring programs provide statistics and item analyses which are helpful in evaluating individual test items. A good technique is to store objective test items on individual cards with item difficulty and item discrimination scores noted on the card. The cards can then be filed by objective to develop an item pool for testing purposes.

Affective instruments. The affective domain is a difficult area to evaluate, since it is hard to specify objectives in clear, behavioral terms. Nonetheless, since all learning involves affective components, it is important to provide for them in an evaluation plan.

Either essay or objective test formats may be used in this area; however, since feelings and attitudes may vary in their intensity, it is important that objective formats allow some provision for flexible responses.

The most common pattern is to request that the student indicate a response on a bipolar scale such as most like me/least like me or agree/disagree. Normally a scale of 1 to 5 or 1 to 7 is used. Longer scales tend to be unreliable while shorter scales do not discriminate sufficiently between levels of response.

A common objective item format would be:

	agree			disagree	
1. I enjoy school.	1	2	3	4	5

while an essay or interview format would ask the open-ended question:

1. What is it that you do or do not enjoy about school?

In either case, it is important to assure students that their responses will not be graded and that they will not be penalized for their responses.

From measuring student affect to rating teacher effectiveness, evaluation plays an important role in the instructional system.

By providing information to the teacher and the students, it keeps the system dynamic. It allows for change, adjustment, and improvement. Evaluative data certifies the success of the instructional system, or if there is failure, suggests what can be done next. Students can adjust their study time and habits; instructors can use more visuals or restructure their lecture notes. With continual feedback, each can make successive approximations to their common goal.

Chapter 7

ENVIRONMENT

Increasingly, high school students are finding that they have a choice of not only whether they will go to college, but which one they will attend. By taking any one of the national scholarship tests, students will receive a number of brochures describing college programs, as institutions use mailing lists and other mass media to recruit students in an ever tightening enrollment market. Many students who take the choice seriously spend hours pouring over college bulletins, talking to teachers and advisors, questioning students who have graduated before them, and even visiting campuses in an effort to decide which school they will attend.

The concerns of prospective students may include the school's academic standards, intellectual climate, national prestige, programs and course offerings, and campus social life. These characteristics of the college are evaluated against the student's goals, values, and self-expectations. By the time students make their choice and arrive for the first day of class, they have a more or less accurate, very detailed image of what the college is like and how they will fit in. What entering freshpeople do informally and intuitively is what researchers and theoreticians on college environment do in a more formal way: identify and describe college characteristics and assess their impact on students.

The great psychologist Kurt Lewin (1951) contended that human behavior is a function of two elements: the person and the environment. That is, a person's traits, values, and preferences along with the characteristics of a particular situation will influence the person's behavior. This position implies that if one is going to influence the behavior of others, it is necessary to describe, identify, and influence the relationship between the person and the environment.

Higher learning is a particular set of behaviors, people, and situations. In order to foster learning (the intended behavior of higher education), the instructor must be able to assess the characteristics of the student and accommodate them in the classroom environment. The current chapter is a continuation of this discussion. Characteristics of the individual student which are likely to influence scholastic behavior are covered in Chapter 5. The intended outcomes or behaviors were addressed in Chapter 3. Three critical aspects of the student's instructional environment, the teacher, the media, and evaluation, were covered in Chapters 2, 4, and 6, respectively.

The present chapter, on Environment, addresses the remaining elements of the student's ecology. Aspects of the campus milieu, the student's social or peer group, and the socio-psychological and physical features of the classroom all influence learning. Some of these environmental characteristics, like some student characteristics, are extremely difficult to change; others are more susceptible to instructor influence. But whether a feature of the environment is a "given" or can be manipulated by the professor, knowledge of this element and its relationship to other elements in the instructional system provides a critical context for learning activities.

The Campus Environment

Colleges have been traditionally defined in a variety of ways. Recruitment brochures are likely to describe their institutions in terms of curricular organization (university, liberal arts college, technical school, etc.), the type of control (public, private, denominational), the geographic region (Northeast, Pacific, etc.), and the homogeneity of the students (coeducational, women's college, etc.). Demographic information such as the size of enrollment, library resources, and faculty-student ratio is also likely to be presented. Although these features are reliable ways to describe and distinguish institutions, these broad descriptors frequently obscure critical differences between colleges which may fall within the same category. Nor is there any compelling reason to believe that these aspects of the campus environment affect student behavior in any direct way. Rather, it is more likely that a campus climate or milieu created by these and other variables does influence students.

George Stern (1970), as the Head of Evaluation Service of the Psychological Research Center at Syracuse University, was the principal proponent and contributor of a "need-press" model of the college environment. His position corresponds to Lewin's in the contention that behavior is an outcome of the relationship between the person and the environment. Aspects of the person are represented by what Stern calls "needs," tendencies that seem to give unity and direction to a person's behavior. Aspects of the environment are represented by the concept of "press," characteristic demands or features of the environment as perceived by those living in it. Needs and press are complementary constructs, represented operationally in common conceptual terms; so that a need for achievement may correspond to a press for achievements. Needs are measured by a device constructed by Stern; this Activities Index (AI) is an instrument of 300 items charting a respondent's personal behavioral preferences. Imbedded within it are thirty scales which range from Abasement to Understanding. They include such traits as Achievement, Affiliation, Aggression, Change, Impulsiveness, and Reflectiveness.

Environmental press is measured by another instrument called the College Characteristics Index (CCI), 300 items which ask the respondent about certain events or activities that occur on campus. The assumption behind this instrument is that consensual or aggregated perceptions of occurrences in the environment are a meaningful estimate of its press. The CCI is composed of thirty scales, each corresponding to the analogous need scale of the AI. Thus, both the person's need and environmental press can be measured in commensurate terms. For example, a need for achievement can be inferred from the response of a person who enjoys taking tests, competing for prizes, competitive sports, and setting high personal standards. A press for achievement is reflected by such things as honors programs and high academic standards.

Stern contends that congruency between a student's need and press would influence such things as academic achievement, satisfaction, attrition, and stability. That is, the greater the extent to which a student's goals, preferences, and expectations fit the demands and expectations prevalent in the environment, the more the student will succeed in college and the more he will enjoy it. However, the evidence from the research to date tends not to support Stern's position. In fact, some evidence indicates more achievement from students with low congruency between needs and press.

There are several problems with this approach to college environment. First, there seems to be a very low statistical correspondence between analogous scales in the AI and the CCI, contrary to the developer's intentions. Secondly, the direction of discongruency, not merely degree of congruency, may influence achievement. That is, if the student's needs for dominance, for example, were *greater* than the press for dominance, the impact on the student's behavior would be different than if the need were *less* than the press. Furthermore, while needs and press are represented by thirty scales, student behavior is inadequately expressed by one or two measurements, such as academic achievement. While one could expect that high congruency between need and press for *achievement* would influence the student's *achievement*, one would hardly expect congruency on other scales, such as Aggression or Impulsiveness, to influence achievement.

A co-worker of Stern's, C. Robert Pace (1969) from the University of California at Los Angeles, abandoned the need-press model and developed the more empirically based College and University Environment Scale (CUES). This carefully standardized 150-item instrument measures five factors of the campus environment: Scholarship, Awareness, Community, Propriety, and Practicality.

Briefly summarizing these categories: Scholarship relates to the intellectual and scholastic discipline and achievement of the college; Awareness refers to concern about social and political problems, expressiveness through the arts, and tolerance of criticism; Community pertains to the friendly, cohesive, and group-oriented aspects of the campus; Propriety relates to a climate that is proper, mannerly, and conventional; and, finally, Practicality characterizes an environment that emphasizes vocational interests, enterprise, organization, and social activities.

Pace used the five scales of the CUES to identify eight types of campus environment, each with a characteristic profile, or pattern, across these scales. These categories and their corresponding characteristics begin to give a sense of what it is like to live and study at these schools. Both selective universities and selective liberal arts colleges, for example, tend to emphasize Awareness and Scholarship; the latter group of schools also tends to rate high on Community and Propriety scales. General universities, state colleges and other universities, and teacher's colleges all emphasize Practicality, with teacher's colleges stressing Propriety, and general universities emphasizing Awareness as well. Denominational liberal arts schools are typified by a climate of Propriety and Community, while general liberal arts schools also emphasize these qualities, though to a lesser degree. Finally, colleges of engineering and science seem to singularly stress Scholarship, while scoring very low on Awareness and Community.

Educational Testing Service's John Centra and his colleague Donald Rock (1971) used an instrument similar to CUES to answer the critical research question: To what extent are excellent graduates due to the excellence of the institution? After controlling for the proportion of the students' scores on the Graduate Record Exam that could be predicted from their entering Scholastic Aptitude Test Scores, these researchers found a number of college characteristics which could distinguish between groups of high achieving schools and low achieving ones. Centra and Rock found that: (1) ratings of faculty-student interaction positively correlated to achievement on the GRE Humanities and Natural Science tests; (2) curriculum flexibility was positively related to achievement on the Natural Science and Social Science tests; (3) students at schools with high scores on cultural facilities overachieved on Humanities but underachieved on the Natural Science test; and (4) challenging schools produced students who scored high in Humanities.

The implications of the work on campus environments for the classroom instructor have been obscured by the fact that most professors are helpless to change the college milieu. The college environment, like the mission of the institution, is essentially a *given*. However, knowledge of prevalent characteristics of the college can aid the instructor in formulating expectations about the outcomes of the instructional process. Some of the characteristics of the environment, especially faculty-student interaction, academic challenge, and others cited as important by Centra and Rock, are within the professor's domain and may be altered to influence student learning.

The Peer Group Environment

Stanford's Lewis Mayhew (1966) assesses the college environment by the extent to which it conforms to the ideal of an institution of higher education. Mayhew epitomizes the ideal college as one where ideas are important in and of themselves, leisure is enjoyed and respected, and academic work is viewed as essential rather than a tedious means to some pragmatic end. People are encouraged to accept the uncertainties of not knowing how things will come out, intellectual and creative effort is valued for itself, both cognition and affection are viewed as valuable forces, and finally, people's lives are changed.

Mayhew provides a set of guidelines for creating an environment conducive to the attainment of the above attributes: (1) the curriculum, the extracurriculum, and the interaction with faculty should be on a sufficiently limited scale that the educational impact can be realized; (2) an ethos, philosophy, or theory which assigns meaning and establishes priorities for educational activities should be provided; (3) the institution should make clear and explicit its expectations for students; and (4) the institution should recognize and support the existence of several student subcultures on campus. This ideal educational community centers around a student peer group which is conducive to learning.

Theodore Newcomb (1962) of the University of Michigan, reiterates the importance of student peer groups, rating them second only to the characteristics of the individual student in impact on learning. Newcomb indicates that the influences of these groups are moderated by several conditions. The effect of group size on the strength of interpersonal relationships will in turn affect the impact of the group on the individual. Smaller peer groups will have a greater impact on their members. The homogeneity of the group in age, sex, social class, and attitudes and the extent to which it is isolated from groups having divergent norms will also moderate the group's influence. Fraternities and sororities which create homogeneous environments by selecting for religion, social values, and scholastic achievement have strong influences on their members.

Rather than have such energies dissipated through mainly social organizations, Newcomb suggests ways to focus the impact of student peer groups on intellectual concerns. He recommends the establishment of formal membership groups of moderate size and relative homogeneity. These membership groups should overlap with the student's living arrangements to maximize opportunities for interpersonal interaction. And, most importantly, faculty members must be included in this environment, either as members of the group, as members of the residence, or both. Such an arrangement will increase the extent to which students discover that ideas stemming from faculty contact are worth further exploration with each other.

Newcomb's work is frequently cited by institutions which are trying to harness student peer group influence for educational purposes through a live-and-learn environment. This approach is a particularly attractive alternative for large institutions which otherwise provide a relatively impersonal, competitive, and confusing college experience.

One experiment using this approach, called the Residential College, was conducted at Newcomb's home institution, the University of Michigan. A dormitory was set aside as a living-learning environment with a student body limited to 800. Although the Residential College shares the objectives of its larger parent college, it has its own curriculum of studies emphasizing the Humanities and Social Sciences. Since it is both a residential and academic community, students and faculty collaborate on all matters of policy, including curriculum. The experiment is an attempt to provide the interpersonal atmosphere of a small college within the setting of a major university.

Lacy (1975) evaluated the Residential College by comparing attitudinal and personality measures of its students with those students who applied to the college but were rejected because of space limitations, and therefore went to the parent college. He found that toward the end of the first year in school, the Residential College students reported more satisfaction with faculty and peers, and described their environment as warmer and more supportive than did the control group. More importantly, this environment with more peer and faculty interactions resulted in greater gains on personality scales of Liberalism, Social Conscience, Cultural Sophistication, Thinking, Introversion, and Autonomy.

However, the encouraging results of this and other studies of residential colleges are difficult to act on in view of some recent trends in higher education. In recent years a higher percentage of the total number of college students has been attending junior colleges and large urban universities which have few or no residential facilities. Coupled with attempts to cater to the adult learner who requires flexible scheduling of instruction, these large universities tend to automate instruction. Since neither of these environments promotes the establishment of student interpersonal relationships, this trend can result in a phenomenon known as the "lonely learner."

Nevertheless, several strategies exist for establishing educationally conducive peer groups within these settings. One approach is to provide a number of small commuter centers where students can go to drink coffee and interact with each other and with faculty members. Another approach is to create a number of faculty-sponsored thematic organizations, such as a physics club or a wilderness club. Such centers and organizations could provide impetus for small groups, supporting members with academic and personal concerns.

The Classroom Environment

The "environment" over which the instructor has the most control is the classroom environment. The social features of the classroom environment such as interpersonal influence, group norms, and intra-group communication, along with physical features such as furniture arrangement and interior design, can influence various aspects of student behavior.

Richard Schmuck (1971) of the University of Oregon identifies aspects of the classroom climate which can have an important impact on students: (1) the manner in which power and interpersonal influence are exerted in the classroom; (2) friendship patterns among students; (3) the norms of the group in relation to educational goals; (4) communication patterns among students; (5) the cohesiveness of the classroom group; and finally (6) the stage of development of the group.

Schmuck presents a particular arrangement of these features which he feels would result in positive affect among students. "...a positive classroom climate is one in which the students share high amounts of potential influence—both with one another and with the teacher; where high levels of attraction exist for the group as a whole and between classmates; where norms are supportive for getting academic work done, as well as for maximizing individual differences; where communication is open and featured by dialogue; and where the processes of working and developing together as a group are considered relevant in themselves for study." (p. 18)

Although the open, unstructured, and egalitarian environment described by Schmuck may sound ideal to many instructors, it is important to note that it is not the best environment for all students. Studies by Dowaliby and Schumer (1973) and Domino (1974) report that while students low in anxiety excel in student-centered instruction, students high in anxiety do better with teacher-centered instruction. Domino (1971) also found that whereas independent students performed well in unstructured situations, conforming students were superior in structured situations.

The instructor may want to take the students' preferences for these and other types of classroom environment into account when planning a course. Table 7.1 provides an instrument describing six types of environments an instructor may want to consider.

David Ausubel (1968) has also focused on the group as the principal feature of the classroom environment, and in his review examines the impact of the group on cognitive learning. The impact of the group on learning is a confluence of the nature

Table 7.1. Styles of Educational Environment.

Using 1 as the environment which you prefer *most* and 6 as the environment you prefer *least*, please rank the following descriptions of educational environments.

	Teacher-oriented environments: classroom setting; seats facing toward the front; teacher located behind or beside a table or lectern; seats may be permanently situated, with small arm tables.
	Automated environments: use of instructional technologies; audio-tutorial instruction; programmed instruction; computer-assisted instruction; educational television, and so forth.
	Interaction-oriented environments: seminar settings; students and teacher face each other; circular arrangements of chairs or chairs located around table; informal setting; comfortable chairs; large, open, multi-use space in a colleagueal setting.
	Student-oriented environments: independent studies; contract learning; student works on his own in a college or university; students makes use of library, laboratory, museum, private room, lounge, and so forth.
	Sheltered experience-oriented environments: creation of simulated experiences such as games, role plays, and instructional simulations; laboratory experiences; apprenticeships- practicum experiences; workshops.
	Experience-oriented environments: field experiences; on-the-job experience; work-study programs; internships; academic credit for life experiences.

of the task, the amount of interaction among members, the size and nature of the group, and whether the measured outcome is a group product or an individual one. Reviewing the relevant research in light of the above considerations, Ausubel came to these conclusions:

For simple tasks, done either with the group or in the presence of the group, the rate of learning is increased. This effect is apparently related to pacing or competition. On the other hand, complex problem-solving tends to take longer in a group. Furthermore, the individual products of problem-solving in a group tend to be no better than if done individually. This effect is moderated by ability; students with low ability will benefit from the tutoring of the group, which will be reflected in their individual product.

A group product of problem-solving is likely to be better than the mean of individual products, due to the pooling of ideas. Evaluations made by a group are likely to be better than those made by individuals; but convergent tasks which require concentration and attention to detail are likely to be better if done individually.

Group size seems to be important only to the extent that students benefit from personal involvement in the task. Larger groups reduce the opportunity for some individuals to participate since the more aggressive members dominate the group.

A review by N.L. Gage and David Berliner (1975) reiterates these findings; while citing the inconsistent nature of the relationship between class size and achievement, they note the impressive impact of class size on the teacher's choice of instructional method. Not surprisingly, single students receive tutoring, programmed instruction, and independent study. Students in groups of 2-20 are predominantly taught through discussion. Groups of 20-40 provide an option for a variety of interpersonal and audiovisual approaches, while groups of 40 or more are typically taught by lecture. This is not to say that the correspondence between class size and method should exist, only that there is an empirical basis for this common belief.

Physical as well as social features of the classroom environment influence learning. However, it seems that features of the physical environment have only a second-order effect. Clifford Drew (1971) reviewed studies which examined such physical characteristics as room color, symmetry, furniture arrangement, and degree of privacy, some of which did make a slight difference in learning. Drew noted, however, that the behavior is probably determined more by the characteristics of the people than by the characteristics of the room.

However, one strong pattern did emerge from his review. If the instructor wants to encourage creative behavior among students, an ideal physical environment seems to be one of subdued colors, with a complex-asymmetrical interior design which is private and secluded, and which has an intimate furniture arrangement that maximizes face-to-face contact. Aside from this unique situation, and short of extremes in temperature, crowding and the like, characteristics of the physical environment seem to be much less important than other elements in the instructional system.

The Faculty Environment

Another facet of the college environment is that created by a professor's colleagues. College instructors have values, traits, and preferences which affect their transactions with each other. Predominant patterns of these characteristics are likely to be reflected in measures of the larger campus environment, since institutions with certain prevailing dispositions are likely to attract and select like-minded faculty. The effect of some features of the faculty environment can closely parallel the effect of the student peer group as described by Newcomb (1962). This is especially true at the department level where the instructor must interact with her colleagues on issues of research and teaching. The lack of a formal organizational structure in college departments leaves more latitude for interpersonal influence. Group norms regarding the tolerance of deviation and the desirability of change, for example, can set a tone which facilitates or interferes with interests of the individual faculty member.

More specific attitudes concerning the nature and importance of teaching are likely to influence an instructor's behavior in this area. These norms are reflected in the reward structure, the nature and extent of communication about teaching, and the existence or lack of support for instructional projects. A department which adequately rewards effective teaching, encourages discussions and seminars on this topic, and supports fledgling efforts at improvement is likely to move its members to value good teaching. A department which ignores or deprecates teaching is likely to extinguish a concern for good teaching or push it underground.

Stanford Ericksen (1976) of the Center for Research on Learning and Teaching at the University of Michigan, contends that a particularly good way for an institution to provide support for teaching is to establish a separate Center for Teaching. Although the range and domain of such a center would vary from institution to institution, Ericksen identifies three functions which would help to create a faculty environment conducive to good teaching.

One of these functions is the dissemination of information. Through newsletters, the center can report on noteworthy instructional efforts on campus, confirming that faculty colleagues are concerned with teaching and doing something to improve it. Such a newsletter could also provide instructors with general information about learning theory and instructional methods and technologies.

Beyond giving "background" information, a center could provide specific advice to an instructor based on a discussion and assessment of her specific instructional problems and concerns. Specific advice might also be disseminated through workshops or seminars. Workshops could provide instructors with specific skills and knowledge needed to implement new ideas in the classroom, while seminars would give faculty members a forum to discuss issues of learning and teaching seldom raised at department staff meetings. Such a supportive milieu could result in changes in values as well as behavior.

Finally, the relatively affluent centers might provide financial support to some instructors who need seed money to try out new ways of teaching, or serve as granting agencies for institutional funds. Given in the form of small grants, this money could go for materials, technical assistance, and production which might not otherwise be available.

The availability of teaching centers and their resources is one way that an institution can demonstrate its concern for good teaching and create a supportive faculty environment. The value of teaching stressed by the department, and the value of learning stressed by the instructor and the student's peer group is the environment of the instructional system. The extent to which this environment supports teaching and learning will largely determine the extent to which the instructor's goals are accomplished.

Chapter 8

IMPLEMENTATION

Professors may sometimes feel that the role of an instructor is minimal. They may believe that the intelligence and motivations of their college students will outweigh any of the subtler aspects of teaching. A semester may seem far too short to root out any student weaknesses resulting from twelve years of prior schooling. They may feel that the financial and logistic difficulties of using media or creating new materials will not be justified by the resultant learning and the positive regard of their students and colleagues. Research indicates that in many situations their choice of one medium or strategy instead of another will not make a difference. In short, there are instructors convinced that they have no degree of freedom, that the situation is overdetermined, and that what they do instructionally will not make a difference. They are satisfied to study and contribute to the knowledge in their field and present this scholarship to their students in a way that will not impede learning, nor elicit a distaste for the subject matter.

While there are a considerable number of constraints and "givens" in the instructional system, the instructor's role is not trivial. The classroom that the instructor walks into on the first day of the term does not predetermine the events that will transpire there; it is not a fixed setting in the way that a basketball court or a restaurant is. A variety of experiences can occur in the classroom. And although students come to class with their own abilities, needs, and preferences, they can still be informed, excited, directed, and inspired by the teacher. Finally, the fact that some media are equivalent for certain situations is as much an asset as a liability. The ability to use demonstration, *or* film, *or* television gives the instructor options which he can exercise according to his own preferences and judgment.

While the content expertise of the instructor is a critical prerequisite for teaching, several important instructional decisions remain which can make a difference in student learning and affect. The balance of this chapter will provide the instructor with ways of implementing the ideas presented in the previous chapters to accomplish this goal. Two alternative models will be described; because these models are more ideal than practical, the chapter will conclude with a set of recommendations which can serve as the "next-best-thing."

The Congruency Model

The previous chapters have identified a number of approaches for describing and analyzing the instructional system. The recurrent and explicit heuristic of these chapters has been that the instructor should seek the proper mix of content, medium, student, evaluation, environment, and teacher. One way to approach this problem might be to assess the situation as it currently stands and try to discern a pattern. As a pattern emerges the instructor may seek to make decisions which refine it and make it more congruous. Those elements which are dissonant could be changed and modified to fit the pattern more consistently.

Three principal patterns are suggested from the foregoing chapters and the work of Chickering (1976), and Bergquist and Phillips (1975): The content-centered situation, the teacher-centered situation, and the student-centered situation.

It is important to qualify these categories by saying they have not been empirically derived nor validated, although they could be. Rather, they are an attempt to fit together some of the independently constructed ideas of the previous chapters in a logical way. Because they have not been validated, nor their impact on learning examined, they should be applied with due caution.

1. Content-centered instructional situations.
The primary feature of this pattern is a predominant concern

for covering the material of the course or discipline in a systematic way. There is structure both in what is to be learned and how it is to be taught.

The instructor in this pattern sees herself as an expert and a formal authority. She is characterized by her deference to her discipline or profession. She teaches what she knows. The field-independent cognitive style fits this pattern—analytical and directive. Teaching behaviors would include: specifying that which is important to learn, providing step-by-step instructions, giving complete and definitive answers to student questions, and making well-organized presentations. In essence, the teacher provides information and certifies that students have learned it.

Subject matter is the accented element in this pattern. It could include a course in the humanities which gives primary concern to "the great works," or a course in the social sciences which stresses familiarity of theories and principles. But this pattern is likely to be predominant in disciplines with a heavy technical or vocational content, such as physics, pre-medicine, and engineering. The skills taught in these courses are in the cognitive domain, ranging from knowledge to application. Psychomotor skills, such as laboratory techniques and equipment operation, also fall into this pattern.

The media in these courses are either one-way or self-instructional, both being highly structured and managed by the instructor. Lectures, books, films, and video presentations predominate. Audio-tutorial and programmed instruction are the most appropriate self-instructional modes.

The primary motive of students in content-centered courses is vocational. They want to acquire skills needed to fill their roles in society. They are also concerned with recognition, social acceptance, and impressing others. Compliant students—those who are task oriented, and want to do what is expected—as well as anxious, dependent students will prefer these courses. Field-independent students tend to select more technical courses; and although these students want the course goals specified, they may not care for structure otherwise, preferring instead to achieve these objectives in their own ways.

Evaluation in these courses tends to take the form of objective exams. The function of evaluation is to certify that the students have learned, and this is determined by the teacher.

The environment can be of two kinds. One is teacher-oriented, with fixed seats facing toward the front and the teacher behind the desk or lectern. The other is automated, using such arrangements as programmed instruction, computer-assisted instruction, or audio-tutorial instruction.

2. Teacher-centered instructional situations.

The concern in this pattern is on intellectual growth as exemplified by the professor. *What* the students are to learn is predetermined, but not *how* it is to be learned.

The teacher is the accented element in this pattern. He is the model of the way to approach the discipline, the profession, and the intellectual process. He is a socializing agent for the intellectual and professional community. He teaches what he is, for he is overtly involved in role modeling the educated person.

The subject matter is both cognitive and affective. Since the source of knowledge is personal inquiry, the cognitive skills emphasized are analysis, snythesis, and evaluation. Affectively, the students must acquire the tastes, the values, and the habits of the professor. And although the teacher of any discipline could be the role model for his profession, the area most appropriate for this pattern is the humanities, with the professor as the personification of culture and intellect.

Media in the teacher-centered pattern can be either one-way or two-way, depending on the instructor's style. The class may be treated to rather eloquent lectures and demonstrations, or involved in teacher-led discussions.

The students who prefer this style may be dependent, participative, or compliant. Field-dependent students will enjoy the personal contact inherent in this pattern but dislike the lack of direction and structure. Field-independent students will favor the freedom of inquiry.

Evaluation in a teacher-centered class is done by the teacher. The product tends to be an essay exam or a written report which is subjectively graded.

The classroom environment is focused on the teacher, but with interpersonal or participative overtones.

3. The student-centered instructional situation.

This pattern also stresses intellectual training but is primarily concerned with the personal and emotional growth of the student. The structure of the course is aimed at facilitating the student's independence.

The instructor's role in this pattern is that of guide and group leader. The students determine their own directions; the instructor helps them get there. In this role he poses key questions, presents dilemmas and paradoxes, and fosters insight. He is likely to be field-dependent, with a concern for the social context and a democratic classroom orientation.

The subject matter is both cognitive and affective. The principal stress is on personal growth—coming to know oneself and others. Cognitive skills are synthesis and evaluation. Courses in the social sciences are heavily laden with this interpersonal content.

The media in this situation are predominantly two-way or self-instructional. Role plays, simulations, contract learning, and independent study are used extensively. Self-instructional modes allow a great deal of student input, but learning contracts are more appropriate than heavily-managed, impersonal systems like programmed instruction.

The learner's role in this pattern is central. What is learned in this situation is greatly determined by the learner. The students tend to be collaborative, or independent, to use Grasha's terms. Witkin's field-dependent learners fit best in this group. They enjoy the personal determination of goals, the interpersonal interaction, but prefer the instructor's guidance.

Although little evaluation typically occurs in these courses, formative evaluation would serve well the purpose of this pattern. Personal assessment as well as subjective evaluations by teachers and peers would provide feedback necessary for student growth.

Finally, the environment in a student-centered classroom is highly interactive. Small classrooms with flexible seating are ideal.

A course may fall within one of these three patterns. To make the course more congruent, a teacher may adjust the media, the evaluation, or the content to fit the predominant pattern more closely. However, some adjustments are easier to make than others. Media and evaluation are relatively simple to change. Subject matter can be changed within some limits. And although changes in the students or the instructor border on psychotherapy and go beyond the domain of this book, less dramatic changes, such as the acquisition of new skills, are feasible.

For example, a professor teaching the concept of motivation in an introductory psychology course may find that most of her twenty-five students are field-dependent, participative, and collaborative—a prototypic student-centered class. However, her preference in the past has been to give lectures and objective examinations. The instructor could make this situation more congruent by employing discussions and role plays, and by using essays or other more subjective evaluations. If she and/or a subgroup of her students are more inclined toward a content-centered approach, some balance could be struck between the two patterns.

The three patterns described above need not be stable over an entire term. An introductory sociology course may move from content-centered theory to interpersonal application. A physics course may move from a focus on current research, with the teacher as scientist, to an emphasis on principles. And an English literature course may move from concentration on Shakespeare's works, through the professor as literary critic, to personal meaning. The instructor who is aware of these potential movements can adjust his teaching accordingly.

The Decision-Making Model

A second approach to improving instruction is derived from some of the literature on instructional design and problem-solving (Gagne and Briggs, 1974; Gerlach and Ely, 1971; Schmuck, Chesler, and Lippitt 1966; Banathy, 1968; and Shavelson, 1976). This is a decision-making model, which identifies the number and sequence of the instructor's decisions, the information needed to make them, and their implications.

This model describes a process which begins some weeks before the start of the term, and continues through the end of the semester and into the next. The instructor sits down with her books and information collected from students during previous terms. Based on these data she plans or designs her course. The course is implemented and additional information gained. The instructor analyzes these new data, makes adjustments, and so on.

The decision-making process can be divided into these four stages: specification of desired outcomes, assessment of givens, selection and design, and implementation and evaluation of outcomes. This model lacks thorough validation although some support may be taken from the large number of authors who have proposed comparable schemes.

1. Specify desired outcomes.

The instructor uses his content expertise to select what the students should learn. This decision could be based on a variety of factors such as the goals of the institution, and the logical and psychological structure of the discipline.

Some of the authors using this paradigm include a prior step called "needs assessment." This method involves collecting information about what skills or capabilities are expected of students who take the course, from colleagues teaching subsequent courses in the sequence, students in the program, accrediting and professional agencies, students' employers, and so on.

Based on this and other data, the instructor plans the curriculum of the course. It could emphasize career, personal, or intellectual development. It could represent objectives from cognitive, psychomotor, and affective domains, and from each level within the domains.

Most authors in this area strongly suggest that the objectives be specified in precise terms. The objectives should have some behavioral component which states what the students should be able to do; they should specify the conditions which accompany the performance, and the criteria for determining their accomplishment.

2. Assess givens.

The instructor next determines constraints or relatively unchangeable elements of the system.

He could begin by collecting data on his students. Although a plethora of questionnaires and other instruments exist, the simple forms in this book should be useful. They will give the instructor information on the students' motivations, and learning and cognitive styles. Giving pretests, such as a version of the final exam, is a helpful way to determine students' cognitive strengths and weaknesses. Both course content and mode of presentation should reflect these data.

A review of the content specified in step one and modified by the amount students already know, can be used to make media decisions. The pertinent stimulus characteristics of the subject matter, such as its visual or audio features, as well as the nature of the students' tasks, such as making visual discriminations or applying principles, can lead to selecting film over lecture, role play over discussion.

A final constraint is the instructional resources available to the teacher. The lack of equipment and funds for the development of materials obviously limits the number of options open to the instructor. An assessment of equipment, materials, and services available will provide the instructor with his maximum number of options. Knowledge of the operation, appropriate uses, and advantages and disadvantages of available media increases the chance that the instructor will apply them fruitfully in the classroom.

3. Select and design instruction.

The instructor next selects the medium and designs the instructional material. Much has already been discussed about the selection of media, but to briefly recapitulate: media should be based on the features of the object to be studied, the task to be performed, the characteristics of the students, the skills of the instructor, and the resources available.

The question asked during the selection process is not "What is the best medium to use?" but "What will work best given the situation?" Frequently, several comparable media will do the job; selection beyond this point can be based on personal preference or logistical convenience.

In addition to presentation of information, the instructor should design for other instructional events, such as providing feedback and assuring retention. These other features of instruction will require the teacher to write study guides, practice tests, worksheets, or homework problems. Although more and more commercially available materials are based on instructionally sound principles, still the college teacher frequently has to design her own instruction, whether a lecture or a slide-tape presentation.

4. Implement and evaluate.

The design process does not end once class begins. Although textbooks are ordered, syllabi handed out, slides developed, and lecture notes prepared, these all represent the instructor's best guess of what will work. The course plan does not come with a guarantee. Information should be continually collected as to the accuracy of the guess—is it really working?

This formative evaluation requires that adequate preparations be made to collect information. Questionnaires on student preference and style can reaffirm that this year's students are basically like last year's. Worksheets and exams can indicate that, indeed, students are learning. Student rating forms can confirm that they enjoy the class and find it worthwhile.

If all did not go well, modifications may need to be made within the term. But to make adjustments, detailed information is necessary. It does not help much to know only that the original plan failed. Detailed or open-ended questions, critique sessions, or informal discussions with students can provide information as to what changes can be made.

An instructor who applies this model to a particular lesson would begin by specifying his objectives. A professor of business administration, for example, may be teaching a course on the management of small groups. His objective for the week is to enable the students to identify deviant behavior, and apply group theory to the control of deviance. Upon examining his twenty-five graduate students, he may find that they cluster into two large groups. One group is participative, collaborative, and field-dependent; the other group is competitive and field-independent. All of the students are very able; many have social science backgrounds and are already familiar with small group theory. He has a small but adequately equipped classroom with access to a variety of media equipment and computer software. The instructor himself is field-independent and prefers a teacher-centered course. He has had fifteen years of experience in management consulting and is an established expert in his field. He feels this background qualifies him as a model for his students to emulate.

Given this situation, the instructor decides to assign readings on small group theory, allowing those already familiar with the content the option of foregoing this preparation. A study guide is supplied, enabling the students that prefer more structure to take advantage of the explicitly-stated objectives and questions. Upon completion of the readings the class is shown a filmed series of vignettes depicting various types of deviant behavior in small groups, with commentary from the instructor. Half-way through the film he begins asking for student comments. For the following class period he arranges with several students to conduct a role play demonstration in which he models ways to handle deviant behavior. He completes the lesson by assigning a brief case study in which the students apply the knowledge they have gained.

The results of the case study, the observation of student in-class responses, and mid-course student ratings indicate the instructor's effectiveness and suggest modifications for future, similar situations.

This four step decision-making model is cyclical, iterative, and self-correcting. The last step leads into the first as course goals and media selections are adjusted to reflect refinements in the instructor's thinking. More information leads to better guesses as successive approximations are made toward more effective instruction.

Next Best Things

The congruency and decision-making models are two of the ways that a teacher can approach instructional decisions in a systematic way. Although each model has some benefits, each also presents problems. First, each is likely to require a whole new orientation toward teaching—a change not made easily or quickly. Secondly, the instructor is likely to be skeptical—with good reason, given the track record of most instructional innovations. Finally, each will require time, cost, and energy.

For these reasons, this chapter and section closes with a number of suggestions and recommendations, which are in keeping with the spirit of the instructional paradigm proposed, but which can be implemented with less cost. In this sense they represent a partial trial of the paradigm. The instructor can test its fit and effectiveness before applying the whole model.

Since these recommendations are meant to be minor departures from the way an instructor is currently teaching a course, they will begin with rather simple suggestions and move through successive approximations toward full implementation. If one of the recommendations is tried and proves useful, the instructor can move to the next more complicated, costly, and hopefully more rewarding level.

1. The instructor should teach to the "average" student. A time honored approach to accommodating student needs is to aim an instructional presentation at the abilities and knowledge of a large cluster of students who fall in the middle of the continuum. The teacher's hope is that the instruction will accommodate most of the students in the class and that the students who need extra help or additional challenges will see her after class. The greatest danger is that the instructor may base the assessment of the class average on subjective impressions. An error in judgment can result in missing the mark altogether. Assessment of student entering behaviors or preferences in teaching style must be based on data. Information such as previous courses taken, achievement test scores, and so on, are better than nothing. The best plan would be for the teacher to collect specific, detailed data from her students using entry quizzes and questionnaires.

2. The instructor should use a variety of media. When it is unclear which approach will work for most students, a "shotgun approach" will do. The selection of two or three media or methods which seem appropriate will give the instructor some added assurances in situations of otherwise low confidence. A lecture giving an overview of the detailed information in the text, augmented by a film, may accommodate most students.

3. The instructor should conduct formative evaluations and stay flexible. Because the instructor is aiming for some hypothetical "average student" he will be wrong on occasion. Periodic formative evaluation will keep a minor error in judgment from becoming a catastrophe. If part way through the course, students can identi-

fy and describe sociological principles but cannot relate them to their personal lives, the instructor may decide to conduct a simulation that was otherwise unscheduled. Waiting until the end of the year to discover this problem would have been too late.

4. The teacher should get to know the content better. The primary responsibility of all college teachers is, of course, to know their discipline. This is a fundamental prerequisite for all scholarly activity. But beyond this basic responsibility there are things that an instructor can do to make this knowledge more consumable by students. Organizing a complex and elaborate body of information into a clear and easily followed presentation is an important task. Taking the logical or psychological perspectives of Bruner or Gagne as suggested in Chapter 3 are two of the ways to do this. Defining the discipline as a specific set of terms, concepts, and relationships to be described, demonstrated, and applied is another approach. Sharing this organization with students can provide meaning and structure to their learning.

5. The teacher should get to know himself better. Many instructors teach the way they do because they have always done it that way. They have not examined their assumptions about teaching. A personal assessment of these underlying assumptions can lead to insights useful in making subsequent instructional decisions.

An instructor can learn more about himself as a teacher by various means. He can talk to other professors about teaching. He can find out their opinions about students, media, and teaching in general, and compare his opinions to theirs. Interaction with fellow teachers may even extend to the classroom: an instructor can invite a trusted colleague to visit his class and discuss his teaching approach. More private ways of self-assessment include self-analysis questionnaires of the type included in Bergquist's and Phillip's *Handbook* (1975).

Students are also great sources of information, for next to the teacher they are the most intimately informed about his teaching. Student ratings, critique sessions, and informal discussions can generate useful insights.

6. The teacher should get to know her students better. The essence of accommodating student differences is knowing what they are. Instructors can easily fall into the trap of treating all stu-

dents the same, or treating them as a "class." In fact, each student has his own motives, needs, and abilities. Knowing what these are can help the teacher prepare instructions. Recognizing a pattern of skills, interests, and preferences allows the teacher to present the instruction in a way that is effective for most students. Deviations from this pattern require the instructor to provide individual assistance.

One or more of the questionnaires provided in Chapter 5, or any of a number of other such instruments, will enable the instructor to acquire this information. Monitoring or charting individual student progress on quizzes and course products allows the teacher to identify and assist students who encounter difficulty.

7. The instructor should get to know instructional media better. Instructors presently have a great number of instructional options available to them. But many of them have been developed only recently and may not have been part of college experience of many of today's faculty members. By increasing their repertoire of instructional skills, teachers can make their presentations more versatile and increase the amount of satisfaction that they and their students will derive from a class. Many institutions now have media or teaching centers which provide consultation and workshops to instructors interested in acquiring additional skills.

8. The instructor should require mastery and have the students iterate until they are successful. If it is unfeasible to make precise matches between students and methods it may be sufficient to require that the student reach a certain level of attainment or mastery before proceeding in the course, and ask him to continue working until this is achieved. As a result, the student and the teacher may try several media and methods, in a trial-and-error fashion, before the right match is found and the student learns. This approach is supported by Block (1971), Bloom (1971), and others.

9. The instructor should individualize instruction. The ultimate way to accommodate individual differences is to individualize instruction. The teacher interviews and assesses each student, tailoring a specific instructional program to meet his or her needs. Characteristics such as interests, entering capabilities, learning style, and motives would be determined and matched for each stu-

dent to a specific set of content objectives, teacher, media, evaluation, and environmental characteristics. Such an arrangement would be designed to compensate for the learner's weaknesses and capitalize on strengths. And although this final stage remains an ideal for all but a very few instructors, it is the logical extension of the ideas implied by the instructional system.

In applying any of the above models the instructor will need to make a decision about which media are appropriate for a particular situation. The following chapters, in Section Two, are meant to supply the instructor with information on a variety of media. It was written as a "consumer's guide" for instructors. In each chapter the medium is described, its advantages and disadvantages cited, and its appropriate uses discussed. If the instructor decides to use the techniques, "how to" information and a list of resources are provided. It is hoped that such information will enable the instructor to make an appropriate match between media and other elements in his instructional system.

SECTION TWO

Techniques and Methods
of Teaching

Chapter 9

LECTURE

If someone alien to our culture asked what "education" looked like, the description would be something like this: a large number of young minds eager for new knowledge gather together to listen to a person of great wisdom profess his discipline and, as a result, become enlightened.

It is almost irrelevant what time period is being described. Archeologists of future centuries who unearth artifacts from present-day classrooms are likely to detect little change in education from the classical Grecian academy. The modernity of the 200 seats, arranged in a semi-circle to focus on the podium, would be betrayed only by a rusted overhead projector. For two millennia, education has been tightly bound to the lecture method. The roots of this approach can be traced to Athens, the rise of the theatre, and Plato's Academy. Oratory was the primary mode of mass communication and central to the Greek democratic process. The tradition evolved into an instructional system in medieval European universities. Instruction took the form of the reading of and commentary on a book (the word "lecture" means "a reading"). Manuscripts being scarce and expensive, the lecturer had the one available copy. The lecture was the only way that the knowledge stored in books could be transmitted to a large number of students.

For good or ill, the lecture hall remains the chief and usual meeting place for teachers and students. Kenneth Eble's (1972) study of seventy colleges and universities led him to conclude that teaching is still largely a matter of a single professor talking to fairly large numbers of students, despite innovative practices found on almost every campus. In the minds of many if not most faculty members, lecture is synonymous with teaching—not in any reasoned way, but because of an association formed from many years of going to lectures during their own education.

Yet, despite the dominance of the lecture, criticism of it as a technique and a system has existed since the Middle Ages. The criticisms sound familiar: the student is passive, inhibited from interaction with the lecturer or the subject matter, and restricted to taking notes which may never be used.

The assets and liabilities of the lecture can better be considered if it is viewed for what it is: a form of communication. The lecture is a medium whereby the teacher can convey a body of knowledge to a large, and with amplification, limitless number of students. As a medium it is essentially verbal and one-way. The students do not interact with the teacher to alter, refine, or pace the message. In these respects the lecture differs from most other forms of instructional communication. Given these characteristics, one is better able to determine the advantages and disadvantages of the lecture, and when it can best be used.

Advantages and Disadvantages

There are major reasons why the lecture has survived the competition from many technological innovations such as the printing press and television. The lecture is inexpensive. The primary cost of a lecture, the faculty member's salary, is much less than an equivalent television production, with its added costs of technical support and equipment. A lecture takes less preparation time than competing media. It also takes less student time to cover the same material than with engagement in a discussion. A lecture can be current in content and easily adjusted to meet changes in subject matter or audience (if they are considered as a group).

Although the above advantages tend to be more logistical than pedagogical, the lecture does surprisingly well when compared with other teaching methods, as seen in final exam scores. In a review sponsored by the Center for the Advanced Study of Educational Administration, Dubin and Taveggia (1968) examined the data from 36 experimental studies comparing lecture and discussion methods. Of these, 51 percent favored the lecture method and 49 percent favored discussion. Similar results were found in comparisons of lecture versus lecture-discussion and lecture versus supervised independent study. Students receiving lecture achieved as much as students in lecture-discussion or independent study groups. The general conclusion was that teaching methods in higher education do not differ in their effectiveness, at least when measured by scores on final exams. However, this conclusion ignores the fact that lectures may be better in some situations than in others, or that they may be better for some students, but not for all. For example, in the conclusions of a more recent review, Costin (1972) states that as the difficulty of knowledge increases, discussion may be more effective than lecture.

The disadvantages of the lecture are also major. The reader is likely to be aware of all of them, as they frequently appear on the rating sheets of any teacher who uses the method.

The primary drawback of the lecture is that it is essentially a unidirectional mode of communication. The listening student, in most cases, has little opportunity to influence the nature, rate, and flow of information. The only control the learner can exercise is to ignore it or turn it off—blank stares and nodding heads. One-way communication offers little in the way of interaction and feedback, which are crucial for learning. If used excessively, as is too often the case, the lecture encourages intellectual passivity, the opposite of learning.

This deleterious effect can be moderated by incorporating forms of interaction into the lectures. Posing questions, even if only rhetorical, can maintain student attention. Encouraging students to ask questions will give the instructor the feedback useful in making adjustments in content or pacing. A few lecture halls around the country are wired with electronic response systems. Such a system allows the teacher to ask quiz-like questions, or student opinions about the interest or format of the lecture. The students respond by pressing buttons at their seats. A distribution of the responses appears instantly at the podium, indicating whether or not the lecturer is on target. An equivalent effect can be obtained by asking the students for a show of hands, or to hold up color-coded cards.

Other drawbacks of the lecture are less easy to counteract. The lecture, as a verbal medium, allows the student no direct experience with the body of knowledge. Although the instructor transmits the subject matter to the students, she may simultaneously serve as a barrier. Not only is it difficult for the student to interact with the lecture, it is also difficult for the student to interact with the discipline—to see what it looks like, how it feels, how it changes when acted upon. As a result, the lecture fails to encourage creativity and problem-solving.

A final disadvantage of the method is its poor effect on retention. Students frequently forget, or never learn, much of what is said. This problem is more pronounced for longer lectures. In a study for the BBC done by Joseph Trenaman (as reported by McLeish, 1976), an audience listening to only the first 15 minutes of a lecture retained 41 percent of what was presented. Those listening to 30 minutes of the lecture remembered 23 percent of the material presented in the first 15 minutes; those listening for 45 minutes remembered only 20 percent. Thus, while the lecture is an inexpensive and easy way to deliver information to students, it is not very efficient. Only a small portion of the total lecture time can be used effectively for learning.

Appropriate Uses

Content. The verbal nature of the lecture puts constraints on the type of subject matter for which the method can best be used. In its basic form, the lecture is most appropriate for the teaching of factual information. Wilbert McKeachie and James Kulik (1975) of the University of Michigan looked at a number of studies comparing the effects of lecture and discussion on student performance. Three different types of learning were examined: factual information, higher-level cognitive learning, and attitude or motivation. In those studies which used factual information as the criterion, students attending lectures did better, in general, than those in discussions. Students in discussion groups did better in higher-level cognitive and motivational areas. The lecture is particularly useful if the information is recent and not readily available in print or other forms.

The lecture can serve as an overview or orientation, preparing students for subsequent learning experiences by providing them with a conceptual framework. It can also integrate previous experiences such as readings, labs, and field work. It can and should be augmented by other media. A brief lecture prior to a film or slide-tape can specify the purpose of the presentation and draw student attention to crucial points. After a game or role play, a lecture can supply meaning and context. When serving such functions, the lecture should present a structure that helps the student understand the various experiences. Presentation of new information should be subordinate to this.

For content other than information, the lecture must be augmented. Accompanying visual aids and demonstrations are useful for the effective teaching of concepts and problem-solving procedures. In such cases, it is necessary that the student see examples. A filmed interview with a schizophrenic patient can do much to elaborate the concept of schizophrenia obtained from a lecture. During a lecture, the instructor can help the student to visualize the concept of static electricity by rubbing a plastic rod with fur and touching an electroscope. The blackboard is useful in showing the students how to solve integral calculus problems.

It has been claimed that the primary affective feature of the lecture is to provide the student with a model. The effective lecture can motivate the learner to emulate the instructor by adopting the values and skills of a scholar. Every instructor remembers the great lecturer who first excited him or her about the discipline. The major drawback of the method in this regard is that the model presented is in a very limited role—that of a lecturer. The other roles of the scholar are only implied.

Students. A lot of work has been done to try to identify the type of student for which the lecture works best. There seems to be some consistency in findings in this regard. Students who need structure and guidance or who have a low tolerance of ambiguity tend to prefer lecture to independent study (Pascal, 1971, 1973). Introverts learn more from lecture than discussion; the reverse is true for extroverts (Beach, 1960). Flexible students perform better with independent study, while the more rigid or anxious student finds lecture more effective (McCullough and Van Atta, 1958). Domino (1971) found that students scoring high on Achievement-via-Conformance performed better by lecture than discussion. In general, the structure provided by lecture can probably accommodate a number of student deficiencies. This can also be said of other structured modes, such as programmed instruction or the Personalized System of Instruction.

The instructor faces at least two problems when trying to act upon these findings. First, student traits of this type are not easily identified. It is possible to systematically check for such traits, using the instruments in Chapter 5 or some others; or the instructor may rely on a more-or-less subjective assessment of his students. Even if the first problem is resolved, it is likely that the instructor will find students of both types in her class. This predicament argues for the use of a variety of teaching methods or some arrangement where students can opt for one approach or another. (See Chapter 8.)

If student preferences are considered, a number of studies have shown that students generally like *anything* other than lecture (McLeish, 1976). This lack of popularity seems to be related to something other than the effectiveness of the method, so caution should be exercised not to base method selection solely on student preference.

Instructor. One aspect of the instructor's personality which contributes most to the successful use of lecture is comfort in the role. An instructor who plans on using lecture primarily or exclusively should be comfortable as the center of attention. Fifteen to two hundred pairs of eyes and ears hanging on every word is bound to stimulate any teacher so inclined. Unfortunately, this same attention is likely to make many instructors uncomfortable. Not all instructors are suited for lecture. The mix of voice, manner, timing, and personality differs for every instructor. Although there are some skills that can be learned in order to improve lecturing, teachers who find a conflict between their personal communication style and the lecture method might be more effective if they used a different approach. Small group discussion, tutoring, or written instruction might be more appropriate.

Environment. Class size is a frequently examined environmental quality. Although there seems to be no difference in achievement between large and small classes, students seem to prefer the smaller group. It is not clear, however, if this is due to the increased likelihood of discussions evolving in the smaller classes, a condition preferred by students (McKeachie and Kulik, 1975).

The fact that many students are gathered to hear the lecture has a great impact on audience participation. An individual student may be embarrassed to ask a question in front of two hundred others. Fear of asking a "stupid question" or having others feel their time is being wasted by one person's ignorance is difficult to overcome. The instructor must go out of her way to encourage questions in such a situation. For instance, she could reserve a time for questions, wait for ten seconds or so before moving on, and praise students who ask questions.

Concern for the physical environment should include acoustics. The shape and size of the room and the arrangement of seats should be such that a person in the back of the room can hear clearly. A less than ideal arrangement might require amplification. Since lecture is an audio mode and the visual mode is the way people gain most of their information, distracting visual stimuli should be eliminated. Overly warm room temperature, dim lights, and other sleep-inducing conditions are also not advisable.

How to Do It

Part of the lecture method's tarnished reputation can be attributed to the fact that many instructors do it so poorly. Lecturing, like most other aspects of teaching, can be improved with training. Practice alone, however, will not lead to polished performance; in fact, it may lead to depression and discouragement. Thoughtful preparation for lectures and the acquisition of some basic skills of presentation can work wonders.

Preparation. A primary concern in the preparation of a lecture is its organization. The first consideration is what should be said. Sir Lawrence Bragg (1966) has commented:

> The value of a lecture is not to be measured by how much one manages to cram into an hour, how much important information

has been referred to, or how completely it covers the ground. It is
to be measured by how much a listener can tell his wife about it
at breakfast the next morning. (p. 1614)

He goes on to say, "Suppose we ask how many main points can we
hope to 'get over' in an hour? I think the answer should be 'one.'"
The organization of the lecture should be built around one main
theme.

Although the standard form for a lecture is introduction, body,
and conclusion, there are two possible variations, principle-centered and problem-centered. Research on which approach is best
for which situation is inconclusive, and the decision is left to personal judgment.

The principle-centered approach is characterized by the old
statement, "Tell them what you're going to say, say it, and then
tell them what you've said." The instructor should begin the lecture with a generalization—a statement of the main point. The
body of the lecture should provide the listener with materials that
support the main point. There are several types of support from
which the lecturer can choose. An *explanation* clarifies and defines
the main point, relating its parts to the whole. An *analogy* points
out similarities between something known and something not
known. A figurative analogy compares two things from different
classes (the heart is like a power plant) and the literal analogy
compares two things from the same class (the comparison of one
town to another). An *illustration* is a factual or hypothetical example of the main point. Various *statistics* or other factual data
can be used to support the lecturer's position. And finally, *testimony* from firsthand observers and experts can be used. The conclusion of the lecture serves to summarize the support and restate
the main idea. (See Figure 9.1.)

The problem-centered mode leads the student from a problem
to the solution. The ideal lecture using this mode would start with
the problem—one which is meaningful to the students—presented
in such a way that the student feels a need for a problem solution.
Then the lecturer would interweave the evidence and examples
leading to her conclusion so that the average student would discover the solution before the instructor pointed it out. It is

Figure 9.1. Organization of a Principle-Centered Lecture.

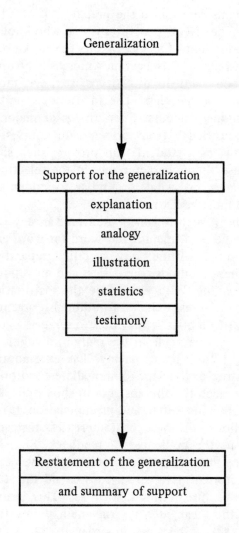

recommended that the instructor organize the lecture to permit the students to involve themselves in the solution to the problem rather than presenting information they can obtain elsewhere. (See Figure 9.2.)

A second consideration in the preparation of a lecture is audience analysis. The effective lecturer is one who knows his audience and can accommodate the message to the background and interests of the listeners. This becomes increasingly difficult for the new student body with its diversity of sex, age, race, background preparation, and social class. The instructor is left to search for similarities among students. Such things as major, occupational goals, prior knowledge from prerequisite courses, and that old stand-by, status as a student, can provide such similarities. The teacher can use these characteristics in the selection of examples and anecdotes to link what is familiar to students with what is unknown and must be learned.

Presentation. A lecture can be delivered in any of a number of modes. It can be read, memorized word-for-word and recited, delivered impromptu without any specific preparation, or extemporized. Of these methods, the easiest and most popular is extemporaneous speaking. With this mode the instructor prepares the lecture with careful research and forethought, organizing it by outline and preparing a brief set of notes to serve as a guide during the speech. Notes can be made in the margin, dividing the speech for the purpose of timing and pacing. The extemporaneous speech allows the instructor to adapt to immediate conditions.

During the lecture, the instructor should be aware of such things as rate, volume, pitch, and pronunciation. It is impossible to give prescriptions for these characteristics. Instead, the lecturer should look to the audience for feedback. Speeches can be recorded for later analysis and subsequent improvement.

The instructor can give verbal cues to aid the student in learning from the lecture. Phrases such as "This is important" and "Now, note this" can identify the main points for the learner. Prepositions such as because, in order to, if ... then, therefore, consequently, etc., emphasize that a relationship is being presented.

Giving the outline of the lecture on the board can help the

Figure 9.2. Organization of a Problem-Centered Lecture.
(Source: Gage and Berliner, 1975, p. 504)

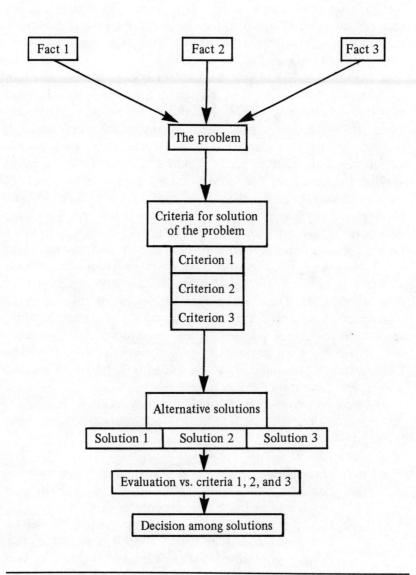

learner maintain concentration. Verbal transitions from one item to the next also help.

Non-verbal expression is also important in the lecture. The lecturer should maintain eye contact, looking from face to face to get feedback on pacing and clarity. Any posture, movement, or gesture can also contribute to the quality of the speech if it does not draw too much attention to itself. Such expression should be subtle rather than grandiose.

A perennial problem for the lecturer is coping with boredom. Attention is greatest in the first ten minutes of a speech. From that time on, attention wanes except for a final spurt at the end. Thus, for 80 percent of her speech, the instructor must constantly struggle to maintain student interest. Several suggestions may be useful. Keep the lecture *active*. The lecturer could be active by varying tone, gesture, and floor position. Involve the students by asking questions, giving them a chance to stretch, or breaking them into buzz groups of four to six people for brief periods of discussion. (This last technique has been used in lecture rooms as large as one to two hundred people.) Keep the lecture *real*—evoke images and use slides or films. The lecture should be *relevant*. Relate it to students' interests and needs. *Suspense and humor* can also be effective. These techniques can be tricky unless they are made part of a natural style. Audio-visual aids can maintain interest as well as provide numerous other pedagogical benefits. While any of the above suggestions can sometimes help, there is nothing like arousing a genuine curiosity and need-to-know in the students —the prime function of the lecture.

The best way to a good lecture is self-improvement. The following questions can be used to review audiotaped or videotaped lectures:

Yes/No 1. Was there a good reason for giving the lecture—no better way the information could have been communicated or the learning accomplished?

Yes/No 2. Did the lecturer begin by saying what the lecture was about and what it was supposed to accomplish? (Where you were coming from and where you were going?)

Yes/No 3. Was there one major idea or governing theme?

Yes/No 4. Was there a parsimonious use of examples, illustrations, facts, and data?

Yes/No 5. Did the lecture address in a novel or problem-solving way a real question or issue for which the students had adequate preparation?

Yes/No 6. At the end did the lecturer tell the student what happened in the lecture?

Yes/No 7. Was he short-winded rather than long?

Yes/No 8. Was there a relatively immediate opportunity in class or shortly after for students to actively use the information or ideas conveyed in the lecture?

Resources

Books and Articles

Allen, D., and Ryan, K. *Microteaching*. Reading, Mass.: Addison-Wesley, 1969. A description of what microteaching is and how it is done.

Bligh, D.A. *What's the use of lecture?* Harmondsworth, Middlesex: Penguin Books, 1972. A general discussion of what lectures are and how to use them.

Costin, F. Lecturing versus other methods of teaching: A review of research. *British Journal of Educational Technology*, 1972, *1* (3), 4-30. A review of lecture, comparing its effectiveness with a variety of other approaches.

Makay, J.J., and Sawyer, T.C. *Speech communication now!* Columbus, Ohio: Charles Merrill, 1973. A book on speech; it discusses the more technical aspects of how to prepare and present a lecture.

McLeish, J. The lecture method. In N.L. Gage (Ed.), *The psychology of teaching methods*. Chicago: University of Chicago Press, 1976. A review of the work done on lecture, including the history of its evolution, ways to improve it, and experimental results.

Using Microteaching to Improve Lecture Techniques

Dr. Ernest Johnson, professor of Agricultural Engineering at the University of Massachusetts, has been teaching a lecture course for several years on the subject of internal combustion engines. He heard about microteaching through the Clinic to Improve University Teaching at the University of Massachusetts: "I have always been interested in improving my teaching. When I heard about the microteaching program, I thought it sounded like a good opportunity to improve my techniques."

Microteaching is a scaled-down teaching situation involving a five- to twenty-minute lesson taught to three to ten students. During the microteaching process, the instructor focuses on a specific teaching skill, which is usually selected as a focus before the lesson is taught. The teacher is videotaped during the session while concentrating on the skill. Following the lesson, the teacher views the videotape, possibly in consultation with an expert. The instructor then reteaches the lesson, incorporating this feedback.

Dr. Johnson was videotaped three times during one semester. After each taping, a trained consultant watched the tape with Dr. Johnson and helped him to focus on certain lecturing techniques that were used: "One thing that I remember, that came as a shock to me, was that I asked questions and then did not allow time for students to think about a response. I realized that there was no use in asking questions if I wasn't going to allow students to answer them thoughtfully. I had not been aware of this problem until I watched my lecture on videotape."

Dr. Johnson also realized that he was having difficulty with the pacing of this lecture. Since the material discussed in the lecture was not covered in the course text, he felt that it was important to go slowly so that students could take notes. Even so, he was concerned that students did not get all of the information or that they became anxious because the pace was too slow. After identifying the pacing problem in the initial videotape, Dr. Johnson decided to provide lecture notes to the students before the lecture. In the later tapings he saw that this technique allowed him to keep a comfortable pace in the lecture without worrying about the students' getting lost or not getting all of the information.

In this microteaching situation, the students were involved along with their teacher, since taping was done during the regular class time. The students seemed to feel that it was a positive experience. They were interested in helping their teacher improve his techniques.

Although Dr. Johnson admits that he was "quite nervous during the first taping session" and uneasy at times about taking a critical look at his teaching style, he felt that the microteaching system worked very well for him: "I would recommend it highly to anyone who is serious about improving their teaching techniques. I have continued to use the knowledge that I gained during the experience."

Dr. Ernest Johnson
Agricultural Engineering Building
University of Massachusetts
Amherst, Massachusetts 01002
(413) 369-4076

Chapter 10

THE BOOK

In a very real sense the book can be seen as the foundation of our entire culture. Most of the greatest thoughts in history were initially expressed, stored, and later rediscovered in books. They have been the basis for law and government, and the prized possessions of the wealthiest people. They have provided fuel for wars, and for fires. They have stirred minds and changed empires. And even with the recent revolutionary advances in mass media, it is difficult to imagine an idea presented via film or video that was not first drafted in print.

Without doubt, books are the foundation of our educational system. Anyone's earliest memories of school are filled with learning to read them. Twelve years of apprenticeship are required to apply them usefully. And the fact that some people finish the apprenticeship less than competent in their use of books is frequently decried as a national crisis.

In higher education, books are the focus of learning. They are both instructional tools and objects of study. Their importance is illustrated by the fact that there is hardly a course, no matter the field, no matter how specialized or advanced, for which a book has not been written. The occasional professor who does claim that there is no book for a course, usually follows by announcing the forthcoming publication of one, for the writing of a book is a high point in the career of any scholar.

With the permeation of books in our culture and schools, it is surprising to find relatively little written on their importance and impact. Two recent reviews (Carroll, 1974; Rothkopf, 1976), however, do add to our understanding of books as instructional tools. Both of these authors articulate definitions of written material.

John B. Carroll (1974), of the University of North Carolina, rejects the definitions of "anything that can be produced by a printing press" (p. 152) and "a string of characters representing verbal discourse" (p. 152), as insufficiently delimiting, and instead prefers to define print with the more descriptive term, "frozen language" (p. 152). Carroll views this aspect of print as its essential characteristic, and the source of both its usefulness and liability. Whereas print is "starkly cold, deadened, unrelated to reality, cut from context, 'irrelevant,'..." (p. 152), it is also stable and enduring, and its use is not restricted to particular times and places.

Ernst Rothkopf (1976), of Bell Laboratories, narrows his concern to discourse, "... that is, connected, cohesive presentations of some matter which, in style, more or less resembles connected speech" (p. 92). He divides discourse into three kinds: (1) general instructional materials, such as textbooks, and didactic expository articles; (2) specific instructional works, such as programmed instruction; and (3) materials that are the collective experience of our culture, such as literature, and scientific and technical works.

The principal characteristics of written discourse as identified by Rothkopf are its content, representation, and form. The content of a book is its purpose or intended meaning. Related features, such as completeness, accuracy, specification of the goal, and the inclusion of additional material, are dependent on the author's purposes for the material. In addition, the completeness and inclusion of extra information will also depend upon the presumed prior familiarity of students with the subject matter.

Whereas features of the content are very much dependent on the author's goals, the representation and form of a book are dependent on the intended audience. Features of representation and form can be changed, short of extremes, without changing the content.

Rothkopf also discusses written discourse from a complementary perspective—reading. This is the process that interfaces the book with the student. As Rothkopf speculates, this process involves the movement of the reader's eyes across the written material, a quasi-acoustic translation of the message, and the concatenation and elaboration of the information to form useful representations. These representations can be used to answer immediate questions and solve problems that the reader may have, or they can be combined with previous information to form more or less permanent memorial representations.

Thus, it can be seen that a book, unlike a lecture, is an active medium, requiring the student's continual engagement in order for the message to be transmitted. It differs, however, from discussion and computer-assisted instruction, in that it is not interactive. The potential for the student to alter the message to fit his or her needs is limited to the search or review of some useful subset of the material that is available. The learner cannot request information or pursue questions that do not fall within the content of the book.

Advantages and Disadvantages

An essential feature of the books, as noted earlier, is that they are frozen. Unlike discussions, or even lectures, their messages are relatively stable and enduring, and as such they can be reliably delivered to all. Because of their stability they can be easily tried out, evaluated, and revised. This malleability is limited to a certain prepublication phase of print; for, once released, books are difficult to modify (an important limitation when the expected half-life of knowledge in some disciplines is five years).

In addition to stability, a book is enduring, unlike media such as video or lecture, which have messages that are transient. This feature provides the student with a number of options. The message can be entered at any point. It can be examined carefully, scanned, skimmed, or skipped, thus allowing the learner to control the rate of presentation (a rate which, in any case, is faster than speech). The added feature of portability is also to the learner's advantage, enabling him or her to use a book without regard to time or place.

The book puts a burden on the learner as well. The reception of a book's message depends on the reader, and the single greatest source of failure to learn is the failure to read. Another burden is imposed by the fact that a printed statement cannot encompass all aspects of an idea. It cannot completely delimit and specify its potential interpretations. As such it simplifies experience (maybe overly so), and it allows—requires—the reader to use imagination to complete the message. This, however, is not a burden uncommon to most media.

While the book requires the active involvement of the learner, it is not interactive. That is, the student cannot mold or shape the direction of his or her investigation beyond the domain of the text's message. Unlike discussion or computer-assisted instruction, the student is limited to the content of the text, and can modify it only to the extent that he or she can select some smaller portion which is relevant to the goal of learning.

As for relative advantages with regard to learning, head-to-head competition between reading and other media is similar to most such comparisons—a draw. Studies by Stanton (1974), Goldberg (1972), Ulrich and Pray (1965), Baskin (1962), and Koenig and McKeachie (1959) show no significant differences in performance between students learning through independent study (principally reading) and either lecture or discussion. McGraw *et al.* (1966) and Bartz and Darby (1966) found texts to be more effective than programmed instruction, but these studies are balanced by the work of Young (1967) and Ripple (1963), who obtained opposite results.

With such inconclusive findings, the strongest support for the use of books remains the testimony of two of educational research's senior statesmen. Ernest Hilgard (Dubin and Taveggia, 1968), of Stanford University claims that, "The objections to the textbook are something like the objections to the lecture, but where there is really something to be learned (like in an anatomy course) everyone would recommend a textbook. Maybe textbooks aren't so bad after all, but in any case they may be so *powerful* as to override differences in teaching." (p. 47) The University of Michigan's Wilbert McKeachie (1976) concurs by saying, "... my years of experience in attempting to assess teaching effectiveness have led me to think that the textbook, more than any other element of the course, determines student learning." (p. 30)

Yet despite these impressive testimonials, ambivalent research results seem to indicate that books are not panaceas. It is likely that the instructor needs to supplement a text with relevant visual and experiential media, and/or alter it to correspond to the instructional needs of the learners.

Appropriate Uses

Content. As mentioned above, the appropriate use of books would hardly be limited by the subject matter of the course, judging by the successful use of them in practically every course taught in college. Carroll (1974) does, however, make some general recommendations about their use. He suggests the use of print for the learning of facts and information already amassed. This kind of content is usefully stored and selectively retrieved in books.

Print should not be reserved, however, for the simpler types of learning. Books allow for the careful study that may be necessary for the acquisition and understanding of complex concepts and relationships. Carroll suggests that print be supplemented by illustrations, and coupled with practical experience.

The learning of psychomotor skills or interpersonal skills might better be done through demonstrations, simulations, or tutoring than through print. Although books exist which are intended to help improve one's golf swing or tennis stroke, the effectiveness of these materials—without coaching or extensive practice—is highly questionable.

Learning which is highly experiential, with its attendant affective component, can be done effectively through direct experience, simulations, and role plays, or even vicariously through films or other visual aids. But books should not be excluded. The affective impact of a good novel is inescapable. And even the student's affect toward more technical content can be influenced by books, as is the case with Skinner's (1948) *Walden Two* and Watson's (1968) *Double Helix*.

Finally, learning objectives which require learners to *apply* complex concepts or algorithmic procedures may require a medium more interactive than books. The extensive practice and feedback required by such objectives would call for the use of such interactive media as programmed instruction, computer-assisted instruction, or tutorials.

Thus, it is easier to indicate the types of content books are less appropriate for than to be explicit about their best applications. Objectives dealing with psychomotor skills, interpersonal processes, and applications of cognitive skills might be best taught via other methods.

Students. In general, studies which compare reading, per se, to other media are extremely rare. More common are studies which examine what is called "independent study." (The term is used differently in these studies than it is used in Chapter 23.) This technique usually relies heavily on reading, but may also couple it with lectures, discussion, or tutorials, thus making it difficult to draw conclusions about one factor in the method. However, this is the source of information on the differential benefits of reading for different students.

It seems that all students can learn well from books, at least within an environment that provides other instructional supports as well. However, if reading is the only source of instruction, effectiveness may depend on personality factors, such as responsibility or anxiety. Other personality factors, including need for achievement and autonomy, are less clearly related to preference for independent study.

It seems more likely that student characteristics may relate more to *how* reading is used than whether it is used. As mentioned earlier, the use of metaphors and similes, or the average sentence length may depend on such student characteristics as prior knowledge of content and need for instructional support. The use of study questions for reading is particularly helpful for students who have poor study skills, as demonstrated by Rothkopf (1972).

Bigelow and Egbert (1968) found that students in a teacher education course who performed better than predicted from prior GPA using the independent study of readings, scored high on personality characteristics of responsibility and intellectual efficiency. Stanton (1974), in a study comparing lecture and the independent study of freshmen, found that students who saw themselves as tense and anxious performed better with independent study. It seems, therefore, that some internal motivational characteristic may be needed to learn well from reading, although this finding may be limited to independent study situations where other instructional supports are limited.

Bartz and Darby (1966) compared programmed instruction and readings in both traditional and independent environments for a beginning mathematics class. They found that textbooks were more effective than programmed instruction in independent situations, but limited their conclusions to the less able students that generally populated the course which they studied. Baskin (1962) found that students studying independently in a variety of courses performed as well as those attending lecture, and concluded that independent study should not be reserved for superior students only.

As for preference, studies by Pascal (1971, 1973) indicate that those students who liked independent study of readings scored high on personality measures of autonomy, thinking, introversion, complexity, theoretical orientation, and practical outlook. Koenig and McKeachie (1959), on the other hand, found that women high in need of achievement preferred independent study to lecture, but obtained *no* interaction between either independence or affiliation and satisfaction or performance in independent study and small group discussion treatments. Their study is confounded with regard to its implications for reading by the fact that both groups also received lectures; theirs was not a test of reading alone.

Instructor. It has been recorded that the sixteenth century faculty of the University of Salamanca protested against the instructional use of printed books because they might be deprived of a livelihood. Since that time, faculty members have become acclimated to the textbook, and little of the resistance shown toward other media is displayed against print.

At least part of the reason for this acceptance can be attributed to the fact that, contrary to films and other media, most professional books and journal articles are authored by college faculty members themselves; being published is an essential aspect of the scholarly role. Also contributing to their acceptance is the fact that faculty members are themselves heavy users of books, and thus would find no dissonance in asking their students to use them as well.

Environment. Unlike films, simulations, or even lectures, there is no special environment or supporting hardware needed for the use of books. A strong advantage is their transportability and endurance. They contain relatively permanent messages which can be accessed and used at any place and any time. If a preferable condition for their use exists, it is probably a well-lighted room subdued in noise and other distracting stimuli.

How to Use It

Typically, the chore confronting an instructor who decides to use a book is choosing *which one* to use, and deciding how it might be supplemented. And although these are common chores for college faculty members, it is unclear that the amount of thought used in making these decisions is commensurate with the instructional burden placed on the medium. Instructor forethought in this regard is as critical to the successful use of textbooks as the students' skill and persistence in study.

Selecting a text. Choosing a text is a task that few instructors relish. Few criteria exist to aid in the rather fine discriminations needed to select one text from the many on the market. Charles Morris (1977) of Denison University proposes a four-step process for selecting psychology textbooks which can be modified to be applicable for any discipline:

1. *Identify objectives.* A textbook is written for the author's purposes and objectives. These may be stated, or only implied. They may or may not correspond to the instructor's objectives for the course. The prime criterion for selecting a text should be the extent to which it matches the goals for the course. Otherwise, attractive features of the text, such as an appropriate readability level, the use of illustrations, and an attractive layout must be secondary to this concern.

Dissonance between the instructor's intent and that of the book can create a good deal of confusion in the class. Disenchantment can arise when a text appears irrelevant or contradictory to the instructor's goals. To a certain extent, this situation is probably unavoidable unless an instructor is using his own text. However, judgments can be made about the relative match of texts with objectives. In general, it is recommended that a text be chosen which needs to be supplemented with additional readings, rather than one which contains extraneous material.

Matching the text with the course objectives requires that both the author and instructor be explicit about their goals. The instructor's half of this task is covered in Chapter 3. Although more and more authors are specifying the objectives of their materials, it is by no means common practice. Texts which do not list objectives will require that the instructor try to ascertain the implied goals embedded in the preface, the chapter headings, and the homework exercises. Once the two lists are compiled and examined side-by-side, the instructor can make a judgment as to congruity.

    2. *Know the students.* Characteristics of students thought to be relevant to college teaching are addressed elsewhere in this book (Chapter 5). The application of these constructs to the selection of a particular text is, however, problematic. First, the selection of a text needs to be made a month or so prior to even seeing the students, thus eliminating the possibility of examining student data for patterns which might suggest some action. Secondly, the implications of student characteristics for instruction lack the precision needed to make fine discriminations between texts.

Therefore, the instructor is limited to making rather gross generalizations about the students likely to take the course, and using these to determine minimum requirements of an acceptable text. The preparedness of the students is one of these generalizations. The number of prerequisite courses, and thus the prior familiarity of the students with the discipline, should indicate the amount of depth and detail allowable for a text. The selectivity of the institution and the general ability of the students should indicate the level of readability and difficulty of the text. Information in the prefaces of texts frequently describes the intended audience in enough detail to make these rather rough matches.

    3. *Read the book.* The importance of a text in a course would certainly justify the time needed to read a few of them before making the final decision. Reviews of textbooks in professional journals can be used to make pre-

liminary selections and to narrow the choice from many to several. The final selection, however, should be based on a careful examination of the remaining candidates. While examining each book, the instructor can assess such aspects as content, readability, human interest, layout, and instructional supports.

Readability is a measure of the reading difficulty of a text. The difficulty is usually dependent on such things as average word length or average sentence length. Of the many formulas used to determine readability, probably the best known is the Flesch (1949) test:

$$RE = 206.835 - .846 \text{ wl} - 1.015 \text{ sl}.$$

Where word length (wl) is the number of syllables per 100 words and sentence length (sl) is the average number of words per sentence or independent clause, the use of this formula will yield a number between 0 and 100. Anything between 50 and 60 is considered fairly difficult (for the average reader) and is at a high school level. Texts with scores between 30 and 50 are college level, and those between 0 and 30 are at a college graduate level.

Flesch also developed a human interest scale. Ratings on this scale are based on the use of "personal words" and "personal sentences." Personal words include personal pronouns, masculine or feminine words (e.g., "brother," "actress"), or group words (e.g., "People," "group"). Personal sentences contain spoken passages: questions, commands, or requests addressed to the reader; exclamations; or grammatical incompletions which require the reader to infer the full meaning. A "minimally interesting" text would contain 3 percent personal words and 30 percent personal sentences.

Gillen, Kendall, and Finch (1977) compared Flesch scores with the subjective ratings of students for twenty-seven psychology text books. They found that the students' ratings for both readability and human interest correlated significantly with Flesch scores. In addition, the Flesch human interest score correlated significantly with the students' overall recommendations for the texts.

Other features of the text, such as layout and instructional aids may also be valuable. Useful headings and subheadings, stated objectives, and study questions can help the student process and store information in the text.

    4. *Assess impact on students.* Few texts undergo systematic evaluation prior to publication. This puts another burden on the instructor—one of determining whether the text *works*.

Several simple techniques may be useful in this regard. Asking students to rate the text will give the instructor some information about its impact. An item analysis of the final exam will also pinpoint those areas for which the text, or the course in general, is weak. Finally, larger classes may justify the use of controlled experiments, providing different texts to different sections and comparing the effect on a common examination.

Assessment of the text's impact is the verification of assumptions made in earlier steps in the selection process. A text proving to be inadequate on this test should be replaced.

Supplementing a text. A text or other written material, such as a novel, may contain the content that the instructor considers critical, yet be deficient in form or exposition. The instructor can modify and improve a text by using several techniques suggested by the work of Rothkopf (1976).

The explicit statement of learning goals, or directions to focus on and remember certain key points have been shown to increase the recall of goal-relevant material. This effect decreases, however, as the number of goal statements per passage increases.

The use of questions embedded in the text has also been shown to increase learning. Questions asked prior to the relevant passage will increase goal-related learning but not non-goal-related learning. Questions periodically asked subsequent to the reading of relevant text will increase both types of learning.

As mentioned earlier, the effects of these supplements is greater for some students than others. Those less familiar with the subject matter, and less adept in study skills benefit most.

The instructor can incorporate objectives, directions, and study questions in a study guide which students can use as they read through the text. This practice resembles one of the features of the Personalized System of Instruction (Chapter 18) and is likely to increase the impact of textual material on student learning.

XIP: Because We Are Unique

John Henzy is now using the Xerox Individualized Publishing (XIP) service for the second year in his sociology course at Gloucester County College. "All community colleges serve unique populations. We have found that the Individualized Reader is one way to speak to this uniqueness. Using this service allows us to change texts as often as necessary to suit the changing needs of our student body."

Xerox Individualized Publishing is a custom publishing service. A teacher who wishes to use this service consults one of the five XIP catalogs: Economics, Education, Sociology, Comprehensive Psychology, and Human Behavior. Each catalog lists articles which have been cleared for publication in XIP readers. A teacher may choose any of these articles for inclusion in the reader and arrange them in any order.

In addition, the teacher may include his original material in the reader, including summaries, study questions, paper topics, course outlines, and original articles. If the teacher wants to include articles not listed in the catalog, Xerox will also try to clear these articles for publication. The minimum order is 500 copies of the reader, and the cost is dependent upon the quantity ordered and the size of the reader. The cost is covered by the price the student pays in the bookstore.

John Henzy uses an Individualized Reader as the core for his course. In addition, the course includes lectures, the BBC film series "Family of Man," a glossary of terms, and a bibliography of journals and books related to material in the reader. Mr. Henzy explains that his use of the XIP reader reflects his goals for the course: "I want to present a conceptual framework, supported by examples and applications. I use readings to provide concrete applications and examples. The readings also serve as a basis for further student research. I ask students to support or refute the view presented in an article, using other articles as resources. The students begin to appreciate the scope and function of professional journals. They also learn the research skills necessary to uncover information to support their arguments."

The reaction of Mr. Henzy's students to this use of readings has been positive. "To an extent, I think that my own enthusiasm about the reader affects the students. I have had to put myself into the reader. (Mr. Henzy spent six months reading over 400 articles before selecting the 40 articles included in the text.) Preparing the reader helped me to focus on my objectives for each class meeting. I had to decide exactly what I expected the students to gain from reading each article. The result was that the reader became a very important part of the course; and the students sense this."

Using the reader was a major change in Mr. Henzy's teaching style, which had formerly been entirely lecture. "I find that the reader requires me to do more planning for each class session. But I have gained much for my time investment. The atmosphere of the classroom is more informal, with more student participation, and more student interest."

Prof. John Henzy
Department of Sociology
Gloucester County College
Sewell, New Jersey 08080
(609) 468-5000, ext. 272

Xerox Individualized Publishing
191 Spring Street
Lexington, Massachusetts 02173
(617) 861-1670, ext. 562 (collect)

Chapter 11

INSTRUCTIONAL TELEVISION

Any discussion of television must begin, but need not end, with the fact that the revolution in postsecondary education once promised by the proponents of instructional television did not happen. The impact of television on learning processes has been profound, but it has taken place in the living room rather than the college classroom.

The May, 1976 issue of *Educational Technology*, "A Second Chance for Instructional Television?," carries an important discussion of failure of the medium to assume a prominent position in American education, particularly higher education. Despite some outstanding success stories exemplified by the extensive use of television at institutions like the University of Mid-America in Nebraska, Coast Community College in California, and Miami-Dade Community College in Florida, the medium's instructional potential has not been realized. George N. Gordon's article, "Instructional Television: Yesterday's Magic" (1976) suggests that the relative failure of television as an instructional medium stems in part from its having been oversold and, perhaps more importantly, from the fact that program formats and instructional techniques have not yet been adequately developed.

Perhaps the most important reason for television's failure is that the medium has not been used in ways that capitalize on its unique advantages. With a few notable exceptions, instructional television has been employed to project "talking faces." The average lecturer in person turns out to be more engaging, if not measurably more informative and effective, than his televised image. Where used simply to multiply and extend the lecture, the medium's special visual potentials are largely lost.

Televised instruction is probably the most thoroughly evaluated of any instructional medium or method. Hundreds of thousands of dollars worth of evaluated programming have shown that measured by end-of-course testing, TV lectures are as effective as live lectures, but that students like them less (Schramm, 1972). It has been suggested (McKeachie and Kulik, 1975) that for conceptual learning, often a crucial component in college courses, television instruction alone is less effective than live interaction between student and teacher.

To date television has been an instructor-dominated medium used by faculty members to deliver instructional content to students. The important learning possibilities inherent in the new portable equipment have yet to be widely realized. Video need not be thought of exclusively as a means for conveying teacher-determined objectives and content, but might instead be used to foster student expression, creativity, and learning. The potentials of student-made videotapes are worth special attention as an alternative to conventional papers and reports. The basic production techniques suggested in the "How to Do It" section below can be employed by students as well as teachers.

Microteaching techniques are another exciting and powerful alternative which has emerged with the advent of portable equipment. As a kind of electronic mirror, videotape can readily be used for improving the individual student's learning of specific skills and behaviors, such as laboratory techniques, counseling, and dance. Microteaching with video is explained in the appendix to this chapter.

Advantages and Disadvantages

The audio and visual advantages of video relative to other media are quite apparent. They may be less apparent when the choice is between video and film. Most of the considerations in this decision are logistical and technical; but, in general, if the instructor wants to show professionally-prepared materials, film is probably the answer. If the instructor chooses to produce a program locally, it will probably be with video.

Although a variety of prerecorded instructional video materials are becoming available in cassettes, they are not yet as accessible as film through uniform listings and distribution networks. It is possible that with the standardization of color videocassettes or videodiscs and increased demand, a nationwide market will result. As it stands, prerecorded video material suitable for a given course may exist but will be hard to locate.

The local production of video materials tends to be easier and quicker than the production of film (assuming the availability of equipment). This is particularly true of what is known as "small format" video. This is 1/2-inch videotape equipment which is relatively inexpensive, easy to handle, does not require elaborate production crews and facilities, and allows for immediate play-back. For these reasons, the "How to Do It" section of this chapter will stress video production.

Videodiscs, a recent technological advance, will increase the capabilities of television (Magarell, 1977). Instead of using a video-tape, the videodisc player uses a 12-inch disc which looks much like a phonograph record. The player interfaces with standard tele-vision equipment, but differs from videotape in capacity and capability. Unlike videotape, it allows for the viewer to access any particular "frame" or still image, which can be held indefinitely. This allows for pages of text to be stored and read via video moni-tors. Surprisingly, 54,000 pages of text or still pictures can be stored on one 12-inch disc. Motion pictures can also be stored and displayed (up to 30 minutes), or music and other audio material (up to 15 hours of material). Stills, motion, and audio can all be stored on a single disc, allowing for a variety of multi-media appli-cations. The videodisc player also allows the viewer to freeze a frame indefinitely, to slow down the motion, or reverse the motion. Videodisc equipment is presently available and the first college courses on videodiscs (developed by the Consortium of Universities of the Washington Metropolitan Area) will be com-mercially available sometime in 1979.

With regard to learning, the relative effectiveness of video has been examined in a number of reviews comparing video with conventional instruction. These reviews show no superiority for either approach. Chu and Schramm (1974), Dubin and Hedley (1969), and Kulik and Jaksa (1977) all show that most studies demonstrate no differences between the techniques. Although a few studies have shown preference for one technique over the other, the number advocating video is about equal with the number selecting conventional instruction. In general, until more precise recommendations exist, the instructor's decision to use video will probably be heavily influenced by practical considerations.

Appropriate Uses

Content. The basic problem in determining which medium is best suited for given content and objectives is that researchers have yet to characterize the range of media capabilities with a sufficient degree of precision. Until such time as sophisticated criteria for matching media, content, and objectives are developed, common sense suggests that there are content and objectives for which television is more suitable than other instructional techniques.

The type of information best communicated by television has a strong visual component involving motion. Since the medium is capable of simultaneously reproducing sound and picture, it is particularly powerful in presenting dramatic performances, documentaries, interviews, or virtually any other action. Whenever the content is most effectively presented with some combination of sound, motion, still pictures, and graphics, television should be considered.

As commercial or entertainment television makes clear, the medium can convey significant social and emotional attitudes as well as dispense information. Series like "Civilisation" and "The Age of Uncertainty" are as effective in cultivating positive attitudes toward art and the "dismal science" of economics as they are in conveying content.

Instructional television can be effectively used for cognitive and affective objectives. Since it can serve virtually any teaching purpose that does not require personal interaction, it would be easy to conclude that the medium is the best one for all such purposes. In fact, there are many applications where still pictures, audiotapes and/or films will be satisfactory, and perhaps preferable, when cost and accessibility are considered.

Students. It is not clear from the research which students learn better from video (or film) than from less visual presentations. One position is that the visual component of video aids those students who are less able to visualize ideas for themselves. A contrary position is that less visually able students will have more difficulty learning from a very complex, visual presentation such as video or film. Snow (1965) found that students previously experienced in learning from films learned more from those shown in a college physics course than students less experienced. This "visual literacy" seems to be particularly important in learning from artificial visual effects such as zooming or slow motion. It seems that, apart from any spatial ability, there may be special skills needed to benefit from complex visual presentations such as video or film. It is possible that students lacking these skills may be aided by the instructor who outlines the content on the board, poses study questions, or points out important parts of the video message in advance.

Televised instruction has been shown to be most effective when viewers are motivated and are required to respond in some way to the program (Ide, 1974). A television program, like a lecture, film, or slides, can all too easily be an entirely passive experience for the student. For video to be most effective, students should be primed to seek or evaluate information. They should be given specific learning goals in viewing the televised materials.

Instructor. In a classic study done on faculty reception of innovation (Evans, 1967), it was found that professors who oppose the use of instructional television rather narrowly focus on what is traditionally academic, and perceive as the greatest threat those forces which might dilute the academic aspects of the university. Instructors who showed a discriminating acceptance of instructional television were generally "more adventuresome, flexible, and mobile" in their thinking and teaching. They evidenced considerable concern with the university's social and community functions as well as with its traditional academic dimensions.

With adequate preparation, virtually any instructor can use television for instruction. Whatever the form, whether it be showing prepared videotapes, instructor- or student-made materials, or interactive video, she must schedule the equipment and, in some cases, learn how to operate it. Guides for the effective use of prepared videotapes are much the same as those for film. The instructor should preview and carefully select the materials that enhance instructional objectives, introduce the material to the class beforehand, and discuss it afterward. Microteaching with video requires special care and sensitivity on the part of the instructor, in addition to adequate technical preparation.

Environment. Television can be used in large lecture rooms, normal classrooms, and individual study carrels, depending on instructional groupings. The environment should include technical support services to facilitate the presentation of the materials, for example, sufficient monitors for convenient viewing and listening. The ideal for a classroom setting is one monitor for each cluster of about fifteen students.

More important than the fact that instructional television can be used in a variety of conventional environments is that television has potential for extending instruction into homes and remote areas; it can give students access to a wide range of visual materials at their convenience. Currently, a sizeable number of state universities are using television programming to teach courses in everything from animal husbandry to art history. The British Open University has perhaps the most varied and elaborate curriculum of this kind, while in the United States, the University of Nebraska's network is the leader in the field.

How to Do It

The instructor should first consider the relevant dimensions of the instructional goals, the learners, the environment, and his own preferences, as well as cost and accessibility. If television appears to be the most appropriate method for presenting a single unit or a whole course, there are a few basic procedures that will enable him to use it advantageously.

Although the instructor will be concerned with the operation and proper use of the equipment, subtle and more important considerations bear on content and production characteristics of the videotape which can affect the intended learning. Whether reviewing prerecorded materials or producing videotapes, it is useful for the instructor to consider the following issues.

An ideal production focuses on the goals of instruction and avoids irrelevant or distracting information. A good production repeats the central content information several times throughout the tape. Thus, repetition (though not simple-minded redundancy), along with built-in opportunities for learners to respond to what they are learning and to receive feedback on their responses, is essential for maximum effectiveness. It is also important that the central visual material be easily perceived by the learner and labeled with words, either seen or spoken—ideally, both.

To be interesting, a production need not be in color, or use clever camera work, animation, special pictorial techniques, or drama. Except where the content specifically requires such techniques, a simple expository presentation will teach content well.

Needless to say, a variety of otherwise useful and desirably prepared videotapes may lack one or more of the content or production characteristics listed above. Only a portion of the tape may relate directly to the instructional objective. Prepared video may lack built-in opportunities for student responses. The material central to the instructor's purpose may not be explicitly labeled.

One or more of these deficiencies in a prepared videotape does not mean that the tape cannot be used effectively in the classroom. Rather, they provide opportunities for the instructor to supplement the tape for the class. For example, a visually superb and detailed tape of cell division with narrations suitable for a high school or introductory college science class might be used in an advanced biology class when the sound track is replaced by the instructor's commentary.

The video monitor and its accompanying tape deck allow a presentation to be started and stopped at any point and sections repeated. The audio portion can be turned down. Thus, the instructor can use only those portions of the material that relate directly to her objectives. She can repeat sections or stop the tape or disc and discuss the information with the class. While the material is running, she can direct attention to and label important phenomena. It is a common misconception that once begun, a video presentation must run from beginning to end without interruption; this practice results in poor usage of prepared television materials and poor learning.

Video materials and live instruction can and should be combined to produce maximum learning. This does not necessarily mean that they must always be combined in a single class session. It is easy to imagine tutorial or discussion sections being used with a scheduled series on public television, for example, Kenneth Clark's "Civilisation." But whether television is being used in the classroom, home, or study carrel, prior to viewing the teacher should motivate students to pay attention to material that relates to instructional goals as well as providing structures for assimilating the content. Following the program, learning can be enhanced with practice, discussion, and by integrating the televised content with other materials and activities in the course. Many prepared television courses and course segments come with instructor and student materials expressly designed to be used in conjunction with the video programming.

Production. Frequently, an instructor who feels that video is the most appropriate way of presenting material cannot find appropriate prepared videotapes for specific content objectives. Even without this problem, some instructors are intrigued by the prospect of producing a videotape. Producing even a modest segment of good videotaped instruction can be time-consuming, and the decision to do so should be carefully made.

If an instructor decides to make videotaped material for a course, the most important step is planning. It is best for a beginner to work with someone from his campus audio-visual or television unit. However, this is not always possible and basic instructional materials can be produced on portable black and white equipment if the following suggestions are considered and incorporated.

In general, the same content and production criteria apply to producing one's own video materials as apply to selecting prepared videotapes. The instructor must have a clear idea of exactly what learning is to be achieved using the medium. The choice of objective(s) will govern the use of repetition, sequencing, questioning, feedback, labeling, and other elements. Strict adherence to objectives will reduce the temptation to include extraneous, less relevant, "dramatic," and allegedly humorous details. Again, except when another method is functionally required to portray the content, a simple expository presentation should be most effective.

Here are a few of the basic steps that may be useful additions to the resources listed at the end of the chapter.

1. Start with an idea.
2. Turn the idea into one or more clearly defined instructional objectives with due consideration for the abilities and interests of the intended student audience.
3. Develop an outline tied to the specific instructional objectives.
4. Write a script.
   a. A script is a shot-by-shot or scene-by-scene listing with accompanying narrative. Along with the words that will be heard, specify what will be seen in the shot or scene. The narration—brief, clear, and straightforward—must enhance the shot or scene. The shot or scene must enhance the narrative. Five to fifteen seconds is a typical, single-idea shot.
   b. Build into the script opportunities for student participation and questions where appropriate.
   c. Estimate the time required for each shot or scene and segment of narration. Then determine the length of the entire production. Pacing is very important. Packing too much information into too few minutes is a frequent mistake. The reverse, dragging things out, can make the production tedious.

Shooting

1. Learn to operate the equipment.
2. Do not make it a practice to pan or zoom from one scene to the next; this makes the audience dizzy.
3. Mix long, medium, and close shots.
4. Include only those parts of a scene that are relevant to what you are trying to show or say.
5. Keep the background uncluttered. Concentrate the camera on one center of interest at a time.

Microteaching with Video

Microteaching with video consists of using video equipment, usually portable, to record some student behavior which is then played back, discussed, and critiqued. In effect, it is instant replay of the learner's performance. Technically, microteaching with video is fairly easy. It requires less preparation and planning than producing content-oriented programming. Psychologically and pedagogically it is trickier.

One example of microteaching with video might be its use in a graduate course in social work counseling. After the students receive a lecture on various theories of social work counseling, they are given verbal and written instruction on basic counseling procedures. They are then asked to practice with each other, with one student role playing the social worker and the other the client. Following this exercise, each pair is videotaped in the role play situation; then, with the instructor and class, they view and discuss their recorded behavior. This method can be used in any course where visible skills and behaviors are among the objectives.

Microteaching with video has a number of advantages. It offers immediate shared feedback. It allows the mastery of complex skills and behaviors to be broken down into a number of components. And it is an individualized method. But microteaching is not without limitations.

Equipment is relatively expensive and the procedure is time-consuming. In some instances, a number of students can be taped simultaneously. Follow-up discussion and critiques need not always be conducted for one student at a time. Because video shows the student an image of herself, it has the power to arouse strong feelings; it is a very potent teaching strategy which must be sensitively handled. Otherwise, it can have discouraging and adverse consequences.

Content. Clearly, microteaching with video is most appropriate for learning which requires specific, visible behaviors on the part of the student. Its application to a calculus course is not readily apparent. In courses such as drama, ballet, or counseling its advantages are evident.

Students. Generally, microteaching with video yields the best results when the discrepancies between the actual level of performance and the acceptable or desired level are not too large. Little is to be gained by videotaping a student's performance the first week of acting class other than to establish his entry level. However, further on in the course, when students have mastered some of the basic techniques, it might be employed to good effect. Microteaching with video should probably not be used with students who have markedly low self-esteem.

Instructor. Using interactive video requires sensitivity. Appearing before a television camera is a new and frequently threatening experience for many students. The entire microteaching procedure should be carefully explained and the student's freedom to negotiate those aspects of the performance she wishes to have critiqued should be emphasized. If the instructor intends to use microteaching with video, it is best if she herself has experienced the technique from the student's point of view: being taped, critiqued, and given suggestions for improvement.

Environment. Microteaching with video is not likely to be successful if there is a high level of anxiety. A psychologically safe environment is essential. The instructor must work to create a positive student attitude toward the experience and give the student a sense of control through specifying those aspects and dimensions of his performance that will be reviewed and for which specific information and suggestions will be given.

Video can be used to record student performances for grading and testing purposes, but this use should never be confused with the use of microteaching as a formative technique.

How to Do It

The instructor should give a complete explanation of the specific behavior to be learned by the students. All students should be given an opportunity to practice the behavior. Next, the instructor should carefully explain interactive video: how the process will work and how it will lead to improved performance. In advance of on-camera performance, the teacher might work out with each student a brief checklist, formal or informal, of those specific aspects of her performance that will be reviewed and for which suggestions will be made. The more highly specified the elements of the performance to be reviewed, the higher the prospects for subsequent improvement.

The student then performs the behavior on camera. Immediately following the performance, the student is given a chance to view the tape without comment from the teacher or other observers. It is important that the student be given an opportunity to become accustomed to his own voice and appearance.

The tape is then played a second time, during which observers can comment on those specific aspects of the performance for which feedback was negotiated. Feedback on aspects of the performance other than those originally negotiated may be requested by the student but should not be volunteered by either the instructor or other observers. The tape can be stopped and parts repeated as desired. The instructor and/or other observers can then offer specific remedial suggestions that the student can use in further practice.

After further practice, the student is taped again and improvement noted. The cycle is repeated with negotiated specifications, feedback, and suggestions until the student has achieved an acceptable level of performance.

Resources

Books

Bretz, R. *Handbook for producing educational and public-access programs for cable television.* Englewood Cliffs, N.J.: Educational Technology Publications, 1976. This basic, practical guide is designed for the video novice. It is useful to anyone seeking to produce televised instruction, regardless of whether it is to be used on a cable TV system, or directly in a school setting.

Mattingly, G., and Smith E. *Introducing the single-camera VTR system.* New York: Charles Scribner's Sons, 1971. Discusses the uses and misuses of television, and gives a detailed functional description of components, maintenance, and operation of a single-camera VTR system.

Stasheff, E., and Bretz, R. *The television program: Its direction and production.* (5th ed.) New York: Hill and Wang, 1977. Provides detailed advice on pictorial composition, scripting, camera angles, and sequence. While written for studio production, the basics can be adapted for single-camera use.

Videofreex. *The spaghetti city video manual: A guide to use, repair, and maintenance.* New York: Praeger, 1972.

Periodicals

Educational Broadcasting. Acolyte Publications, Los Angeles, CA., 90049. Bi-monthly magazine which carries articles on video and other media applications in education. Features include an editorial, meetings, news briefs, and new products.

Educational and Industrial Television. C. S. Tepfer Publishing, Ridgefield, Conn., 06877. A monthly magazine covering the more technical aspects of video application, production, and operation.

Places

National Information Center for Educational Media (NICEM), University of Southern California, University Park, Los Angeles, CA., 90007. The objective of NICEM is to catalog and store in computerized form current and comprehensive data on all types of non-book educational media: motion pictures, filmstrips, recordings, videotapes, and similar materials. They publish a catalog entitled *Index to Educational Videotapes.*

Great Plains National Instructional Library, Box 80669, Lincoln, NE., 68501. The Library offers college (and other level) course materials in art, business, data processing, humanities, and psychology. Most courses are available on 3/4" videocassettes. The library publishes a catalog of its materials.

Indiana University, Audio Visual Center, Bloomington, IN., 47401. The Center distributes film versions of television programming including that from the Public Broadcasting Laboratory, National Instructional Television Center, and National Education Television.

Video for Architectural Simulations

Lester Fader, Professor of Architecture at the University of Michigan, has developed a unique application for video in architecture. "What I have been developing is a way of pre-experiencing architecture and the environment with scale models, a way that would more closely approximate reality. The best medium for doing this is, of course, video."

Mr. Fader and his students construct small-scale models of the physical environment—ranging from single rooms or buildings to city blocks. Using specialized optics fitted to surveillance video cameras, students "travel" through their models as if they were driving or walking, and view the result on a video monitor. "The real advantage of video is that people are already cued to see the whole world on the tube. It stands for reality. In other words, it is not difficult to experience the video version as a full-scale simulation, whereas it is in many ways difficult to imagine a direct view of a model as a scaled experience."

Video also has the advantage of providing immediate feedback to the student. If the design is not satisfactory, students can quickly change their model and evaluate the results. Mr. Fader has also developed a studio which can be physically altered. The studio helps to make the video simulations more realistic. "Lighting quality can be controlled by a grid ceiling that can be raised or lowered. Also, scenic images can be rear projected on translucent surfaces to simulate views outside of windows. We can study the effect of many design variables on space quality."

While Mr. Fader's prime concerns are with educating architects, urban designers, and landscape architects to work together on design development, he explains that video-simulated environments can also be a tool for involving the public in design decision-making. "We have

made several successful video presentations to planners
and other concerned community people. I can see a day
when many large group presentations will be through
video projection systems. The audience can comprehend
and experience the proposal immediately. Again, the
benefits of video are obvious in terms of cost, immedi-
acy, and being able to get visual access into remote
modeled spaces with lighting and movement that approximate a real world experience."

Prof. Lester Fader
Architecture
University of Michigan
Ann Arbor, Michigan 48109
(313) 763-0039

Chapter 12

MOTION PICTURES

"Sticky My Fingers, Fleet My Feet," "How to Save a Choking Victim: The Heimlich Maneuver," "Roots," "How Solid is Rock?," "Infinite Acres," ... These are film titles representing subjects ranging from middle age illusions of youth to introductory calculus. Through motion pictures students may witness a powerful documentary on a mental institution, an interview with Carl Sandburg, or a presentation of the symbiotic relationships of animals and the African Baobab tree. They may watch actual experimental subjects in the Milgram experiment on obedience and see documentation of the aftermath of the bombing of Hiroshima. Nursing students may view a silent film loop on how to give an injection until they feel confident about attempting to perform the injection themselves. Students of literature may see an enactment of a Hemingway short story, while astronomy students can witness the death of a star.

Despite newer technological developments in videotape, live television, programmed learning, multi-image slide projection, and three dimensional holographic representations, the motion picture persists in its richness, variety, sensitivity to conflict and current issues, and aesthetic appeal. The distinguishing feature of the motion picture is the wealth of audiovisual experience it can bring to the classroom. Films combine sound with visual effects such as the close-up, panorama, split screen, zoom, and animation which cannot be easily replicated by most other media, or even real life.

191

Thus, they constitute a significant resource for faculty members in higher education.

Advantages and Disadvantages

Surprisingly, the generalization that one instructional technique is about as good as any other can be applied to comparative research on motion pictures. However, there are specific situations where film has an advantage relative to other media.

In the case of motion pictures, comparative studies were conducted in depth prior to 1950, but since that time there has been little interest in the area. In summarizing the results of film research from 1918-1950, Hoban and van Ormer (1951) identified individual studies which showed that the use of motion pictures could contribute significantly to usual methods of instruction, that films alone could be as effective as good instructors, and that for dynamic content, films may be superior to print.

While motion pictures can be as effective as direct teaching by instructors, it is generally not appropriate to use films for the same purpose as the lecture. Films should be used to present visual information involving change or motion. Most often they present processes or demonstrations of activities which could not be presented easily or economically by the instructor directly or would not otherwise be available. Lectures, on the other hand, can be superior to films in presenting very current and highly verbal information, since they do not require elaborate visual production techniques. Slides can be as effective as motion pictures for many purposes which do not involve explicit motion, and they have the advantage of flexibility, easy up-dating, and low cost production.

Miller (1969) found that film had no more impact on student learning or attitudes than did a still presentation, although the students preferred film.

The impact of salient visual, audio, and motion characteristics is generally not understood. There are, however, technical capabilities of films which make them appropriate for presenting certain types of content. Motion pictures, like television, can record live demonstrations, lectures, interviews, and discussions in which predominantly verbal material is presented. Comparison studies indicate that, in general, there is no significant difference between the live and recorded versions (Chu and Schramn, 1974). However, for activities which are difficult to repeat, film or videotape recordings can be used for convenience.

There are many comparisons which can be made between motion pictures and television productions and some have not been systematically documented but may be very important. For example, motion pictures are normally shown on large screens, under theatrical conditions, to large groups of students. It is possible that this creates a shared experience, a kind of common bond, that may not be possible when small clusters of students view individual monitors in a semi-lighted room. On the other hand, since television is capable of presenting live programming perhaps it is subjectively more believable. Personal viewing of a small screen might make television a more intimate medium than film. Perhaps the television viewer feels more of a one-to-one relation with respect to the program than with film. At the same time, the large screen and full sound of the motion picture may engulf the audience and produce emotional responses which are not possible with television. In either case, these effects have not been specified or documented.

Marshall McLuhan has hypothesized that the motion picture and the television image are fundamentally different (McLuhan, 1964). Motion pictures are "hot." Television is "cool." "Hot" media are lower in participation by the audience than "cool" media and consequently have different effects on an audience.

Appropriate Uses

Content. Although all disciplines may be represented in a film catalog, the selection of a film for a specific objective is more problematic. Films tend to deal with introductory or general content. Thus, in psychology, films are available on the work of Jung, Piaget, and Skinner, among many others. In engineering, industrial processes are presented. In literature, the works of Shakespeare, Hemingway, and Twain are performed and discussed. What often are not available are films on abstract, subtle, or rapidly changing aspects of content which are often stressed in college courses. Faculty members may often find that many films are available in their discipline; however, few are available in their specific area of interest or which relate to a particular course objective being taught.

Motion pictures have been used to accomplish instructional objectives in cognitive, affective, and psychomotor domains. In cognitive areas, facts are often presented, processes documented, and concepts illustrated. Since the motion picture is a one-way medium, the presentation of this type of information is very efficient. Often the information is visual and would not otherwise be available, as in documentary footage of a volcano erupting or on the village organization of certain Indians of South America. Motion pictures, like television productions, tend to be most powerful when they present content which is visual and which involves motion or change. Since motion pictures present information in a continuous linear sequence, they can be used effectively to present processes or information where sequence, continuity, or cause-effect relationships are important.

Motion pictures have been produced to influence attitudes and to motivate students. Films such as the epic series, "Roots," the documentaries "Let My People Go," and "The Inheritance" are designed to influence student and public attitude through favorable identification with the subjects. Many times, films are used to interest students in subject areas or to motivate discussions. The power of film editing, music, and camera work as well as content development are often designed to play on viewer emotions.

To accomplish psychomotor objectives, motion pictures serve as models for analysis and repetitive viewing. Films have been produced to teach equipment operation and physical skills such as handball, gymnastics, and other athletic skills.

Students. In general, the amount learned from motion pictures is associated with a number of student traits, although higher ability students tend to score higher on tests after viewing a film. Lower intelligence groups have been shown to have greater increments in learning from films (Hoban and van Ormer, 1951). On the other hand, Allen (1975) concludes, based on his review of the research, that students of higher mental ability may benefit more from motion pictures or television than those of lower ability. Cronbach and Snow (1977), however, found no interactions between verbal ability and learning from motion pictures in a study by Snow (1965).

Snow (1965) and Vandermeer (1949) found indications of more learning from films for those students with prior experience with films as an instructional resource. Hoban and van Ormer (1951) also found studies which indicated a positive relationship between prior content learning and learning from films.

It is hard to make firm generalizations based on sometimes conflicting or vague conclusions drawn from the research. However, it does seem that some students need assistance in learning from films. This is supported by the work of Witkin and his colleagues (1977), who have found that field-dependent students (see Chapter 5) have difficulty in deriving structure or meaning from perceptually complex fields. An instructor might assist these students by providing a structure for them to use when viewing a film. This can be done by furnishing a study guide, writing questions on the board, stopping the film to stress a point, or otherwise aiding these students in processing complex information. Furthermore, since prior knowledge of the subject may be important in learning from films, an instructor should carefully teach any prerequisite skills and introduce the content prior to the showing in order to equalize the background of the students.

Based on the evidence to date, instructors should anticipate that students will have divergent responses to most film experiences. Where convergent types of learning are required, the instructor will have to employ techniques of introducing content and following up presentations with content-related activities.

Instructor. The way an instructor shows a film can be a powerful variable in film learning (May and Lumsdaine, 1958; Hoban and van Ormer, 1951). Directing attention to parts of the film and repeated showings of the film can contribute to the overall learning experience.

In general, instructor traits which are recognized to contribute to learning, such as the ability to motivate students, to present information clearly, and to conduct discussions, contribute to the ability to utilize film effectively. Instructors should carefully plan introductory and follow-up activities so that students are motivated for viewing and have a clear concept of the content of the film.

At the same time, a good motion picture can be of help to an instructor who has difficulty making presentations and motivating students. Films may be selected which present content with more clarity than the instructor could. Films which are designed to produce emotional responses in students can be used as motivators for discussions. Such "trigger films" can effectively stimulate responses which instructors could not elicit alone.

Motion pictures can be incorporated into a teacher's present pattern of instruction. Content-centered teachers who are basically concerned with making clear, effective presentations of subject matter will most likely be comfortable using films which present information clearly. Person-centered instructors may rely on films to focus attention for discussions or to stimulate interest in a subject for discussion. Moreover, instructors who wish to individualize instruction may use motion pictures in independent study settings for reference by individual students. In general, instructors need not change patterns of instruction when utilizing films, and the use of motion pictures does not place demands on the instructor for significant role changes as would adopting PSI or audio-tutorial systems.

Environment. The physical environment has not been shown to be a powerful variable in learning from projected media (Wilkinson, 1976), although inadequate light control, poor acoustics, and inadequate image size can interfere with student perception of the images.

Since projection is largely a technical matter which is dependent on the availability of appropriate equipment and facilities, motion pictures are most conveniently used in schools which have organized audiovisual centers to provide equipment or projection services. Moreover, the acquisition of films can be costly on both a rental and purchase basis; budgetary support is often necessary. While an individual faculty member can use film effectively, strong administrative support is required to provide films on an institutional level.

How to Do It

Motion Picture vs. Television. An issue of concern to producers of media and educators alike is when to choose motion pictures and when to select television, since the media have so many attributes in common. In making this decision a number of factors should be considered.

First, there are technical features which are not held in common. Since videotape offers immediate playback of visual and sound, it can be used to evaluate scenes on location or in the studio, thereby avoiding costly retakes at a later time. It can also be used for instructional objectives that involve self-evaluation of performance. The gap in this regard between video and film may be closing with Polaroid's introduction of an instant motion film system. Such a system has many of the same advantages of video with less cost in equipment. On the other hand, motion picture film can be used to produce slow motion, time lapse, and animated effects which are not possible with existing portable video technology. Motion pictures incorporating these techniques can be recorded on videotape and played back on television.

Both media can be used to communicate visual content involving motion. Films are more economical to use with large lecture groups of students, since a single large image can be shown with one projector. Utilization of videotapes requires at least one large monitor for each 15-25 students or an extremely expensive color video projector. Videotape may, however, be recorded on film through a process called a kinescopic transfer, but at additional cost and with a loss of technical quality.

Videotapes can be distributed to many locations simultaneously via cable or broadcast and can be incorporated into study carrels through videocassette technology. A highly developed rental distribution network exists for films; videotapes currently have limited loan or rental distribution, although library distribution of videocassettes is developing.

Videotape production can combine various camera views, effects such as split screens or superimposures, and media such as slides and film segments into a single final production with relative ease in a well-equipped studio. It is therefore preferred over film production when all of the resources can be assembled at one time.

Film, on the other hand, is preferred for location use and complex editing involving sound and picture. There is, however, new television editing and videotaping equipment which is as convenient to use as film and retains the advantages of videotape.

In any comparison of film and video it is important to recognize that television production equipment is constantly being improved to overcome traditional limitations. At present, however, many technical advantages exist on both sides, and selection of the most appropriate medium should be based on a complex of factors including production, distribution, and utilization requirements.

Selection. The first step in effective film utilization is logistically the most difficult and time consuming. It is to identify and select appropriate films for use. Ideally, faculty members should be as familiar with the motion pictures in their field as they are with the textbooks in the field. This is seldom the case. Journals which regularly review literature do not always include reviews of films. Consequently, the faculty member who begins to investigate the resources which are available normally does not have specialized references in his field to guide selection.

What is required, then, is a survey of catalogs and standard references. University film rental libraries generally make their catalogs freely available to faculty members, and local audio-visual centers often have collections. A very comprehensive *Index to Educational Films* is published by the National Information Center for Educational Media (NICEM), along with other media indices. Such listings, however, provide only catalog descriptions and producers' or distributors' addresses. They constitute a first level of selection, from which an instructor can identify titles which might prove relevant to her instruction.

The next step is to secure additional information on the films. When professional journals are available which review motion pictures, they should be consulted. In addition, there are two standard reviewing services to which many audio-visual centers subscribe. The Educational Film Library Association (EFLA) and the Landers Film Reviews both provide evaluative ratings of films in addition to content summaries. Colleagues should be consulted when possible. The producers can be contacted for additional descriptive literature. Occasionally, study guides are produced which detail film content and suggest related activities and resources.

Preview. At some point, the instructor will need to isolate the title that she wishes to preview for use in teaching. There is no substitute for personal preview. Faculty members, like students, react in highly individual ways to films. The problem here is that unless there is a local film library of some depth, the films are not made available for free preview. Producers will make prints available to media centers without charge for preview with intent to purchase but will not do so for evaluation prior to rental. University film distributors generally charge for all off-campus uses. This is perhaps the most difficult hurdle for a faculty member to overcome. If funds are available, an instructor can rent the films, preview them, and use them if they are acceptable. It is more likely, however, that funds will be very limited and the instructor cannot risk wasting them on inappropriate materials. Teachers must be resourceful in seeking out the materials. University film libraries will normally permit previewing on the premises. Faculty members should consider visiting their center if one exists, for the purpose of previewing materials. Film preview sessions at conventions should be exploited when available.

Motion pictures should be evaluated with specific instructional objectives in mind. Since the use of a motion picture normally requires a large commitment of class time, it should never be done without an instructional goal in mind, and it should be clear how the film contributes to accomplishing the goal.

Since the power of the motion picture is in its capacity to present visual information involving motion, careful attention should be given to the visual impact of the film. A presentation which is primarily verbal would be more efficiently communicated through audio or print media. Since it is probable that the students will remember the pictures they see, they should be directly relevant to the instruction desired.

Since audience responses are variable, the instructor should try to place himself in the position of a student viewing the film. He should look for confusing or misleading points and be sure to note any vocabulary or concepts which need to be presented prior to the film showing.

The instructor should pay close attention to the rate of development of information in the film. While she may follow it easily, the students may not.

In general, motion pictures do not have to be elaborate productions to be effective. In fact, irrelevant production techniques such as unusual camera angles and editing techniques can interfere with the efficient presentation of content.

The instructor should look closely for stereotypes of minorities, women, older persons, or any other group which might be communicated by the film. He should watch for technical inadequacies such as poor focus, inaudible sound track, and unreadable graphics. Not all motion pictures will meet the faculty member's expectations. Poor films should not be used just for the sake of instructional variety.

Utilization. Once the motion picture has been selected, the instructor must incorporate it into a lesson plan to achieve instructional objectives. May and Lumsdaine (1958) have demonstrated that the simple expedient of directing attention to the parts of a film which should be learned will significantly influence the degree to which students respond to the film in the desired manner. The instructor can put a list of open-ended questions on the chalkboard to be considered during the film, or simply announce the content students should notice. He might give a short quiz prior to the film on content which will be covered in the film. Any of a variety of techniques can be used, including repeated showings of sections of the film or the entire film. The instructor may wish to stop the film at points to provide additional information, to summarize information, or to redirect attention to new content. The film should be considered as the teacher's tool, to be handled as he sees fit. Moreover, he should follow up film showings with discussions, related activities, or readings.

To a great extent, utilization patterns will be dictated by the films themselves. If an instructor is using an expository film, he may wish to introduce it with a short lecture on the content and then follow up with questions and answers. With a documentary film, he may wish to direct students' attention to problems through open-ended questions, introduced prior to the film showing and discussed afterwards. And if the instructor is using a film designed to evoke discussion, he may wish to break the class into small groups to facilitate participation in the discussion by all the class members. He may wish to assign responsibility for certain areas of discussion prior to the film showing. In general, it is extremely important that the content in the film be reinforced by some subsequent learning activity.

The instructor may wish to experiment with innovative patterns of film viewing. After showing the film in class, she may have it placed on reserve in a preview center for a short time to allow students to review it individually. The instructor should try to organize a series of subject related films for enrichment showings outside of class. She may be able to schedule a sequence which parallels the content being developed in class.

Faculty members should list locally available films on the course bibliography and encourage students to treat the films as instructional resources.

Projection. All of the instructor's efforts in previewing, selecting, and ordering films, and designing lesson plans will be to no avail if the film does not make it to the screen. It is wise to place an order as far in advance of use as is possible to insure availability, and to order equipment and/or a projectionist early as well. Then the instructor should double check the arrangements during the week prior to use. Close attention to the logistics of ordering the film, equipment, and projectionist services will greatly reduce the possibility of error at the time of the showing.

Even though a teacher may utilize a projectionist, he should pay close attention to the quality of projection. Sound should come from the front of the room. When possible, it should appear that the sound actually originates at the screen surface. Volume levels should be adjusted to provide comfortable listening in all audience seating areas. This may require walking around the room to check levels in areas away from the projector and screen.

The projected width of the image should be roughly one-sixth of the distance between the screen and the last row of seating. To evaluate visibility, the instructor can stand at the back of the room to see if the image is large enough. If adjustments cannot be made at the time, for the next showing a larger screen and a wide angle lens might be requested. Care should be taken not to compel students to sit extremely close to the screen or at wide angles to the screen. The base of the image should not be lower than 3-4 feet from the floor to permit easy viewing by students in back rows of seating.

If a projectionist is assisting, he or she can be instructed to stop the film, to project sections a second time, and to start the film at any time during the class period without running through leader count-downs, focussing the image, and adjusting sound levels in the presence of the class. The instructor should make the need for quality projection known to the projection service ahead of time.

If handling his own projection, the instructor should *never* assume that he can operate an unfamiliar projector. He should ask for training in the operation of the equipment or request a model that he is sure he can operate. If possible, he should try out the film ahead of time to make sure that it is on the reel correctly, and that the can will open. Most good projectionists operate under Murphy's Law, "If anything can go wrong, it will." However, careful preparation and attention to detail will avoid projection failures.

Resources
Books and Articles

Index to 8 mm motion cartridges, and *Index to 16 mm educational films.* National Information Center for Educational Media (NICEM). Los Angeles: University of Southern California, University Park, Los Angeles, California 90007. Annual publication listing annotations and sources of educational motion pictures. Subject index and addresses of sources.

Leifer, A. D. Teaching with television and film. In N. L. Gage (Ed.), *The psychology of teaching methods: The seventy-fifth yearbook of the national society for the study of education. Part 1.* Chicago: University of Chicago Press, 1976, 302-334. Discussion of the teaching capability, the implications on learning, the content, design, production, and use of television and film in education.

Limbacher, J. L. *Feature films on 8mm and 16mm* (5th ed.) New York: R. R. Bowker, 1977. Annotated directory of feature films available for rental, sale, and lease. Directors' index and distributor listing.

Periodicals

Educational Communications and Technology Journal (formerly *AV Communication Review*), Association for Educational Communications and Technology, 1126 16th Street N.W., Washington, D.C. 20036. A journal published quarterly which emphasizes research on audiovisual media. Features book reviews and research abstracts.

Landers Film Reviews, Landers Film Reviews, P.O. Box 69760, Los Angeles, California 90069. Published monthly except June, July, and August. Reviews of educational motion pictures. Subject and title indices.

Previews, R. R. Bowker Company, 1180 Avenue of the Americas, New York, New York 10036. Published monthly. Reviews of educational media. Feature articles on media.

Places

The American Film Institute, 1815 H Street, N.W., Washington, D.C. 20006. A center organized to educate, research, and publish; to develop an archive of American film; and to provide aid to filmmakers. Emphasis is on history and aesthetics.

Educational Film Library Association, Inc., 17 West 60th Street, New York, New York 10023. Sponsor of the American Film Festival and reviewing service for educational motion pictures.

Consortium of University Film Centers (CUFC), Visual Aids Service, University of Illinois, 1325 South Oak Street, Champaign, Illinois 61820. Professional organization. Source of information on non-commercial distributors of educational motion pictures.

Motion Pictures: A Unique Application

Larry Michaelsen has been using motion pictures in a unique way in his organizational behavior course at the Business School of the University of Oklahoma. Feature films such as *Flight of the Phoenix* and *The Sting* are shown to students as a part of the final examination of Mr. Michaelsen's course. Students are given general areas to think about as they watch the film. The film is shown two or three times before the exam. In the exam students are asked six or eight questions which require them to apply theories of organizational behavior to the situations and/or characters in the motion picture.

Mr. Michaelsen has used this technique instead of case studies, which are commonly a part of the curriculum for organizational behavior courses. "I prefer this method to case study because it forces the student to collect the relevant facts, rather than relying on the case-writer to do this. The film also provides an opportunity for the student to apply his knowledge to a life-like situation."

Mr. Michaelsen has used this technique in other learning situations as well. In adult education courses he has used the feature film as a focus for class discussion. For instance, the class may find situations in the film that support or contradict the theory being presented in class. He has also used the technique at the end of one or two-day seminars, as a summarizing technique. "Because it is a different medium, I find that the motion picture can hold the attention of participants even at the end of a seven hour session."

The student reaction to this technique has been extremely good. Students feel that the feature film ties concepts together and helps them to remember the theory at a later time. "Another interesting thing that develops is that groups of students often hold impromptu sessions after the film has been shown to review theories and help each other learn the concepts. They be-

come excited enough to want to spend some of their
own time talking about the course material. There is no
way to generate that kind of interest by using a case
study.''

The main disadvantages of this technique are cost and
logistics. Of course, there must be equipment and facilities available in order to show a motion picture. Prints
of feature films (usually 16 mm) must be rented from
private rental agencies, since they are not available for
purchase. The cost is usually $25 to $50 for a short-
term rental. Mr. Michaelsen suggests that if cost is a
problem, novels can be used for the same purposes. He
has used *The Great Escape, Serpico,* and *The Godfather*
successfully.

"The great advantage of the motion picture is that
the non-verbal behavior can be observed. The viewer collects information from the film at a faster rate than
from a printed page. In this sense, the motion picture is
closer to real life than the printed media."

Mr. Michaelsen explains that perhaps the most rewarding aspect of this technique is that students become
more analytical in their approach to motion pictures as
a medium as a result of their experience with feature
films in his course. "Students are eager to suggest other
motion pictures for me to use in the course. They say
that they can't just sit back and passively watch a movie
anymore. They find themselves analyzing it; and thus
taking a more active role in the experience." The technique seems to have given students a new perspective on
a medium that has often been taken for granted in their
lives.

Prof. Larry Michaelsen
317 Adams Hall
University of Oklahoma
Norman, Oklahoma 73069
(405) 325-2651

Chapter 13

STILL PROJECTION MEDIA

The chalkboard more than any other device can be identified with traditional teaching in higher education. It is used with large and small groups alike to present information, to solve problems, to outline points made in a lecture, to present diagrams, graphs, and charts, and to summarize discussions. The applications are endless. The chalkboard has many real advantages in the spontaneous presentation of written and graphic information. It is completely within the control of the instructor. As long as the chalk can be found, it always works. Material written on the chalkboard will almost certainly be copied into students' notebooks. But it also has severe limitations. Presentation of the material depends on the instructor's printing and drawing skills. It is for the most part impossible to prepare in advance. Presentations cannot be reused. It cannot be used to present pictures. Since lettering on a chalkboard has to be large and bold to be visible, chalkboard space is at a premium in most classrooms and auditoriums.

Still projection media such as slides, filmstrips, and overhead transparencies can be used to overcome some of the limitations of the chalkboard.

Advantages and Disadvantages

In general, the research indicates that with the exception of content which explicitly involves motion or change, there is no difference in learning between still and motion picture presentations (Levie and Dickie, 1973). For the instructor in higher education, this is a clear indication that effective visual presentations can be developed using slides, filmstrips, or overhead transparencies at a fraction of the cost required to produce motion pictures or television programs. In addition, through the use of still media, the instructor can control sequence and rate of presentation of information; and slides and overhead transparencies are flexible and can be updated easily. The use of such media with live commentary by the instructor or with recorded narration written by the instructor personalizes the presentation of the content. On the other hand, visual materials have been shown to be more effective than audio materials alone when other than verbal information is involved (Levie and Dickie, 1973).

Projected materials tend to focus attention in group presentation on the information on the screen. They permit the inexpensive use of color and are flexible means of presenting content which is changing from semester to semester. A slide can be produced at a fraction of the cost of preparing handouts for a large lecture group.

Slides are easier to update than filmstrips, easier to produce, and less expensive for single copies. Filmstrips have a fixed sequence, are very convenient to store and project, are less expensive than slides for quantity distribution but are difficult to update. Both filmstrips and slides are capable of presenting pictorial, graphic, and printed content, and can be used with audiotapes and programmed for automatic projection. In general, slides are preferred in higher education due to their flexibility, ease of updating, ease of production, and the limited need for compact storage and wide distribution of the materials.

Overhead transparencies are used primarily for the projection of printed or graphic information. The overhead projector may be used for the spontaneous presentation of information by writing directly on transparencies in front of the class. Both overhead transparency and slide presentations can be prepared in advance and can be reused, slides being preferred for full color pictorial content. Both lend themselves to presentations in partially lighted rooms for note taking, and with either presentation the instructor can remain in front of the class to retain eye contact.

Appropriate Uses

Content. Since still projection media are most often used in conjunction with lecture presentations, the media have been used extensively in all subject areas. Visual disciplines such as art history, architecture, and natural resources have used slides extensively to present pictorial and graphic information. Other disciplines use media to present charts, graphs, outlines, and other visual organizers to supplement verbal presentations. The media are most effective in the presentation of information, facts, and processes which are visual and which are interpreted through verbal commentary. The media, then, present visual content directly and facilitate the learning of verbal information through the presentation of visual and pictorial organizers.

The power of still media is in the area of transmitting factual knowledge, but they can be motivational as well. Multi-image slide presentations in particular are often designed to accomplish objectives in the affective domain, or at least are designed to produce positive responses among students to the formal content presented.

Students. Although it is reasonable to assert that students in general profit from good visual presentations, two specific groups have been identified for which visual treatments are especially important.

Field-independent learners tend to provide the mediators necessary to learn relatively unstructured content. Field-dependent learners, on the other hand, are likely to have difficulty doing this (Witkin *et al.*, 1977). When instructional presentations are designed to utilize visual organizers and verbal cueing techniques, the structure which the field-dependent learners are unable to generate on their own is provided, and the result is that field-dependent and independent students should not differ significantly in their learning.

A second specific group which would benefit from advance organizers, outlines, and directing attention to content cues are students with low mental ability (Allen, 1975). Students with high mental ability also benefit from these techniques, provided they are of sufficient complexity and rapid development. Students of low general ability may profit from substituting other media for verbal presentation, while it will probably neither help nor hurt students of high general ability (Snow, 1977).

In summary, the use of still projection media to present pictorial and graphic content can be effective with all learners. They are especially effective with low ability students when they provide visual organizers for verbal presentations. They are effective with high ability students when they are perceptually rich, complex, and incorporated into presentations where the rate of development of content is rapid enough to be challenging.

For the most part, still projection media are used in the context of a lecture pattern of instruction which would tend to be best suited for dependent learners. There are, however, many applications where these media may be used to individualize instruction. Sound/slide presentations are frequently used in independent study settings. Such applications can potentially place the student in control of the rate of development of content and thus are particularly appropriate for highly motivated independent learners.

Instructor. Content-centered instructors who are concerned with the communication of facts, principles, and concepts would probably feel most comfortable using slides or overhead transparencies. These media are potentially rich in pictorial and graphic detail concerning visual aspects of the content, and they are effective in communicating the organization of the content.

Visual materials can be particularly helpful to instructors who are not comfortable lecturing. While the pictures and graphics serve as visual references and organizers for the students, they serve much the same function for the instructor, giving him a structure from which to work. Less verbal instructors can then prepare materials which help them communicate and consequently help the students learn.

It is likely that student-centered instructors will not rely heavily on still projection media, since they tend to avoid formal presentations. Nonetheless, the media can be used in informal settings with considerable student interaction. The student-centered instructor may emphasize and use the motivational attributes of the media.

Since all projected media require some handling of equipment, instructors need to feel at ease with projectors. Still projectors are simple to operate in general but are occasionally subject to mechanical failures. Instructors who are uncomfortable with audio-visual equipment should rely on qualified audio-visual assistants either to handle the projection or to check out the equipment prior to use and to instruct them in the proper operation of the equipment.

Environment. Either a classroom or study carrel must provide adequate visibility for the projected image. Severe viewing angles, small screen size, and lack of image contrast have been shown to interfere with visual discrimination tasks (Wilkinson, 1976). While in any given situation, proper image size will depend on the nature of the visuals being projected, a rule-of-thumb is that the image width should be no smaller than 1/6 the distance between the screen surface and the last row of seating. For a normal classroom, this might be 5-6 feet. For a large auditorium, it might be 15-20 feet. Students should not sit closer than two image widths from the screen. Under optimum conditions, they should sit directly in front of the screen, but they can normally be seated at up to a 45-degree angle to the screen without adverse effects. Individual student sightlines to the projected image should be clear, and seating should be comfortable. The room should darken sufficiently to permit good contrast and color saturation in the image. Normally this is possible while retaining a light level which is adequate for note taking. An optimum projection environment, then, takes these variables into account in order to facilitate the projection of instructionally retrievable images which are easily viewed by all students in the audience area.

The use of projected audio-visual materials can be greatly facilitated by strong central administrative support. In addition to adequate classroom environments, there are requirements for equipment maintenance, distribution services, projection services, media distribution centers, and production services in order to make optimum use of still projection media.

Faculty members who share teaching responsibilities for similar courses or different courses in the same content area can pool their resources. Since slides of pictorial or graphic materials or charts and graphs presented on overhead transparencies can be used by different instructors or incorporated into a variety of presentations, cooperative sharing of resources can make materials available for departmental use which otherwise would have only occasional individual use.

How to Do It
The production and presentation of visual materials are facilitated by using appropriate equipment. For example, to project a picture, graph, or chart from a book for a one-time use, the easiest way is to use an *opaque projector*. This piece of equipment will project acceptable pictures from textbooks or other printed sources in a darkened room. Care must be taken that the image is large enough to be seen, since textual materials are not designed for projection. Because of the heat generated by the light source, the projector should be equipped with a heat filter to insure that valuable texts will not be damaged.

Slides
Production. The use of a 35mm single lens reflex camera with a macro lens, close-up lenses, or extension tubes and a photographic copy stand with tungsten lights is sufficient for the production of slides from pictures and graphics appearing in textbooks or other printed sources. Care should be taken not to violate Copyright restrictions on published works; however, single copies produced for instructional presentations generally will be considered within the "fair use" guidelines of the Copyright laws (AECT, 1977). Both black and white and color originals can be photographed on a variety of color films. When processed, the photographs are returned as mounted slides suitable for projection.

In addition, original artwork can be photographed, including charts, graphs, diagrams, and titles. It is important to note that the preparation of artwork for projection is different from its preparation for publication in a journal. In general, projected images should be bolder and simpler in design and should be laid out in an area with a height-to-width ratio of 2:3 to conform to the aspect ratio of a 35mm slide.

Projection. The use of 35mm automatic slide projectors with remote control of focus, forward, and reverse functions makes slide projection extremely convenient. Projection trays may be loaded ahead of time and tried out to insure that the sequence is correct, the slides are not upside down, and the left/right orientation is correct. The instructor can then set up projection confidently and can control the presentation remotely from the front of the room while maintaining eye contact with the students.

Often instructors will wish to use the chalkboard at the same time that slides are projected. This is greatly facilitated by placing the screen in the corner of the room so that it does not cover the chalkboard area, which is normally on the front wall. Room lights can be adjusted to permit easy viewing of the board, note taking, and viewing the projected image, since new projectors are bright enough to be used with lights only partially dimmed.

Expository Approach. Normally slides will be projected in a fixed sequence, and the instructor will act as a narrator. The important consideration here is that with a group of both high and low ability students, he should control the rate of content development so that it is not too fast for the low ability students but so that it is rapid enough and of sufficient complexity to maintain the interest of the high ability students.

Instructors normally want students to recall visual information and to be able to discuss it intelligently. In a review of the literature on learning from pictures, Goldstein (1975) concludes that traditional learning objectives are related to the number of fixations which the student's eyes make on the picture. This takes time, and students should be permitted to explore the visuals systematically to maximize learning.

Moreover, visual memory does not always work in isolation from verbal memory. The verbal connections and cues which you provide as an instructor are important in the student's memory process (Levie and Levie, 1975). As far as possible, the instructor should use content outlines, diagrams, flow charts, and other content organizers, since they are important mediators for field-dependent and low ability students.

Inductive Approach. The use of slides does not have to be expository. Students can be encouraged to "read" still pictures. This teaching technique involves asking prompting questions which require students to examine visuals for cues to content. The procedure is one of Socratic questioning of the students. For example, a chemistry professor might project a diagram of two chemical compounds which are geometric isomers of each other. Rather than pointing out the similarities and differences between the compounds, the instructor asks questions such as: "What elements are in each of these compounds?," "What are the bonding patterns?," "What are the geometrical arrangements?"

Sound/Slide Presentations. When a series of slides and an accompanying narration have been formalized into a standard unit or when the instructor wishes to produce sound/slide modules, it is a simple matter to record a narration on an audiocassette (Chapter 14). The cassette may then be programmed to advance an automatic slide projector. Only one side of the cassette can be used, and a cassette visual/sync recorder is required. Programming is a simple operation and the resulting slide/cassette program can be used in lecture much like a film, or it can be placed in a study carrel for individual review by students.

Multi-Image Presentations. Most audiovisual media present information in an essentially linear sequence. While it is possible to stop the sequence and to go back over the sequence, these presentations generally present one image at a time. It is technically possible to produce split screen or multiple image slides, motion pictures, or televison images, but these techniques have the limitation of reducing the size of the visuals and require special production equipment.

There may be occasions, however, when the instructor wishes to compare or contrast visuals or to show a sequence of visuals simultaneously from left to right rather than one after the other. Multi-image presentations offer this potential. An instructor may wish to compare and contrast a German expressionist and an impressionist painter. Rather than showing a slide of one, talking about it, and then projecting a slide of the second work and talking about it, the instructor could heighten the contrast by projecting both slides simultaneously. All that is required is a second projector and screen to provide dual image projection.

Multi-image projection usually refers to the potential to project three or more images simultaneously. These presentations require an elaboration of equipment which would be difficult for an instructor to handle alone. There is, however, equipment available which can program multi-image presentations and can produce a variety of visual effects such as dissolves, fades, cuts, and super-imposures. Such equipment is not in common use on campuses, and often different models are not compatible. The programs can take a great deal of time to develop, but some people feel that they are highly motivational and present visual content in unique ways. While they are considerably more expensive than single image shows, they can be much cheaper than films or television productions. They are more difficult to project than single image media, and require larger screen surfaces. Consequently, they are normally used in auditoriums or lecture halls.

The pedagogical advantages of multi-image projection have not been demonstrated, but it is possible that for some content the presentation of simultaneous comparisons or the sequencing of multi-image presentations has a unique instructional potential and can be motivational and aesthetically pleasing.

Overhead Projection

It is possible to write spontaneously on acetate with permanent or non-permanent overhead marking pens and pencils. Felt pens are available in a variety of colors with narrow or broad tips. Using instruments that are made for writing and drawing on acetate produces bold, sharp lines that resist fading.

To prepare transparencies ahead of time, the faculty member may work directly on acetate with overhead pens, or prepare masters for producing transparencies. It is important to learn the type of masters required to make transparencies on various types of copiers. Electrostatic, infrared, or diazo copiers will all make transparencies, but each requires individually prepared masters. Several color line or color tinted films are available for most copiers.

Some copiers will make transparencies directly from book pages. Since printed originals normally have lettering which is too small for adequate projection, often published originals will have to be redrawn or used with careful explanation of any content which is difficult to read.

In general, overhead transparencies should be kept simple. The use of bold lettering and color emphasizes content. The instructor can also use overlays and combine prepared transparencies with spontaneous underlining, pointing, or cueing with marking pens.

Projection for overhead transparencies should meet normal standards for image size, brightness, viewing angles, etc. Since the image is projected from directly in front of and normally at an upward angle to the screen, some distortion is common with overhead projection. This distortion causes the top of the image to be wider than the bottom and makes it impossible to have the entire image in focus at the same time. To correct for this distortion, the top of the screen should be mounted away from the wall, and the base of the screen pulled back. Where this is not possible, the instructor should adjust the focus as she calls attention to various areas of the transparency.

Holography

This method of recording a three-dimensional image on photographic film permits the viewer to see true depth in the visual; that is, the viewer has to refocus his or her eyes to view background objects, and with some limitations it is possible to rotate the image by changing the viewing angle. At present, however, the production of quality holograms is very expensive and projection is inconvenient, requiring special apparatus. The medium holds great potential, however, for presentation of three-dimensional models or objects which are either not available or too expensive to show directly. A chemistry professor might use a hologram of the atomic structure of a compound and be able to show the three-dimensional configuration without using expensive, difficult to handle, and hard to store models. In fact, a whole library of such holograms could be conveniently available where a like number of models would be impossible to store. A professor of anatomy could use a hologram of the human skeleton and students would be able to see the three-dimensional relationships of the body parts. Solid geometry concepts could be presented in three dimensions on holograms.

Even though it is not clear that seeing objects in three dimensions is pedagogically more effective than two-dimensional slides, it is likely holograms will be used appreciably in higher education. Just as the color image has largely replaced black and white in projected films, it is possible that at some point the three-dimensional holographic image will replace the standard two-dimensional image simply because people will prefer the image which maintains the closest fidelity to the original.

Resources
Books and Articles

Allen, W. H. Intellectual abilities and instructional media design. *AV Communication Review,* 1975, *23*(2), 139-170. Summary of relevant research and implications for the design of media for high and low ability students.

Bright ideas in overhead projection: A guide to more effective meetings. St. Paul, Minnesota: Visual Products Division, 3M Company, 1976. Although not directed specifically to faculty, this pamphlet contains much useful information on the infrared process, masters, lettering, color, framing, and presentation techniques.

A guide to overhead projection and transparency making. Holyoke, Mass.: Scott Graphics, 1974. Pamphlet on the diazo process for manufacturing overhead transparencies. Includes information on preparing masters, lettering, color, mounting, and projection.

Index to educational overhead transparencies. Index to educational filmstrips. National Information Center for Educational Media (NICEM), University of Southern California, University Park, Los Angeles, California 90007. Annual publications of annotated listings of materials. Subject index and addresses of sources.

Kemp, J.E. *Planning and producing audiovisual materials, 3rd ed.* New York: Crowell, 1975. Information on planning for audiovisual productions and step-by-step instructions on producing audiovisual media.

Minor, E., and Frye, H. R. *Techniques for producing visual instructional media.* New York: McGraw Hill, 1970. Step-by-step instructions in technical processes including illustrating techniques, mounting and laminating, lettering and printing, coloring, and producing transparencies. Includes a source list and glossary.

Wittich, W. A., and Schuller, C. F. *Instructional technology: Its nature and use* (5th ed.). New York: Harper and Row, 1973. Basic audiovisual textbook for teachers. Chapters include techniques of utilization.

Periodical

Audiovisual instruction, Association for Educational Communications and Technology, 1126 16th Street N.W., Washington, D.C. 20036. Published 10 times a year. General emphasis on applications of audiovisual technology in teaching. Includes new product information and literature reviews.

Places

Kodak, Motion Picture and Audiovisual Markets Division, Rochester, New York 14650. Source of information on slide production, 8mm film production and technical areas of photography. Index to Kodak publications is available.

Association for Education Communications and Technology, 1126 16th Street N.W., Washington, D.C. 20036. Professional association of media specialists and educators. Emphasis in publications and conferences is on audiovisual media.

The International Visual Literacy Association, Center for Visual Literacy, Gallaudet College, Washington, D.C. 20002. Organization created to promote, develop, apply, evaluate, and disseminate information and research on visual literacy.

National Audio-Visual Association, Inc., 3150 Spring Street, Fairfax, Virginia 22030. National trade association for the audiovisual industry and publisher of *The Audio-Visual Equipment Directory,* a comprehensive listing of equipment including pictures and specifications.

Photography: Stretching the Medium to Its Limits

Students enrolled in introductory microbiology courses at Ohio State University are asked to report to an auditorium for their first class session. There, instead of finding the typical session where the syllabus is handed out and the course requirements are discussed, the students participate in a multi-media experience. The presentation is an introduction to microbiology; the medium is 35mm slides and 16mm film projected on three screens and synchronized with a stereo sound-track. The presentation lasts for a full class period of fifty minutes.

Patrick Dugan, who was Chairman of the Biology Department when the multi-media presentation was conceived, explains the reasoning behind the presentation: "We want students to have an understanding of the breadth of the microbiology field; and to be aware of its implications for all kinds of situations." The slide/tape presentation includes many subjects; from bacteria, to water pollution, to cancer research, to nutrition. The sound track consists mainly of interviews with professionals who are working in fields related to microbiology.

On course evaluations students often refer to the slide show as one of the most meaningful aspects of the course. "The presentation seems to captivate their interest. Many students comment that the presentation makes them aware of the extent of the microbiology field."

The slide/tape presentation also has a certain amount of flexibility. The slides can be changed to update the presentation. Faculty members have also used the presentation at regional professional conferences and received favorable response.

One disadvantage of this production is that it must be used in a large auditorium, to accommodate the three screens and the audio-visual equipment. There is also a necessary time investment involved in setting up the equipment. The presentation can be altered to overcome these obstacles, when necessary. "We have produced a single-screen version of this presentation, requiring only two projectors, which could be used in a regular class-room. This version is used during some semesters when it is not feasible to set up the larger production."

This type of presentation takes a great deal of time, expertise, and resources to produce. The investment seems worthwhile, however. "Many students who enroll in the introductory microbiology courses have heard about the slide/tape presentation from their friends. The presentation has such a good reputation that students are disappointed if we do not use it." Certainly, it is not feasible for everyone to follow the example set by Ohio State in this area. It is worthwhile, however, to consider the potential of photography as a medium when it is stretched to its limits.

Dr. Patrick Dugan
College of Biological Sciences
Ohio State Unviersity
Columbus, Ohio 43210
(614) 422-5211

Chapter 14

AUDIO

The advent of compact, battery operated tape recorders has made audio one of the most versatile of available media. Sound recordings can be used in automobiles, on commuter trains and buses, at home, in formal settings such as language laboratories and classrooms, and in any other convenient location where the student has access to a recorder. In addition, the use of telephone communications has introduced the potential for live transmission of audio directly into classrooms, with provision for student feedback, discussion, and question and answer.

The use of local FM radio stations to broadcast special programming to specific audiences has inexpensively made audio instruction available to a wide variety of students outside of normal class hours. Audio media have permitted individual student access to verbal and other sound materials and have delivered these materials to remote locations where instruction would not otherwise be available.

Outside of reading, writing, and practice drills, sound accompanies virtually all instructional presentations. Either the instructor provides commentary in lecture or audiovisual presentations, or the students question and discuss material. All of these involve sound. This instructional component is used extensively with other instructional media, but it can also be used in isolation for a variety of instructional purposes.

Advantages and Disadvantages

For the communication of essentially verbal information, the textbook has most often been shown superior to audio because of the control which the reader has over the materials. However, there are some short term memory objectives which are better accomplished with audio (Levie and Dickie, 1973). The use of handouts, programmed materials, and textbooks can be superior to many audio presentations when facts or concepts are being presented verbally. But when students are simply being given instructions to follow in sequence, audio may be a better medium, particularly in laboratory settings where the student's hands must remain free to handle apparatus.

In studies comparing audio and live lectures, the achievement of students taught by audio has not differed significantly from that of live lecture groups (Popham, 1961, 1962; Menne *et al.*, 1969). Similar results could be expected for a comparison between audio and video recordings.

In general, when content is non-verbal, visual media such as sound/slide presentations, videotapes, or motion pictures have been shown to be superior to audio-only presentations (Levie and Dickie, 1973). Audio is an inexpensive format for the communication of verbal content. This content might on occasion be best communicated by print media; however, audio is most appropriate when inflections, dramatic pauses, and other variables which are lost in print are important to the communication of the content.

The primary reason for selecting audio over other media is, of course, the importance of the audio aspect of the content. Analyzing a concerto or the interviewing techniques of a case worker are pertinent examples of such applications. Audio recorders also allow the students to evaluate their own performance in these areas.

The audio aspects of the content need not be paramount for the instructor to choose this medium. When visual information is not necessary, audio recordings are much less expensive than video recordings.

Audiotape recorders and record players permit students to start, stop, and go over audio material. This control has been shown to be an important element in the student's affective reaction to the materials (Burford, 1971). In addition, students can learn more when they have control of the recorder (Senour,

1971). Since students control results in a more positive response and more learning, recordings are superior to live telelectures and radio broadcasts for many types of objectives.

Telelectures can be nearly as effective as face-to-face lectures and have been used successfully to make experts available to consult on problems unique to students in off-campus locations (Parker and Riccomini, 1976). Telelectures have provision for feedback and questioning by the students and are, therefore, a more interactive medium than broadcast radio or recordings. They are limited to use in settings where phone lines have been installed, however.

Broadcast radio has the advantage of permitting the inexpensive, simultaneous transmission of audio to diverse locations. It is a one-way medium and not within the control of students. In general, audio recordings would be preferable to radio for pedagogical reasons. Nonetheless, there are economies in broadcasting which make it desirable for instruction in remote locations. As such, it has been used extensively in developing countries.

When radio and telelectures are used, it is often because the real alternative is no instruction at all. Under these circumstances, it is entirely possible for students to profit from the audio presentations. They are especially relevant when the content is very current and of immediate concern to the students.

Appropriate Uses

Content. Audio recordings have been used extensively in higher education in the teaching of languages and in music education. These disciplines reflect the type of content which most relates to the use of audio, since they are directly involved with sound. Students are required to recognize and discriminate between sound and to reproduce sounds. Other examples of sound-related content are the teaching of voice control techniques to speech students, the teaching of speech correction techniques to special education students, and the teaching of wildlife calls to natural resources students.

A second application of audio is to communicate essentially verbal information. Audio has been used in social sciences such as psychology, sociology, and political science, and in history, medicine, and nursing to present lecture material. Programs are available which range from poetry readings to historical radio broadcasts, such as FDR's Fireside Chats and Inaugural Addresses. Audio recording of plays, dramatic radio programs, and interviews and discussions on a wide variety of subjects with contemporary leaders and controversial figures are available.

While audio has been used extensively to present information in cognitive areas of knowledge and concept development, it is also an important tool in teaching speech, language, music, and sound-related skills. Because of the capacity for immediate playback of audio recordings, audio can be used as a feedback and self-appraisal tool in improving language skills, discussion techniques, interview techniques, musical performance, or other sound-related performance objectives. Audio is also appropriate for more complex objectives, where the student or instructor wishes to focus on the audio dimension and exclude non-verbal and visual aspects of the performance.

Radio broadcasts have been used to present lectures, panel discussions, and interviews in many subject areas and to transmit musical performances. The classroom use of radio has been largely replaced with the use of audio recordings or television. The medium, however, has great potential for low cost transmission of verbal information to remote locations.

Telelectures have been used in continuing education programs in pharmacy, medicine, nursing, agriculture, and business. Normally the objective is to bring current information and expertise to bear on issues and problems which are directly related to students interests.

Some dramatic audio programs have been produced to arouse emotional involvement in the subject. Recordings of lectures can influence attitudes, but objectives for utilizing audio are normally not related to affective goals.

In general, content which is not inherently visual, which does not require personal interaction, and which is directly related to sound can be communicated effectively through audio media.

Students. A wide variety of students has used audio to learn specific content. Certain groups, nonetheless, can be identified for which audio has special advantages. Audio materials may be used with students having low reading proficiencies, with the visually impaired, and with students who are home-bound due to illness or infirmities.

Although audio materials do not require reading skills for understanding, they do require listening skills; students who posses these skills will benefit most from audio presentations. Just as students may be expected to vary in their ability to read or to understand visual presentations, they will vary in their abilities to comprehend verbal material presented in audio formats.

Aside from special populations and students with special aptitudes for verbal learning, those who can profit most from audio are independent learners. Audio is most often used in settings where the student must pursue the learning activity independently, such as a language or listening laboratory, or where the student must be motivated to listen to late night radio broadcasts, attend a telelecture in an extension center, or listen to an audiocassette while commuting back and forth to work. Moreover, audio learning requires concentration, since visual stimuli are not available to help focus attention.

Instructor. Since audio is normally used to communicate content or to practice specific skills, the content-centered instructor will probably be more comfortable with its use. However, the audiotape can be viewed as serving the same function as a lecture—providing one-way verbal information. Therefore, its most advantageous use may involve a less traditional instructional arrangement. Individual learning stations or home-study assignments will allow the instructor to use this medium to extend her capacity to provide students with verbal information. The instructor considering these alternatives may want to use audiotapes.

Environment. An important characteristic of audio is that it can be used in a wide variety of settings. All that is normally required is a recorder or receiver and earphones or a relatively quiet listening station. Audio may be used in classrooms, laboratories, automobiles, living rooms, or any other location to which students have convenient access. Irrelevant and distracting visual stimuli should be eliminated if possible.

How to Do It

Radio. It is unlikely that a faculty member will ever use a radio broadcast in class. He might, however, wish to have his lectures broadcast on radio or to prepare special programs for radio broadcast. In this case, the instructor should contact the station which would broadcast the materials to determine what assistance it can offer in production. Broadcast standards are quite high; since writing for radio is a skill which differs from writing lectures, the help of a producer is important.

Telelectures. The use of a telelecture is largely a problem of making arrangements with the local telephone company representative and coordinating the speakers involved. This work is not to be underestimated, and it should be started early so that logistical and technical problems can be overcome. Phone lines will have to run to the classroom, and the phone company will have to provide a special amplifier for the receiver. In a lecture room or auditorium, it should be possible to run the phone conversation through an existing sound system coupled to the telephone amplifier. It would also be possible to record the telelecture. Since the phone company services are not without charge, budgetary support from the department will be necessary.

The telelecture should be treated much like a guest speaker or any other audiovisual device. It should be introduced with a brief indication of the content to be covered or by posing a number of questions to be answered by the lecture. During the lecture the instructor should monitor both the content of the lecture and student reactions to it. He should note any content which appears to confuse students or any points which appear not to have been communicated. In addition, he should note inconsistencies, misconceptions, or errors to be clarified later. Students should be encouraged to ask questions, since they may be reluctant to do so on their own. The instructor should demonstrate interest in the lecture by responding to it with questions or comments. After the telelecture, he should clarify any areas of concern and address any issues of controversy. He should lead a discussion concerning the points which he wants the students to retain.

Recordings. Audiotapes or records should be previewed prior to use. Consult standard catalogs for information on programs and distributors. (See Resources.) Many distributors are reluctant to make audio materials available for preview, since they are so readily copied. The faculty member should assure them that he will observe and protect their Copyright. If the actual programs are not available for preview, he may request study guides or content summaries to evaluate. Normally, recordings must be purchased rather than rented or borrowed, so they must be selected carefully.

When using recordings in a classroom, the instructor should make sure that the recorder or record player has a sufficiently powerful amplifier to deliver quality sound to all areas of the room. Small battery operated cassette recorders normally have only a one watt output and are not adequate for classroom use. They distort sound when the volume is turned up to the level required for most rooms. In a lecture hall or auditorium, it should be possible to play the recording through an existing P-A system. The recorder must play the correct speed and track configuration for the tape.

He should try to eliminate distracting noises from venetian blinds rattling in the wind or noisy air conditioners. For a large room, using an external speaker gives better sound distribution.

The recording should be introduced like any audiovisual medium. Playing the recording in segments allows for questions and comments. Recordings are more effective instructional tools when they are in the control of students, so provision should be made for student interaction.

It is difficult for an audio medium to maintain student attention. This is particularly so if other stimuli, especially visual, compete for attention, as in a home-study situation. A handout outlining the content of the tape can help the student focus his attention.

Students should not be assumed to be good listeners or note takers. Notes on the chalkboard help focus attention on the content of the recording. The teacher can also emphasize content through discussion or by elaborating on the content at regular intervals.

When a recording is used in class, the instructor should try to place a copy of it in a listening area afterwards for independent review by students. It is also helpful to record lectures for later review by students.

Production. An acceptable speech recording can be made with any good quality cassette or open reel recorder. The main technical difficulty is that often the microphone which is provided with the recorder is not appropriate for all recording purposes. Used in a quiet room and placed approximately 8-12 inches away from the mouth, a standard microphone would be adequate to record verbal material for placement in a listening center. It would not be adequate for most broadcast purposes and it might not be adequate for producing quality duplicates. For broadcast quality materials, arrangements should be made for recording in a studio on professional equipment.

In personal recording, it is important to remember that normal microphones are made to be spoken directly into. The further away the speaker is from the microphone, the poorer quality the recording will be. When she walks "off mic," the volume of the recorder must be increased to keep the voice recording at an audible level. This tends to increase the volume of background sounds which are recorded on the tape. Even with very sophisticated filtering equipment, it is difficult if not impossible to remove these noises from a final recording, and they often interfere significantly with understanding. As a practical matter, they normally cannot be removed.

An improved voice recording of a "live" lecture can be made by using a neck mic (lavalier). This microphone is not sold with regular recorders but is available as an accessory. The lecturer wears the microphone, so that as he uses the chalkboard or walks around the room, he will always be "on mic." If a P-A microphone is normally used, it should be possible to record through the existing system.

In standard recording situations, questions to the speaker will not be heard on the tape. They should be repeated before answering so they will be recorded.

On most recorders it is a simple matter to copy records, other tape recordings, or sound tracks from films or television programs. These are normally flagrant violations of Copyright, however, and should not be done without appropriate clearance from the Copyright holder.

When a battery operated recorder is used, the batteries must be fully charged. Recordings made with discharged batteries will often play back at a speed too fast to be understood. It is not always possible to correct this in playback.

Normally master tapes are produced on open reels at 7 1/2 inches of tape per second to maintain as high a quality as is possible. (The faster the tape, generally the better the quality of sound.) Cassette copies can be made for distribution to students. A good cassette master can provide acceptable duplicates. For the most part, a faculty member will not have occasion to use stereo formats or to produce records. If he has an application for more complicated recording or distribution formats, he should secure professional help in evaluating the technical and economic implications of the alternatives. One simply cannot produce professional quality audio without professional tape equipment and personnel.

Speech Compression

Much as it is possible to vary the speed of playback of motion picture images to give slow motion or time-lapse effects, it is possible to vary the speed of a recording to either compress or expand the sound. On normal equipment, increasing the speed of recorded sound raises the pitch and results in a chattering sound, while slowing the speed down lowers the pitch so that voices tend to groan. Special equipment is available which minimizes the change in pitch and results in intelligible speech at either a faster or slower rate than the rate at which it was originally spoken.

Slowing down sounds may have some application in the analysis of speech or other recorded sounds and in facilitating the transcription of recordings. Speeding up the playback of verbal recordings, that is, compressing the speech, can be a more efficient way to listen to audio material. Speech can be compressed up to 50 percent without significant losses in comprehension (Jester and Travers, 1967; Orr, 1971). It is possible, therefore, to listen to material in roughly one-half the time it took to speak it. If normal speech is in the range of 110-120 words per minute, and a person can listen to material at about twice that speed, it is possible for audio material to be transmitted at about the average reading speed of 250 words per minute.

Speech compression has a direct application in providing audio materials to blind students in that it will reduce the time required to listen to tapes. Similarly, an instructor who records lectures for subsequent review by students could make them available on variable speed audiotape recorders. Students could then control the rate of playback and review material in half the original time if they wish or listen to it at original speed if they wish to take notes.

Audiotape equipment which plays back at variable speeds or sophisticated recording equipment which compresses speech for playback or normal equipment is not generally available in equipment loan pools. To experiment with this technique will probably require funding. Listening to compressed speech requires concentration, and students will have to adjust to it. Moreover, students tend to learn the material in their notes, rather than the content of the entire lecture. The notetaking process may counteract the time gained due to speech compression for some students. At the same time, others may find it to their advantage.

Resources

Books and Articles

Index to educational Records. Index to educational audiotapes. National Information Center for Educational Media (NICEM), University of Southern California, University Park, Los Angeles, California 90007. Annual publication of separate listings of records and audiotapes and sources. Subject index and addresses of sources.

Forsythe, R.O. *Instructional radio: A position paper.* Stanford, California: ERIC, 1970. Review of the research, status, and application of radio in education.

Parker, L. A., and Riccomini, B. *The status of the telephone in education.* Madison, Wisconsin: University of Wisconsin, Extension Communication Programs, 1976. Proceedings of the Second Annual International Communications Conference. Reports on a wide variety of applications.

College Credit via Radio

Purdue University has been broadcasting college courses for credit since 1969. Richard Forsythe, now Director of the Office of Materials Development, was instrumental in initiating this open university via radio program. "Up to June, 1976, thirty-three different courses have been offered to 9,523 students who informally registered to monitor the broadcasts. Of these known listeners, 2,691 established university credit by examination." The Purdue courses are broadcast over WBAA, the University radio station. During some semesters as many as ten different courses have been offered.

The courses taught by radio in a particular term are generally the same courses that are taught on campus. In fact, for many of the radio courses, the classes are recorded as they are taught on campus. In other instances, however, the format of the course is altered to accommodate the medium. "Classes which utilize discussion formats are kept small and are recorded in broadcast studios because of the technical problems involved in multi-microphone recording."

What makes this system unique is that the student does not enroll formally in the course. She sends $5.00 to the Division of Continuing Education and receives a syllabus and related materials. The course text can be purchased at a local bookstore. Many Purdue students take advantage of the credit-by-radio program. Credit for courses is established by exam. Full-time students may take exams for radio courses at no charge. Anyone else who wishes to establish credit for the course is charged a $25.00 examination fee. Compared to the $75.00 charge for on-campus courses, the charge for radio courses represents a substantial savings to these students.

"Another attractive feature of the radio courses is that there is no penalty for failure under this system.

Failing grades are not recorded and the student is free to either take the examination at a later date, or enroll in a regular section of the course." Because of the many attractive features of this program, students who participate feel very positive about it.

Evidence also indicates that radio instruction is effective. "Successful radio students tend to score higher on the same examinations than successful students in regular sections of the courses. This is explained, in part, by studies of particular courses which show that radio students tend to have higher grade-point indices than non-radio students."

As an outgrowth of the open university via radio program, Mr. Forsythe is now developing learning centers where tapes of radio courses are stored for individual use. Students who miss a broadcast may go to a learning center at the main or regional campus to listen to the tape of the broadcast. Students can also complete the radio course in a shorter period of time by studying independently at the learning center.

Richard O. Forsythe
Director
Office of Instructional Materials Development
Purdue University
W. Lafayette, Indiana 47907
(313) 749-2381

Chapter 15

DISCUSSION

The traditional metaphor of college is "Mark Hopkins and a student at two ends of a log." This image is frequently used to describe the ideal exchange of ideas and attitudes between the professor and his student. And although it implies a more private tutelage, the closest most students will come to this ideal exchange is a small group discussion.

Next to lectures and textbooks, small group discussion is the most widely used technique in higher education. It plays an important role in classroom teaching, for while lectures and texts impart information, discussion allows the student to become actively involved in learning. While lecture requires the student to listen, discussion allows her to question, probe, and respond.

Discussions are typically of two sorts: instructor-centered and student-centered. This division is based on the instructor's role in the discussion and the amount of structure provided.

The instructor-centered discussion, as the term implies, focuses group attention on the teacher. The students may control the agenda and pace of the discussion, but the principal source of information is the instructor. This form of instructor-centered discussion is common before mid-terms and finals, for it gives the students a chance to ask questions and clear up misunderstandings.

The questions do not have to originate with the students in an instructor-centered discussion. The professor can serve as the focus by asking a logical series of questions in Socratic fashion, leading to a predetermined solution.

233

Finally, an instructor-centered discussion can take the form of a recitation. In recitation the instructor asks convergent subject matter questions usually based on the assigned readings or lectures. The instructor calls on students to give answers in what amounts to an oral quiz. With all three of these versions the instructor is the source of information and the adjudicator of truth.

The student-centered discussion increases student talk time and diminishes the role of the instructor. Questions and comments are directed to other students more than to the instructor. The responsibility of the discussion is turned over to the learner and, as a result, the students become more active and directive in their own learning. There are two modes of student-centered discussion, although they are not mutually exclusive. In the problem-solving mode, students are given a question or problem and must rely on their own resources and ingenuity to come up with an answer or answers. The role of the instructor is limited to setting the task (although another option would be to let the group set the task). The group decides how it will reach its solution.

The second mode of student-centered discussion is the open-ended discussion. The primary purpose of this mode is to have students share experiences, feelings, and opinions about a topic or issue, without concern for resolution. These modes can complement each other by using the open-ended mode to clarify positions on an issue and then moving to the problem-solving mode to resolve the difference.

With either mode, students are the source of information. They may bring diverse experiences and perspectives to bear on a common problem, or present a range of reactions to a shared experience, such as a reading, film, or game.

Advantages and Disadvantages

Probably the greatest advantage of discussion, at least over lecture, is that it is responsive to student needs. If a student misunderstands and needs clarification, requires an illustration of a point, or would like one position compared with another, all she need do is ask. Thus, the student becomes actively involved in learning; seeking out information and opinions.

She also has an opportunity to respond; she can share her position as well. She can nod her consent, raise an objection, or contribute new ideas and attitudes to the discussion.

This interaction among students presents the group with a variety of perspectives, opinions, and options, a condition which can lead to the students' personal development.

The basic problem with discussion is that it is very unreliable. Apart from the times it may become aimless or boring, it is usually haphazard even when done well. That is, because discussion is a less structured activity, not all of the important points may be raised, nor all of the information be accurate, nor all of the students' needs met. Although Hill (1969) presents a systematic discussion procedure which may alleviate this problem, a discussion is very much what the students make it, even when the instructor is an able and experienced group leader.

Another problem with discussion is that a significant amount of class time is required to maintain the group (Stanford and Roark, 1974). This is particularly true for the first several class periods, when the group is in its early stages of development. Students are primarily interested in getting to know each other and learning how to function as a group. This tends to be a less productive, low task-oriented period, but can be an important process if the goals for the course are the acquisition of interpersonal skills.

Despite some of its drawbacks, the discussion method has generated a great deal of support among faculty members. The research results, however, pick no favorites. In examining forty years of research comparing discussion and lecture, Dubin and Taveggia (1968) looked at student performance on final examination and found approximately half of the studies favored discussion, and half favored lecture. Yet to conclude that it does not make any difference whether one uses lecture or discussion would be an overgeneralization. A more recent review by Costin (1972) indicates that while lecture is probably more effective for learning information, discussion may be better for more difficult learning tasks. Furthermore, students seem to prefer discussion to lecture (McLeish, 1976).

Direct comparisons of discussion with other methods are less frequent. Dubin and Taveggia (1968) found fewer studies comparing discussion to independent study, but the results were the same as with lecture. Comparisons of discussions with games and role plays are difficult, since discussion is typically a component of these activities. However, discussion would seem to have a critical supplemental effect for these techniques.

Appropriate Uses

Content. Although some educators believe that discussion is more appropriate for teaching the humanities and social sciences, a review by Gall and Gall (1976) found no support for this position. The effectiveness of discussion is more likely to be related to the nature of the learning task than to the discipline.

Discussion seems appropriate for the application of concepts and the acquisition of problem-solving skills. This is supported by the Gall and Gall (1976) review and a recent study by Smith (1977), who found that classes that engaged in student participation, instructor-encouragement, and peer-to-peer interactions were consistently positively related to critical thinking. Gall and Gall (1976), on the other hand, found that instructor-centered recitation is effective for recall of facts.

Group discussion also seems appropriate for instruction intended to change attitudes. Attitudes can be affected by bringing the pressure of the group to bear on its members. They can also be changed by having the members raise and investigate alternative stands on an issue. This presents a number of positions as being legitimate and may lead to members' overcoming their present biases.

Discussion seems most appropriate for learning interpersonal skills. Skills such as speaking, listening, sharing, and leading are all abilities that can be fostered through group discussion.

Students. There seems to be some support for the differential effect of unstructured discussions on students with different characteristics. Less anxious students achieve more in discussion than in more structured situations (Dowaliby and Schumer, 1973). Students scoring high on tests of Achievement-via-Independence do better as well (Domino, 1971). It seems as though the unstructured learning environment created by student-centered discussions creates a challenging situation for these independent, less anxious students. On the other hand, these same studies show that students scoring high on tests of Anxiety and Achievement-via-Conformance do better in more structured situations, such as lectures.

A group leader who is familiar with the characteristics of her students can adjust the structure of the discussion from time to time to fit the needs of various members. For example, an anxious student can be given structure and brought into the discussion by asking a specific non-threatening question, such as, "Which character in the novel did you like best, Ralph?"

There is also some evidence (Witkin *et al.*, 1977) that field-dependent students (those who view their environment in global as opposed to analytical ways as explained in Chapters 2 and 5) are more suited to group discussion, especially if some guidance is provided by the instructor.

Instructor. The effective use of the small group discussion techniques requires a great deal of skill and experience on the part of the instructor. Although the ideal situation would require a minimal input from the instructor, the students typically lack skills necessary to conduct a successful discussion. This puts the pressure on the instructor to facilitate discussion by compensating for the lack of student skills, while diverting attention from himself to the students. The technique thus requires the instructor to attend to two things at once—the content of the discussion and the dynamics of the group.

The teachers best suited for discussion are probably similar to those students best suited for it, although there is no research on this topic. Teachers able to tolerate ambiguity and a low degree of structure would probably be more comfortable with this technique. Using Axelrod's (1973) taxonomy (see Chapter 2), these qualities would correspond to the "person-centered" or "intellect-centered" instructor. "Instructor-centered" would probably prefer instructor-centered discussions, and "content-centered" teachers would probably prefer discussion the least of these types.

Environment. Environmental requirements for discussion are similar to those for role play and other small group techniques. The room should accommodate up to twenty students. Flexible seating should be arranged so that students face each other in a circle or horseshoe configuration. The teacher, if involved in the discussion, should not stand or sit at what might be considered the apex or head of the group, but rather sit among the students.

Discussions held in large lecture halls pose more problems. Students could be asked to form groups with those sitting around them. After discussing a topic for a limited time, students can report their ideas to the whole class and the instructor.

Students should perceive the psychological environment as being safe, open, and accepting. The instructor should see to it that students are not put down or embarrassed, and that everyone has a chance to talk. For this reason, the composition of groups could be initially based on friendship patterns or student preference.

How to Use It

Any instructor who has used discussion has at least occasionally experienced the excitement that can be generated by students when they "catch fire." Making this more than an occasional occurrence takes considerable skill on the part of the instructor. This is especially so in a student-centered discussion if the students are inexperienced or unskilled in the techniques of discussion. The instructor must walk the fine line between too much and too little control. He must compensate for the students' lack of skills in order to make the discussion productive yet avoid drawing attention to himself and monopolizing the discussion. Skills necessary to make a discussion a productive and enjoyable instructional experience are covered in this section.

Starting. The way the instructor begins the discussion is critical. If it is done correctly, the students will know what is expected of them, will understand the rules of discussion, and will feel comfortable in expressing opinions, doubt, or ignorance. If done poorly, the start of a discussion can be its finish. The instructor can affectively close off discussion and make students feel defensive and threatened.

The instructor should begin by stating the objective or goal of the discussion session. This can be done by asking an open-ended question, stating a problem, or describing a potential outcome of the discussion. The task should be written on the board, along with any rules of discussion that the instructor might find appropriate for the occasion (e.g., "criticism suspended for the first ten minutes"; "always give evidence to support your position"), and a termination time. The instructor should avoid asking questions that have only one answer, giving her opinion, or stating the question too broadly (e.g., "what did you think of the movie we just saw?").

After stating the question, the instructor can walk away from an experienced group, leaving the students to their own resources. With less experienced groups, however, the instructor will have to be more directive. She should wait for a voluntary response to the question (while silently counting to ten), before tactfully directing the question specifically to one of the members. From this point on, the instructor should withdraw until one of the other leadership functions must be served.

Contracting. An optional function of the instructor is to involve the students in constructing a group "contract." This is more important in an ongoing discussion group than for an *ad hoc* discussion. The instructor should get the group members' opinions as to what will be the goals, roles (i.e., what is expected of the instructor and members), criteria (i.e., how the group will know when goals are met), and reward (i.e., what the members will get out of the group). Goals can be elicited using a technique called "problem posting." The instructor can ask the group what problems should be addressed by the group, and list without evaluation any and all suggestions. This list can serve as the group's agenda for the term. It is important for that group to know that it can rewrite its contract at a later time.

Listening. It is important for the instructor to listen attentively to the discussion. This is important for all of the group members, but it is a skill that many people lack and others abandon as they press to have their views heard in a heated discussion. The instructor can serve an important modeling function by following these rules:

- Look at the person who is talking, and at everyone from time to time (attending to non-verbal messages).
- Turn toward the person who is talking: lean forward; smile; nod or say "yes," "right," "uh-uh."
- Restate an important point for emphasis.

- If a statement is unclear, say so; restate the point and ask for correction or clarification.

Information management. If the instructor selects to remain in the group, and if the group is inexperienced, the group may try to reinstate the instructor as the leader and convert what would otherwise be a student-centered group into a teacher-centered group. The device typically used to accomplish this changeover is to return the information management function to the instructor. Students may direct their opinions or experiences to the instructor rather than to each other. They may ask the instructor for the "right answer," for his opinion, or for some crucial missing data. It is important for the instructor to resist this effort. Statements or questions directed toward the instructor should be redirected to other group members. The instructor should provide information only if not providing it would abort the group. The instructor should encourage students to seek critical information from each other or from external sources.

As the discussion develops and the instructor can become a member of the group without fear of being reinstated as an authority, this rule can be relaxed and the instructor can provide information and opinions as would any other member of the group. There are certain group exercises in which the instructor's function is to act as an outside expert or consultant. In such cases, of course, the instructor would provide needed information on request.

Responding to feelings. Sometimes the specific topic of a discussion will be to relate feelings about a situation or experience. But even in task-oriented discussions some feelings may emerge. It is an important function to see that members who express their feelings are protected or encouraged. The instructor may decide that nothing can be done about the feelings or that they are off-target or counterproductive. In such cases the feelings may merely be acknowledged, or handled later outside of the group. The feelings could be restated empathically and the person told that the feelings are understood and that she has a right to them. If the feelings are central to the topic or if they obstruct group progress, the instructor may allow an elaboration of the feelings and group response to them. It is critical that the instructor maintain a safe, open environment during the discussion.

Handling conflict. At the heart of any spirited discussion is conflict or disagreement. Conflict has the potential to further learning if handled well; it should not be automatically diffused. If handled poorly, it can be counterproductive and possibly destroy the group. It is important that the instructor maintain composure and respond fairly to all sides.

When a conflict emerges, the instructor should have either the opponents or non-participants restate the positions. If the disagreement is factual, it should serve as the basis for a library assignment. If the debate is one not yet resolved in the literature, the discussion could be turned to how the issue could be tested. If the conflict is based on values, the instructor should lead the students to realize the values involved. To reverse positions and argue the opponent's cause may give the students an appreciation of the values of others.

If the argument is one of group maintenance (e.g., membership, rules, goals, etc.), several means of resolution are available. The instructor may seek a compromise position or appeal to group harmony or commonly-held values. It may be necessary to table the issue until tempers cool, or to reach an agreement to disagree. Although a vote is possible, it is best for maintenance to seek consensus. If a decision is reached in which there are "losers," it is important that they be reinvolved in the groups as soon as possible.

A conflict may require that the group contract be renegotiated or that the original task be modified.

Focusing. A frequent problem in discussion is that the direction will go off topic. When this happens the instructor may wait to see if the group redirects itself; if not she may remind the group of the task or the goal. Another technique used to train the group in keeping on target is to interrupt from time to time and ask someone to restate the point currently discussed and relate it to the goal.

If the instructor finds that he is frequently focusing, the topic may be producing too much anxiety or too little interest. The instructor may want to confront the group with its behavior (see Confronting) or reconsider the assigned topic.

Gatekeeping. Another frequent problem in discussion is its domination by several people to the exclusion of others. The gatekeeping function helps all members to participate by limiting the comments of monopolizers and encouraging the more passive members to contribute. The instructor should scan the group, looking for non-verbal cues from non-participants which indicate a willingness to talk. Voluntary contributions of under-talkers should be praised. Any limitation on over-talkers should be accompanied by invitations to non-participants. In general, if a question is to be asked of a specific person, direct it to one of the under-talkers. Directed questions should be ones for which there is no wrong answer (e.g., "How do you feel about ...?") because fear of being wrong is a frequent reason for nonparticipation.

Giving feedback. In addition to removing barriers to progress by focusing and gatekeeping, the instructor may also give the group feedback about how they are progressing toward the goal. This function may be served by periodically summarizing the group's accomplishments (see Summarizing) and/or by praising contributions as they are made. Praise may be overt (e.g., "Good point, Laurie.") or covert (e.g., paying more attention, smiling, etc.). Behaviors praised may be on-target comments or facilitative group behaviors (i.e., those discussed in this section). Praise should be given as soon as possible after the behavior is exhibited and can be used to "shape" behavior. If the desired behavior is to increase participation by under-talkers, for example, shaping would mean the instructor would initially praise any comment, no matter how brief, and eventually reserve praise for more elaborate comments.

Confronting. It is occasionally necessary to confront the group or an individual concerning behavior that conflicts with the assignment or with agreed-upon behavior. If the group persists in off-target discussion or some or all of the members consistently break rules, it becomes necessary to point out the behavior. When confronting the group or a member, the instructor should be relaxed and make brief comments in a nonaggressive tone, stating the agreed-upon behavior and the inconsistent behaviors. It may be necessary to repeat the confrontation gently but firmly. The desired result of a confrontation would be to have the group or members reaffirm the agreed-upon behavior and commit themselves to reducing the discrepant behavior. An alternative result may be a renegotiation of the group contract.

Summarizing. At the end of a discussion, learning is facilitated and reinforced by pulling the pieces together. A discussion may take a very convoluted course to its resolution, and the logic may not be apparent. Another possibility is that several important points were made, but remain disconnected. The instructor may summarize to terminate a phase of the discussion or to provide closure or transition. When summarizing, the instructor should briefly restate the points made, identifying contributors, and draw generalizations or relationships across the points. It would be best to list these points on the board either in summary or at the time they are made. This contributes to the students' sense of learning, something which is sometimes lacking as the result of a discussion. It would be preferable to have the students themselves construct these statements.

In general, it would be better to have the students perform all of the functions described above. Ideally the instructor could relinquish the group manager functions as well as the source-of-all-knowledge function and become a co-learner. One of the most powerful reasons for using discussion is to promote interpersonal skills. If discussion is a predominant mode of instruction in a course, it is suggested that early sessions be centered on group skill building. The students should come to feel that the success of the group and their own learning is their responsibility rather than that of the instructor.

Resources

Books

Bertcher, H., and Gordon, J. *Techniques of group leadership.* Ann Arbor, Michigan: Manpower Science Services, 1972. A training handbook for group leaders. Although it is targeted to employment counselors, the skills are generalizable.

Hill, W. F. *Learning thru discussion.* Beverly Hills, California: Sage Publication, 1969. Description of a particular approach to discussion which is coordinated with Bloom's (1956) taxonomy.

Maier, N.R.F. *Problem-solving discussions and conferences.* New York: McGraw-Hill, 1963. A detailed presentation of a large number of discussion techniques useful for solving problems.

Olmstead, J. A. *Small-group instruction*. Alexandria, Virginia: Human Resources Research Organization, 1974. Both research and "how-to-do-it" for a large number of small-group techniques including buzz sessions, case studies, and role play.

Sharan, S., and Sharan, Y. *Small-group teaching*. Englewood Cliffs, New Jersey: Educational Technology Publications, 1976. A comprehensive description of small-group teaching techniques. While many of the authors' examples are expressed at the elementary and secondary school levels, most are readily transferable to the college and university setting.

Stanford, G., and Roark, A. *Human interaction in education*. Boston: Allyn and Bacon, 1974. Detailed treatment of student-centered discussions. Includes exercises that can be used to improve student group skills.

The Agree/Disagree Discussion

H. Norman Wright is a professor at Biola College in California, a small Christian liberal arts college. In the early 1960's he observed a teacher using a discussion technique called the agree/disagree discussion. Since then, Mr. Wright has made extensive use of the technique and has applied it to many learning situations. "I haven't found anything that gets people thinking as much. It creates a high level of interest in students and forces them to clarify what they believe and what they think."

The technique is a simple one. Mr. Wright has taught it to counselors, ministers, and lay teachers. Typically it is used at the beginning of a class. The teacher has prepared a list of statements relevant to the material to be presented in the class session. Students indicate individually whether they agree or disagree with each statement. They indicate this by raising hands, standing up, or by moving to a particular side of the room. The students are then divided into groups to discuss their reasons for agreeing or disagreeing with each statement. Often a time limit is set on this discussion period.

During the class session, information relevant to the statements is presented to the students so that they can make judgments about their decision to agree or disagree. Students often change their opinions during the class sessions.

Mr. Wright has used the technique with all age groups from high school to senior citizens. He has found that the technique works well in a variety of courses that he teaches: Marriage and Family, Organization in Education, Christian Education, Mental Health, Counseling, and Bible study courses.

Mr. Wright has also found other ways to adapt the technique. "Sometimes I give students a list of statements at the beginning of a unit. The statements pertain to subject matter that will be covered over a six- or eight-week period. Each week I deal with one question. The agree/disagree discussion serves as an introduction to the unit."

The students also learn about communication through this technique. "They begin to realize that to communicate, people must have a common interpretation of the question being discussed. Some disagreements occur because people do not agree on the meanings of terms." The reaction of students to the agree/disagree discussion has been quite positive. "At first students are apprehensive when they are asked to stand up or to stand on one side of the room to indicate their opinions. Once they are accustomed to the technique, however, they all agree that it is stimulating and useful."

Prof. H. Norman Wright
Graduate Program in Marriage and Counseling
Biola College
La Mirada, California 90639
(213) 944-0351

Chapter 16

ROLE PLAYING

On Sunday, August 15, 1971 nine college-age males began a social-psychological experiment—they were arrested! Each had volunteered for a two-week-long experiment which would examine the effects of a simulated prison environment on "prisoners" and "guards."

The "prisoners" were informed of their rights, booked, finger printed, and incarcerated in a jail constructed in the basement of Stanford University's Psychology Department building.

The first day passed without incident. On the second day the prisoners rebelled, barricading themselves inside the cells, and cursing at the guards. The guards met force with force, breaking into cells, spraying the prisoners with fire extinguishers, and putting the ringleaders in solitary confinement.

On Monday night the first "prisoner" had to be released from the experiment, suffering from acute emotional disturbance, disorganized thinking, and hysteria. On Friday the entire experiment had to be discontinued—it was no longer an experiment.

In a debriefing one "guard" said, "I was surprised at myself ... I made them call each other names and clean the toilets out with their bare hands" (Zimbardo, Haney, and Banks, 1971, p. 9), and a "prisoner" said, "I began to feel that I was losing my identity ..." (p. 12).

Although this was an experiment rather than an instructional use of role play, it does demonstrate the potential power of this technique to affect feelings.

In its simplest terms role playing is "acting as if." In an instructional role play, a situation is presented to a group of students, and some members are asked to assume roles and act out the situation. The remaining students observe the role play and note specific behaviors related to the goals for the session. When the play is completed a debriefing takes place where players, observers, and the instructor can relate feelings experienced and discuss behaviors displayed.

There are basically two types of role plays. In the first type of role play, the players relinquish their usual patterns of behavior in exchange for the role and patterns of another person. This other role may be that of a real person (e.g., some famous person in history, a roommate, or "I'll be you and you be me") or may be entirely fictitious (e.g., a business executive, someone on welfare, a tormented lover). The role players attempt, as far as possible, to speak, think, behave, and feel like the person they are playing. This allows the student to identify and empathize with other people and their problems. The Zimbardo prison simulation is an example of this type of role play. A second example is the use of the technique by students in a social work treatment course. Having students portray clients allows the students to develop an empathy that would help them to deliver services in a more humane way.

In the second type of role play, the players retain their own roles and behavior patterns, but act as if they were in a different situation. This would be a situation in which one or both role players are likely to find themselves at some time in the future (e.g., applying for a job, interviewing subjects in an experiment, health professionals examining patients, other professionals consulting with clients). This type of role play is useful for the training of specific interpersonal skills (e.g., counseling, teaching, interviewing, handling conflict, persuasion, etc.). Role playing done in this way can be used in conjunction with modeling. The instructor, another professional, or an exemplary student can demonstrate a particular technique while other students can then practice it in a role play. An example of this type of role play is a journalism class where the instructor wants to have the students practice getting information from a reluctant news source.

Role play provides students with an opportunity to experience feelings and practice interpersonal skills in a lifelike situation without running the risks that failure incurs in real life. It also allows students to get feedback that they may not otherwise receive in a real life situation.

Advantages and Disadvantages

Little research exists comparing role play to other classroom methods. Therefore, the relative advantages and disadvantages of role play are left to a more subjective assessment.

Role plays differ from simulation games in their lack of rules and competition. They are also more focused and less open-ended than games. Because the roles, situations, and goals are more precisely defined, one might expect role plays to be more effective than simulation games for teaching specific interpersonal skills.

A comparison between lecture and role play is likely to favor the role play for instructional objectives within the affective domain. The lecturer tends to talk about feelings and behavior rather than elicit them. Everyone can recall a particularly inspiring lecturer or lecture, but it would seem role play would be more reliable in evoking the emotions necessary to bring about attitudinal change. Although it is difficult to completely separate discussion from role play, the dramatization component of the role play is likely to make it more effective than discussion for this objective.

Film and television are frequently used to teach affective objectives. Although these media have the disadvantage of being passive media, the more controlled visual effect may result in dramatic impact equal to or greater than that of role play. Fay (1973) found that groups of architecture students using either role play or film/ discussion were more likely to change their attitudes toward barrier-free designs than an information-only control group. However, role play has the distinct advantage of personalizing the emotions because of the active involvement of the players. Role play has the added advantage of requiring no expensive production or supportive hardware or software. Film and video would be best reserved for large audiences where role play would be infeasible or threatening.

The biggest disadvantage of role play is the artificiality of the situations. As with simulation games, the safety of the environment reduces the reality of the situation. Yinon, Shoham, and Lewis (1974) found that students facing a real life problem tended to choose a lower risk alternative more often than students role playing the same decision.

Furthermore, it seems that the changes in attitude resulting from role plays are either socially desirable responses or short-lived, for they do not translate into action. Ingersoll (1973) found that a role play dealing with voting in campus elections did lead to a change in attitudes about the behavior but not to an increase in a non-reactive measure of voting behavior. Fay (1973) found that architecture students who role played disabled people confined to wheelchairs, or who watched a film and discussed disability, changed their attitudes toward barrier-free designs more than a control group. However, designs of building entrances in a subsequent course did not demonstrate differences in the use of barrier-free designs between groups. Thus, it seems that role play is useful to practice interpersonal skills or to explore different attitudes, but attitude changes may not be stable and do not necessarily translate into behavior.

Appropriate Uses

Content. Because role playing is a technique which involves two or more people interacting, it is best suited for those content areas that deal with interpersonal subject matter, and the feelings, attitudes, and skills that accompany them. Some courses taught in the departments of Communication, Geography, History, Political Science, Psychology, and Sociology and almost all professional schools, are likely to have such subject matter.

However, the technique must be used with specific goals in mind. These goals might include social skills such as expressing oneself, persuading others, resisting persuasion, and so on. Role play can also be used to diagnose interpersonal situations to determine those for which certain skills are appropriate. Probably the most common reasons for using role play are to affect attitudes, or to increase awareness of interpersonal problems and issues inherent in a given situation.

For the reasons given above, role play fits well for courses which stress the personal development of students. It allows them to express feelings and try on new "roles" in an atmosphere of safety and support. Both of these conditions are necessary for student development.

Students. Because role playing puts the spotlight on students and requires them to perform in front of their peers, it is important that the students approach the technique openly and without anxiety. The same student qualifications for discussion probably apply to role play as well. The less anxious and more independent students would probably achieve more using role plays. Although there is much an instructor can do to reduce anxiety (see "How to Use It"), a student who remains anxious should not be required to participate.

For role plays involving skill development and improvement, it is important that students have a basic knowledge of the skills prior to the role play; the emphasis is on practice. Best results will be obtained in enactment and debriefing if this rule is followed. Prior knowledge is less important in role plays involving attitude change.

Instructor. Optimal results are obtained by an instructor who is familiar enough with the content to translate theory into everyday life and back again. Because role playing deals with the application of theories and principles, the instructor will continually be pressed to explain the subtleties of the concepts.

As with discussion, the instructor must be comfortable with the technique. To create the safe environment necessary for an effective role play, the instructor must be familiar with the application of the technique. Although role play is more structured than student-centered discussion, it is probably still necessary for the instructor to handle ambiguity, for role plays often take unexpected turns. Most importantly, it is necessary for the instructor to be able to react to such occurrences without anxiety.

Instructors who characterize themselves as "person-centered" or as "intellect-centered" are more likely to function well with role play. "Instructor-centered" teachers would probably be comfortable using role play to model the application of their expertise. "Content-centered" instructors would not find role play a very efficient way to deliver or demonstrate knowledge.

Environment. The physical environment for role playing should accommodate a group of up to twenty members, yet be intimate, comfortable, and private. Flexible seating is ideal, for it allows room for a variety of role play situations, and a semi-circular or circular audience arrangement.

The personal environment should be trusting, psychologically safe, and accepting of failure. Role playing should not be attempted until the members of the group are familiar and friendly with each other. The membership of the group should be stable, although not necessarily homogeneous (in fact, the group may benefit from the diversity of perceptions of a heterogeneous group).

The group should not feel rushed or anxious. The instructor can contribute to an environment of safety and comfort by having the role play well planned, and by displaying patience. The instructor should reserve 30 to 60 minutes of class time even for a brief role play.

How to Use It

As mentioned earlier, instructor knowledge of and experience with this technique can help in assuring its successful use. Information on the planning, starting, playing, and debriefing of a role play will be covered in this section.

Planning. The instructor should begin the planning of a role play by determining the objectives of the experience. What new interpersonal skills or attitudinal influences are being imparted to the students? How well are the students to perform the skills and in which real life situations? Answers to these questions can help the instructor construct a successful role play and shape the students' experience.

Occasionally the instructor may want to prepare materials for the role play. Handouts explaining the roles, backgrounds, and attitudes of players and describing the situation may be useful, especially in more complex or elaborate role plays. Separate handouts for each player can be used to create a situation where the roles of each player are not immediately apparent to the other players.

Props may also be prepared in advance if their use heightens the realism and dramatic effect of the play. Props should be simple and kept at a minimum, as excess detail may detract from the primary purpose of the role play.

Some preparation may be required of the students. If the students have not done any role playing before and seem anxious, the instructor may want to accustom them gradually. Less structured role plays or "creative drama sessions" could be used as warm-ups for the students.

Starting. The instructor should begin a role play session by describing the role play process. Students should be reassured of the safety of the process and otherwise put at ease. The instructor should emphasize the fact that no lines have to be learned, although each student should try to portray the role assigned. The instructor should discourage behaviors that would detract from the role play, such as overacting or clowning.

The specific role play should be described in detail. The purpose and problem should be described, along with the situation and the roles. One option is to have students research the roles and situations before class. Another option is for the instructor or some other expert to model the appropriate behaviors. The audience (i.e., the remainder of the students who are observing the role play) should be told what to look for. Different students may be told to look for specific things to report back to the class. Finally, the instructor should state what criteria will be used for ending the role play.

Playing. During the role play the instructor should take notes on the behaviors of the players. Interventions in the play should be used to keep the players in role and to keep the action moving, or to make a point to the players or the audience.

The instructor should stop the play if it becomes unmanageable or threatening to one of the players. The play should be stopped when the objective of the play is reached or otherwise after three to six minutes.

Debriefing. Debriefing is a critical aspect of the role play. It is when attitudes and behaviors can be examined and clarified.

The debriefing should begin by de-roling the player. The instructor may want to make the distinction between how the character felt and how the actor would have felt. Reference to the character should be made in the past tense.

The players should be allowed to respond to the role play first. The instructor should help them express their feelings and relate the experience to the objectives of the session. Subsequently the audience may be asked to express their feelings and observations.

The instructor should summarize the role play's critical events, issues and/or solutions evoked by the play. Behaviors of the players may be praised or critiqued. Audio or videotape playback is useful at this stage. Finally, the instructor may want to repeat the play using the same students in the same roles, in different roles, or different students in the roles.

Resources
Books

Bertcher, H., Gordon, J., Hayes, M., and Mial, H.. *Role modeling, role playing: A manual for vocational development and employment agencies*. Ann Arbor, Michigan: Manpower Science Services, 1970. Covers the practice and theory of role playing and modeling. Although targeted for employment counselors, techniques are transferable.

Chesler, M., and Fox. R. *Role-playing methods in the classroom*. Chicago, Illinois: Science Research Associates, 1966. Extensive coverage of the use of role playing as a classroom instructional technique. Although it is targeted at elementary and secondary teachers, the technique transfers to higher education.

Olmstead, J. A. *Small-group instruction*. Alexandria, Virginia: Human Resources Research Organization, 1974. The theory and practice of role playing is only one of many small-group instructional techniques covered in this book. Consequently, coverage is brief.

Role Play: Students' Involvement in Learning

Carina Christian has been using role play as a teaching method in a variety of courses over the past ten years. "I have always tried to get students involved in their learning. Role play has become one of the many techniques I use to increase this involvement." Dr. Christian has used role play as an occasional method in Introductory Science and History of Science courses; and in other interdisciplinary courses, such as Science and Society: The Ascent of Man. Typically it is used once or twice during a semester.

Two general formats are used in the role plays. One format is the re-enactment of a historical situation; for example, the trial of Galileo. Students who play the roles are required to research the historical situation so that it will be portrayed accurately. A second format is the debate. Students are asked to assume opposing viewpoints that historically surrounded an issue. For example, students might research various theories of the origin of the universe and debate these viewpoints. Viewpoints held at a particular time in history may be debated; or viewpoints held at different times in history may be debated.

Because students must become personally involved in role play, this method can convey many kinds of learning that are difficult to teach using traditional methods. "The student has an opportunity to explore both sides of an argument. As a result he becomes aware of the danger of one-sided thinking. He can also experience an emotional involvement in his learning. I think that involvement and excitement is a major ingredient in learning. Many of my students are inspired to do further research as a result of the role play experience."

The success of role play depends, to some extent, on the personalities of the students. "Some students are inhibited by the situation. They worry about their acting ability and are embarrassed to participate. With this type of group I find that role play works better as a spontaneous event than as a planned activity." The success of this method also depends on the ability of the students to pick out the important points in the situation to be portrayed. "Whenever possible, I rehearse the role play with the students in my office prior to the class meeting. If important information or opinions have been omitted from their presentation, I can correct it at this time."

One disadvantage of this technique is that there is only a limited amount of creativity required of the student. "Students are quoting someone else's opinion in the role play. They are not forced to generate new ideas or unique approaches to problems." Role play can also be a more time-consuming method for presentation of new material than the traditional lecture format. "Although some teachers may see this as a disadvantage, I don't look at it that way. Lecturing may be a more economical use of time, but I am really more concerned with the quality of the time spent with students. Presenting compact packages of facts is not my way of teaching."

When considering role play as a method, many teachers reject it because it seems incompatible with the subject matter of their courses. Dr. Christian points out that the use of role play is really only limited by the teacher's imagination. "Once I began using role play I was surprised at the number of situations I could create using this method. Now I believe that teachers in almost all disciplines could adopt this method for their courses. Teachers concerned with increasing student involvement in learning might want to give some thought to the possibilities presented through role play."

Dr. Carina Christian, Project Director,
Institutional Development, Chaminade University,
Waialae Avenue, Honolulu, Hawaii 96816
(808) 732-1471 ext. 144

Chapter 17

SIMULATION GAMES

An old woman trying to continue her daily activities is increasingly frustrated by her declining physical mobility, shrinking material resources, failing memory, and the loss of her friends. With much difficulty she contacts an agency set up by the government to meet her needs. She finds that, in spite of the good intentions of the social workers, they are unable to help her because of limited resources and bureaucratic rules and regulations. Frustrated again, she is left alone, sitting, waiting for death.

Although this could easily be a description of the unfortunate plight of many of this nation's elderly, it could just as likely be the description of the feelings of a participant in Frederick Goodman's "The End of the Line." This activity was designed to help persons who work with the aged become more sensitive to their needs and to generate more effective and humane ways to deliver services. It is also representative of an emerging new class of learning activities —simulation games.

Although people have been playing games for millennia, their use for instructional purposes is quite recent. Because everyone has played games, they are easy to identify, but they remain difficult to define, and even more difficult to design.

As one of the leading proponents of the educational use of games, Goodman (1973) defines a game as a set of activities governed by two sets of rules—move rules and termination rules. Move rules indicate the choices a player may make in the game, while termination rules specify the outcome of the play. An additional requirement of a game is that there be at least two players, one of whom may be fictitious. That is, one of the players may be a non-person (e.g., chance, nature, a machine, etc.) which makes choices and receives payoffs.

A distinction is often made between simulation games and non-simulation games. Non-simulation games deal with content for which there is a high degree of consensus and incorporate, by reference, rules from other domains. Thus, spelling bees and math games include as rules of the game the "rules" of spelling and math.

Simulation games include rules from domains that are less clear and for which there is less consensus. They are meant to represent reality, rather than include it. A simulation game should allow the learner to experience the structure and process of some aspect of the real world. However, a simulation game need not look like reality—only act like it. So, a game on the American electoral process need not replicate reality in total, with its political parties, personalities, and outcomes; but it should include some critical aspects of the structure and process of American electoral politics.

Frequently, simulation games require the players to assume roles and behave in some hypothetical situation. Such roles might include that of mayor, prisoner, taxpayer, farmer, or school board member. The players are given situations and problems appropriate to their roles and asked to make decisions. The rules of the simulation game are designed so that the players experience the life-like consequences of their decisions. Therefore, game decisions that represent sound real life decisions will result in winning the game; while decisions which are analogous to poor real life decisions will result in losing the game.

There are such things as non-game simulations. They include all-machine simulations (such as computer models of electrical systems), person-machine simulations (such as driver-training simulators), and all-person simulations. All-person simulations, or role plays, require learners to take roles and make decisions but, unlike simulation games, have few or no rules and no "winners."

Emphasis in this chapter will be given to simulation games and, to a lesser degree, non-simulation games. Machine related non-game simulations are covered in Chapter 21, on computer-assisted instruction. All-person simulations are covered in Chapter 16, on role playing.

Advantages and Disadvantages

The obvious advantage of simulation games is that they actively engage the student. The learner is drawn—compelled—into the game. No nodding heads and blank stares are seen during the play. Such activities seem to increase the student's interest in the subject matter.

The students are not only actively involved with the subject matter, but also with each other. Student talk increases and the atmosphere becomes more relaxed.

The activity of the students more closely approximates activities required by real life—no quizzes and term papers, but decisions, negotiations, and compromises. Simulations represent real life processes. Students experience these complexities in a diversity of situations, increasing the likelihood that what is learned can be transferred, integrated, and applied in real life.

Simulations have the added advantage of being less expensive than their real life counterparts, not only in preparation but in consequences. Students can witness the results of their decisions without experiencing their costly, and sometimes dangerous and immutable consequences. They are also able to make repeated attempts, something that life does not always allow.

However, while simulation games *approximate* real life, there are some serious shortcomings. Simulation games can be too simplistic, leaving the learner with an incomplete or stereotyped view of reality. The lack of real life consequences can distort the decision process. Students can be cavalier in their strategies because they believe they do not count—or, worse yet, that the decisions do not matter in real life.

There is also a lack of accountability with simulation games. Since outcomes vary with different plays and roles, the instructor cannot be sure of who has learned what. The fun of the play may overshadow all else, and the student may walk away unaware of what, if anything, was learned.

Simulation games have logistical problems as well. Although some games are made from common materials, others are expensive to buy and require the replacement of consumable parts. Frequently games must be modified to fit a specific set of objectives and on occasion must be designed from scratch. Needless to say this requires a great deal of preparation time.

Simulation games also require a considerable time to play, thus reducing the amount of material covered. (One must remember, however, that "coverage" does not equal "learning.") Furthermore, it is difficult to be precise about what is learned from a game. What a particular student learns may depend on which role is played (a "mayor" may learn something different than a "taxpayer") and how it is played (someone who wins may learn something different than one who loses).

The most critical problem that remains for simulation games is that they have not been shown to be more effective than other media, even when the criterion is achievement of higher order skills. Although there is an appalling lack of research on the relative effectiveness of games in higher education, what little that has been done seems inconclusive.

In two studies, one at the University of Southern Mississippi, and one at Xavier University of Louisiana, Louis Mancuso (1974, 1975) compared lecture-computer simulation with lecture and case study. The game used, BROADEC, is a marketing simulation designed to teach principles of management. In both studies, Mancuso found no differences on exam scores between the group using the simulation and those students using lecture and case study.

Marianne Bonds (1974) found no differences on the examination of economic concepts between groups using games and simulations, instructional television, programmed learning, and lecture-discussion. While Chartier (1972) found simulation with discussion to be better than discussion alone, Wentworth (1972) found lecture-discussion to be superior to simulation games. So while simulation gaming remains an exciting and intuitively attractive mode of instruction, the burden remains with its proponents to demonstrate its advantages over other approaches.

Appropriate Uses
Content. Advocates of simulation games frequently claim that the strongest case for their use in instruction is that they teach

higher order skills and influence student attitudes and values. There is a certain logic to this, for rather than simply presenting information, simulation games involve students in a process. The students must make decisions and bear their consequences. As a result, learners are likely to acquire problem-solving and decision-making skills. They are also likely to learn the process involved in the simulation, as well as the concepts on which the model is based.

Many simulation games portray social situations and dilemmas. As such they are likely to teach interpersonal skills like negotiation, compromise, and communication. Playing the role of another person, as is required by social simulation games, can lead to empathic understanding of other social groups and result in changed attitudes and values.

Changes in attitude may even include those concerning the learning situation. Games may foster positive feelings toward the discipline, the instructor, and the educational process.

There is less consensus over whether or not simulation games are effective for teaching factual information. One position is that in its construction a simulation simplifies reality, usually at the expense of detail, so that things may look different or be called by different names than they are in reality. Therefore, students are less likely to learn factual information. On the other hand, it can be argued that the contingencies of the game increase the utility of knowing certain facts (i.e., they are needed in order to win the game), so that students are more likely to learn them. This argument is stronger for non-simulation games than for simulation games. The need to know certain mathematical facts in order to win a math game is inescapable.

Several of the claims made by simulation game proponents are supported by evaluative research. Most of the few studies identified used attitude change as a dependent variable. Several studies (Boags, 1970; Boocock, 1968; Edwards, 1971; Feldbaum *et al.*, 1976; and Wilson, 1974) showed increases in general attitudes such as efficacy, confidence, or subject matter interest. Two studies (Chapman, 1974; and Livingston, 1971) showed changes in specific attitudes, such as more positive attitudes toward blacks and the poor. Livingston noted, however, that these attitudes were not sustained over time. Two other researchers (Hart, 1970; and Heinkel, 1970) showed that more extreme feelings resulted from the play of a simulation game. Only one study identified (Bazen and Bowles, 1975) showed no change in attitudes.

The results of studies which examined the increases in cognitive learning are not as numerous. Three studies (Boocock, 1968; Feldbaum *et al.*, 1976; and Heinkel, 1970) showed an increase in knowledge learned via a game. One study by Hart (1970) showed no such increase. Only one study tested for the impact of a game on higher order skills. Kidder and Guthrie (1972) showed that students who played a simulation game were able to apply behavior modification techniques successfully in the training of mentally retarded children.

In general, simulation games seem most appropriate for changing student attitudes and knowledge. Their impact on higher order abilities has not yet been firmly established.

Students. Few writers on the topic of simulation games address the issue of the differential effects of the technique on student subgroups. One statement which does emerge is that shy, withdrawn, or underachieving students may learn more from simulation games than other students. The argument goes that the intrinsic motivational aspects of games serve to engage such students in the learning of the subject matter. However, a study by Michael Inbar (1968) indicates that degree of previous interest in the topic of the game accounts for more of the students' enjoyment than any general interest in games.

A study by Mancuso (1975) showed that a simulation game was no better than lecture-case study for minority students. Edwards (1971) showed that low ability students were no more likely to say that games provided them with special learning opportunities than high ability students. And while Braskamp and Hodgetts (1971) found an inverse relationship between grade point and performance in a simulation game, it is unclear that this relationship would hold when testing for generalizations and principles learned from the game. In general, it has not been shown that simulation games have more advantages for one type of learner than another.

Instructor. No research has been found on the relative effectiveness of simulation games when used by various types of instructors. However, there are a number of statements that can be made based on the nature of games and classrooms.

Simulation games are likely to change the role of the instructor in the classroom. A faculty member considering the use of this technique should be aware of, and amendable to, such a change. Being experiential in nature, a game draws the focus of learning toward the process being simulated and away from the instructor. The instructor does not serve as judge or as the source of information, but as facilitator and director.

Instructors who use games should probably have what psychologists call "tolerance of ambiguity." It is frequently difficult to figure out exactly what is happening during a game—what is being learned, and who is learning what. Control momentarily transfers from the hands of the instructor to the contingencies of the game. Formality decreases; noise and movement increase. This condition may arouse anxiety in the unprepared instructor.

There are also certain prerequisite attitudes and skills that may be preferable for faculty members using this technique. The instructor should be convinced of, or at least open-minded about, the efficacy of games; she should consider games as serious and intellectually valid approaches to learning. It is also probably helpful for the instructor to be experienced with running games and using discussion techniques.

Environment. Because simulation games are a group activity, it would not be surprising to find that their effectiveness is influenced by the social environment and that they in turn affect the environment.

A study by Inbar (1968) showed that the enjoyment of a simulation game was less in large groups than in small. He proposed that as the size increases, interaction and participation drop. There is probably an optimum size for a game, but it probably varies from game to game.

The effects of games on the social environment is suggested in a study of younger learners by David DeVries and Keith Edwards (1973). The researchers found more use of peers as tutors and more positive attitudes toward the learning environment with the group using games than in a control situation where students were periodically quizzed.

The physical environment of a game may also be important. Because games are sometimes noisy and informal, it would probably be best to conduct such activities in isolated and informal settings where students can feel free to get excited without bothering other classes.

How to Do It

There are two situations an instructor can find herself in once simulation games are chosen as an appropriate medium: (1) she finds a commercially available game which suits her needs, and she merely conducts it with her class; or (2) finding no games which suit her needs, she must design a game or drastically modify someone else's. Given limited time and resources, the first situation is usually preferable. Although both running and designing games are covered in this section, it is strongly advised that only a very experienced gamer take on the design task, and even then it is best to get advice from an experienced designer.

Running a Game

1. *Preparation.* Selection of the proper game is the critical first step in preparation. A game should match the learning objectives, the size of the group, the experiences and interests of the learners, and a desired level of abstraction. A simulation too close to the student's own situation may inhibit play; one too abstract may appear irrelevant. If the instructor has not played the game, information for such a match can be gained from those who have done so, or from reviews of the game.

The instructor can begin the preparation for running a simulation game by preparing himself. Although it is probably best to play a game before running it, the instructor can get its flavor by walking through it. He can organize his thoughts by checking its parts, scoring, room setup, roles, sequence of play, and so on. As he goes he can create a check list that can be used during play.

Much preparation is required of the simulation itself. Slight modifications of scenarios, roles, and rules may be made to fit the class or situation. Equipment should be checked, and lost or consumed parts replaced. Handouts can be prepared to explain the rules, roles, and procedures, and finally the room should be set up and the roles cast.

Students should also be prepared for a simulation game. A game which is sprung on the students as they walk in—notebook in hand—is off to a poor start.

2. *Conducting the game*. The instructor can begin the game by giving an overview or a briefing. The purpose and issues can be stated and the timing and sequence laid out. The rules and moves can be explained and demonstrated, but it is best that the students not be overprepared. The excitement of discovery can be drowned in the minutia of rules and options. A practice round is a good idea, and rules can be explained as the game progresses.

If time permits, the game can be played twice. The first time could be a simpler form to stimulate interest, and a second time to use what was learned.

The students can be involved in redesigning the game for the next play. This practice has been institutionalized by Frederick Goodman in the concept of a frame game. A frame game is a loose format for a game which the participants can alter to fit their own notions and situations. Goodman contends that learning is more likely to occur in the design of a game than in its play.

The instructor can expect to be busy during the play of a game. Frequently he must be the game overall director (or G.O.D.), passing out information, manipulating devices, and scoring rounds. He can adjust the pace of the game: speeding it up by introducing crises or new situations, and slowing it down by calling meetings or holding mid-game debriefings. The instructor should feel free to modify rules as the play requires. He can circulate, listen, observe, and take notes but should keep meddling to a minimum. If his presence inhibits play, it might be best for him to leave the room for a while.

The game will terminate according to the rules, or at the option of the instructor as the game peaks. Termination should be done in a way that does not skew the players' strategies, unless this is part of the instructor's plan.

3. *Debriefing*. There are several functions for the debriefing or

post-game discussion. The instructor must correct any misunderstandings that resulted from a particular way the game was played. She must also make the students aware of what they have learned and how that can be transferred to other situations.

The discussion can begin by concentrating on what happened during the game—who did what to whom? What was the best strategy? What were the effects of various decisions? How did strategies and game rules interact?

The students should be encouraged to express their feelings and values. What values were reflected by the game? Did they match the students? How did a student feel who violated her values?

Once the basic reporting is complete the instructor should lead the students into an analysis of the real life situation which the game represents. What were the situations represented in the simulation? Who were the people? How do they behave in the real world? Why do they behave that way?

Finally, the discussion could turn to the game design. As suggested previously, the intent of the instructor may be to have the students redesign the game. Issues involved in a critique and redesign are: Do the components of the game—the roles, situations, props, and rules—adequately represent the real world process? How could they be changed? What effect might such changes have on the play of the game?

The instructor can conclude the game activity by asking the students to list the things that they learned during the game. Such a summary can serve to stress the instructional benefits of the game and increase student awareness of their own learning.

How to Design a Game

The design of an effective simulation game is not a trivial matter. Indeed, this section is included only after much consideration by the authors, and is meant not as a guide to design (many books have been written on the topic) but to give the instructor a sense of what is involved in the design of a simulation.

1. Define the problem area to be simulated. This could be an organization or a set of social problems, and should be determined by examining the instructional goal of the teacher.

2. Define the objective and scope of the simulation. Next, the

designer specifies what is to be learned by students who play the game.

3. Define the people and organizations involved. The designer identifies the roles and situations that the players will encounter.

4. Define the motives and purposes of the players. The designer must identify and try to represent the real life motives of each of the roles. These motives are operationalized through rules and constraints of the game.

5. Define the resources available to the players. Resources such as money, property, authority, and information should be identified and distributed to the roles in a way that reflects reality.

6. Determine the transactions to be simulated and the decision rules to be followed. Games are composed of rounds of play, and these center around the transaction of the players and their consequences. The designer must determine the type of transaction that will occur (e.g., buying, selling, negotiating, planning, etc.) based on the type of decisions required by the process being represented. The extent to which chance operates in the transactions should also be determined.

7. Formulate the evaluation method. As mentioned above, all games must have termination rules. The designer must list the event or events that will result in the termination of the game and what consequences these events will have on the players. These may be completion of a certain number of rounds, or some critical occurrence such as a goal achievement or the exhaustion of resources by one or more players. The termination may represent some real life occurrence or it may be a contrived convenience.

8. Develop simulation game prototype. At this step the designer constructs the game materials. The designer may choose a board format, a role play situation, or a combination. Any devices and props that represent rewards, resources, and transactions must be constructed.

9. Try out and modify prototype. Finally the game is played. The designer gets a chance to see if what he made works and what changes are needed. The designer should observe and collect information on amount of time taken, the pacing, the operation, the consequences of the play, and the reactions of the players. Such

information can be used for the subsequent modifications that are frequently necessary in game design.

Finally, it should be remembered that game designing is an art. As such it is difficult to codify reliably in a step-by-step fashion. Following these rules is no guarantee of success. Accumulated experience in game design is the best source of guidance for this task.

Resources

Books and Articles

Horn, R. E. (Ed.) *The guide to simulations/games for education and training* (3rd ed.). Cranford, New Jersey: Didactic Systems, Inc., 1977. A directory of games for all levels and areas. Descriptions include goals, playing data, costs, and editor's comment. The volume also contains several articles on conducting and designing games.

Livingston, S. A., and Stoll, C. S. *Simulation games*. New York: Free Press, 1973. An introduction to simulation games which describes the instructional use, design, and research of games.

Seidner, C. J. Teaching with simulations and games. In N. L. Gage (Ed.), *The psychology of teaching methods*. Chicago: University of Chicago Press, 1976. Conceptual introduction to instructional simulations and games, which reviews research and discusses classroom applications.

Stadsklev, R. *Handbook of simulation gaming in social education*. (2 vols.) Tuscaloosa, Alabama: Institute of Higher Education Research and Services, University of Alabama, 1975. Volume 1 has a number of articles on what simulation games are, and how they are designed and played. Volume 2 is a directory of social education games, centers, and bibliographies.

Periodicals

Simulation and Games, Sage Publications, Beverly Hills, California 90212. A journal published quarterly which emphasizes theory and research on simulations and games. Features include meeting announcements, and reviews of books and games.

Simulation/Gaming/News, Box 3039, University Station, Moscow, Idaho, 83843. A bi-monthly newsletter published by

NASAGA, contains articles on developments in the field and regular features reviewing new materials, and announcing meetings.

Places

Center for Multidisciplinary Educational Exercises (COMEX), University of Southern California, Los Angeles, California 90007. The Center designs and adapts simulation/games, evaluates programs, presents demonstrations and lectures, guides research studies, and assists faculty members in integrating simulation/games into the curriculum.

Extension Gaming Service, University of Michigan Extension Service, 412 Maynard St., Ann Arbor, Michigan 48109. An organization which makes the University's gaming resources available to community, educational, and professional groups. Services include consultation, workshops, and modification and design of simulation/games.

Organizations

International Simulation and Gaming Association (ISAGA). Richard Duke, University of Michigan, Ann Arbor, Michigan 48109. A professional organization aimed at facilitating communication among gaming specialists, and between specialists and users of games, regarding research and application of simulation/games.

North American Simulation and Gaming Association Conference (NASAGA), COMEX Project, University of Southern California, Los Angeles, California 90007. A professional organization of educators and specialists in design and use of simulation/games.

Simulation Gaming—Everybody Wins

Donald Valdes has been using simulation gaming as a supplementary activity in an introductory sociology course and in an introductory anthropology course at Denison University. In sociology he is using SIMSOC (developed by William Gamson at The University of Michigan); and in anthropology he is using "The Hunting Game," a game that he designed himself. "I feel that affective learning is extremely important. Gaming allows the student to actually feel experiences rather than just read about them. Because of this affective involvement, I think that my students have become more receptive to cognitive learning."

Dr. Valdes spent a great deal of time and energy in creating "The Hunting Game," which he has been using for two years. "I wanted to see if students in a class could build a culture. The class becomes a hunting and gathering society. They learn that organization is necessary for survival; and they begin to understand the concepts of division of labor and exchange theory."

Dr. Valdes explains that there are a few disadvantages to using the gaming technique: "It is very time-consuming in terms of class time. As an instructor you must be committed to the idea that teaching students processes is just as important as teaching them facts." He also pointed out that for the large games, like the two that he is using, it may be necessary to find additional staff to help direct the game.

Especially with the game that he created himself, Dr. Valdes noticed that he felt more ego-investment in this technique than he had felt with traditional lecture methods. "I felt a bit threatened at the prospect of having the game fail. I was very concerned that the game should go smoothly and that the students would get the maximum learning from it. The rewards made the risk worthwhile. I feel that the technique is not only useful, but also fun."

Students seem to feel the same. They are enthusiastic about using a non-traditional technique. They are anxious to take advantage of this opportunity to inter-act with other students. "I typically have forty-five or fifty students in a class. It is rewarding to hear students say that this is the only class they have where they know everyone who is in the class." Dr. Valdes points out that using simulation gaming has been a welcome break from the routine for students; and a very profitable break for both students and instructor.

Simulation gaming has allowed him and his students to focus on the affective learning process—an area that is rarely developed through traditional teaching methods. "I now realize that the learning process becomes more meaningful when an interactive activity like gaming is included. We take so many things for granted when we learn them from books or through lectures. It is a very enlightening experience to be confronted with the feel-ings that accompany a set of facts."

Dr. Donald Valdes
Anthropology Department
Denison University
Granville, Ohio 43202
(614) 587-0810

Chapter 18

THE PERSONALIZED SYSTEM
OF INSTRUCTION

On an evening in late March of 1963, in front of the fireplace in his New Jersey home, psychologist Fred Keller and his friends J. Gilmour Sherman, Rodolpho Azzi, and Carolina Martuscelli Bori planned a course which Keller described in his diary as "one of the most exciting and most radical ever given in a university setting" (Keller, 1974, p. 147).

The first course taught using the system was an introductory psychology course offered at the University of Brasilia, where the founders were establishing a new psychology program. Their intention was to build an instructional system that would reflect the reinforcement theory of psychology which they all advocated.

Students are more likely to perform well if they find satisfaction in their studies. This common sense observation has been formalized and empirically substantiated by reinforcement theorists. The theory asserts that the consequences of learning are important instructional contingencies. In the most general terms these consequences may be classified as either positive or negative and either internal or external.

Positive consequences (rewards) such as instructor praise, good grades, or feelings of achievement are generally considered to be much more effective facilitators of learning than *negative* consequences such as boredom, failure, or other forms of punishment. External rewards such as instructor praise or good grades are important, but for adult learners they are not nearly as important as the general internal rewards of feelings of achievement, satisfaction, or accomplishment. Such internal rewards have the advantage of relying on the individual's own sense of fulfillment rather than on contrived and temporary external systems.

The Keller Plan, or the Personalized System of Instruction (PSI), is based on these principles. That is not to say that every instructor who uses PSI is a "behaviorist." In fact, many instructors are attracted to the plan for its "humanistic" features. In addition to specifying instructional objectives and providing reinforcement for their successful achievement, PSI provides the student with more options and opportunities for personal interaction than traditional instructional systems.

Keller first publicly announced the details of his plan in 1968. There are five basic components essential to any PSI course:

1. *Mastery*. Each student must demonstrate a required level of achievement of each unit of the course before being allowed to proceed to the next unit.

In a normal course where students are allowed to progress through content regardless of their performance on quizzes, midterms, or papers, it is not surprising that there are large discrepancies in performance at the end of the course. In a PSI course, each unit must be mastered individually and sequentially so that at the end of the course all of the content has been mastered.

This component assumes that there is a core of content in the course which should be learned by everyone and that neither the instructor nor the student should be satisfied with anything less than mastery. Mastery is normally demonstrated by performance on a unit quiz. It places unique demands on the instructional system, however. To expect students to master unreasonable or vague objectives, to master poorly taught content, or to perform well on unfair quizzes would not insure the feelings of accomplishment which are evoked when a student demonstrates mastery. Passing the unit quiz is a major positive consequence of the system.

2. *Self-pacing*. Each student is allowed to proceed through course materials at her own pace. Thus, a student may elect to take a unit quiz at her convenience or when she is most ready to demonstrate mastery, rather than at a time common for all students which is dictated by the instructor.

This feature provides for individual differences in rate or preference and is essential if the level of achievement is held constant. In essence, it is not possible to hold both level of individual achievement and rate of completion constant. In a normal lecture course, rate of completion is held constant. The mid-term and final are given once to the entire class. Papers, lab reports, problem sets, and readings are due on specific dates for the entire class. The result is that performance in the course varies from individual to individual, and grades or scores on tests have a wide range. On the other hand, in a PSI course the tests can be taken at any time (but must be taken in sequence) and can be repeated if required. The result is that while the normal student evidences a steady progression through the course, at any one time individual students will be working on different units and taking different tests. Thus, the level of achievement (mastery) is held constant while the *rate of learning* (pacing) is allowed to vary.

3. *Written materials.* All instruction is conveyed by written materials. These can be self-instructional, programmed texts, or regular textbooks. Written study guides are prepared to identify objectives to assist the student in using the text, and to help the student prepare for unit quizzes. The study guides take the place of lectures and constitute a major line of communication from instructor to student.

4. *Student proctors.* Students, usually ones who have taken the course before, act as proctors to score quizzes, discuss answers, tutor students, and provide feedback to the instructor on the general progress of students through the course and problems with the written materials and test items. The proctors are a vital component of the system, since they constitute the personal contact between student and system. Proctors provide immediate feedback to students. If a quiz item is marked as incorrect, the student can attempt to justify his response. The proctor has authority to give credit if the student appears to understand the item tested, even though the quiz response may be incorrect due to some minor error. At the same time, the proctor can discuss correct responses with students to determine whether or not the item content has actually been mastered or whether the answer has been guessed or arrived at for incorrect reasons. The proctor is a primary source of external reward for the mastery of content.

5. *Lectures.* Lectures are used for enrichment rather than information. The information which in a normal course would be conveyed by lecture is conveyed through study guides and the text. Lectures in a PSI course give the instructor an opportunity to demonstrate the excitement of the discipline, while giving the students a chance to see an experienced professional at work. Similarly, films or other special events may be arranged. These events are never used to convey critical information that would be required for a test; rather they serve a supplemental function.

In a normal PSI course, class meetings are devoted to quiz taking, studying for quizzes, and tutoring by proctors. A student will be oriented to the course plan through written materials and is likely to begin the first unit by receiving a study guide. The study guide introduces the unit and describes what the student will be expected to know. It also asks some study questions drawn from the unit and provides some suggested procedures for determining the answer to the questions. The students can do their work at home, in the library, or during the regularly scheduled class period. The work consists mainly of reading and answering study questions. If students encounter difficulty, they can consult a fellow student, a proctor, or the instructor. The proctor may clarify instructions or provide some additional suggestions for self-study. When each student feels she has a sufficient knowledge of the material, she may request a unit quiz. Upon completing the quiz, the student takes it to the proctor to be checked. The proctor may request elaboration or defense of an answer, whether right or wrong, and score the test. If the student's performance is less than perfect, she is required to review the unit materials and repeat the quiz until mastery is obtained. Students proceed through the remaining units at their own pace—completing two units one week, skipping the next week to study for an exam in another course—until all units are completed or the term ends. The students take a final exam and receive a course grade based on final exam performance and number of units completed.

Advantages and Disadvantages

McKeachie and Kulik have summarized the evaluative research

on the Personalized System of Instruction in the 1975 *Review of Research in Education:*

1. The Keller Plan is an attractive teaching method to most students. In published reports, students rate the Keller Plan more favorably than teaching by lecture.
2. Self-pacing and interaction with tutors seem to be the features of the Keller courses most favored by students.
3. Several investigators report higher than average student withdrawal rates for Keller sections.
4. Content learning as measured by final examinations is adequate in Keller courses. In published studies, final examination performance in Keller sections always equals, and usually exceeds, performance in lecture sections.
5. Students almost invariably report that they learn more in PSI than in lecture courses, and also report expending more time and effort. (p. 173-174)

An excellent review by Kulik, Kulik, and Smith (1976) documents most of the research on PSI. Most comparisons using PSI have been made with lectures. In 39 studies which compared final exam scores, 38 showed PSI superior. In 34 of the studies, the differences were statistically significant. In 9 out of 9 studies that compared retention, PSI students did significantly better. In the five studies that examined grades in subsequent non-PSI courses, the PSI students maintained their edge over their counterparts. Finally, in 8 out of 9 studies that compared PSI courses to lectures, the students rated the PSI course higher.

One study compared PSI with a discussion section and an independent study section (Spencer *et al.*, 1974). The PSI sections fared best on end-of-course measures; the discussion section was next, and independent study proved least effective.

Although head-to-head comparisons have not been made between PSI and other methods, such as programmed instruction, computer-assisted instruction, audio-tutorial instruction, and instructional video, Kulik and Jaksa (1977) examined how each of these fared against conventional instruction. They found that PSI was consistently better and produced greater differences in achievement over conventional instruction than any of these other techniques.

Each of the components of PSI has also been examined to determine the extent to which it is critical to the success of the course (Kulik, Kulik, and Smith, 1976). The features of small unit size, immediate feedback, and mastery seem to be critical to final exam performance. Interaction with proctors, self-pacing, and use of lectures seem less critical. It is likely that most traditional courses could be improved by including at least one or two of the critical PSI features.

Appropriate Uses

Content. PSI has been used in a large number of courses. Although it tends to be used more often in physical or social science courses such as physics, chemistry, or psychology, it has also been used in such courses as poetry, philosophy, and technical writing (Hess, 1972).

Its best use may be in courses with convergent goals, for the instructor must be able to identify content which should be mastered by every student. Courses where students are expected to select content on their own or to work with other students and the instructor in the formulation of course objectives are not appropriate for PSI.

It is also best suited for courses which have interdependent skills or concepts. In such courses the mastery requirement insures that the students will have learned the necessary prerequisite skills before beginning subsequent units.

PSI is most appropriate for content which can best be communicated through written materials. Content objectives which require discussion, gaming, computer-assisted instruction, or audio-visual methods would require some modification of this technique. Nor is PSI appropriate for courses where subject matter changes quickly, thus outdating written materials.

Since the majority of PSI students receive "A's," the method is not appropriate for courses which must create grade distributions to filter students into subsequent courses. It is not appropriate in courses where the level of expertise cannot be judged by an undergraduate student proctor, e.g., foreign language pronunciation.

PSI seems no more nor less appropriate for different levels of cognitive learning. It has been used for objectives ranging from the learning of simple facts to creative problem-solving. While it has not been used extensively for psychomotor learning, it would not be inappropriate, providing the proctors could give feedback on the skills. PSI has not been used for affective learning and probably would not be appropriate. Affective goals are most often divergent and often require extensive, open-ended personal interaction between students. While there is personal interaction between proctors and students, it tends to be limited to discussion of specific content and unit quizzes.

Students. There have been two positions regarding the type of student who benefits most from PSI. One position states that it is best for more able students because the lack of structure does not limit them. On the other hand, the less able students might have difficulty with reading and study problems which would be exacerbated by the system. The second position states that PSI would be best for less able students because of the self-pacing and proctor assistance, while it would be unchallenging for the more able student.

Although studies have been found which support both positions, Kulik and Kulik (1977) reviewed nine studies and found that on the average the effects of PSI seem to be equally strong on high and low aptitude students.

Pascarella (1977) found, however, that achievement in a PSI course is associated with motivation; those with higher motivation did better with PSI. It is unclear whether success in PSI courses requires highly motivated students, or the successful students become motivated because of the frequent feedback they receive about their success.

While PSI courses are tightly structured in that objectives are precisely formulated, units specified and requirements for mastery prescribed, the self-pacing component poses problems for some students. Students who work well independently may be best suited for PSI courses, while dependent students often have difficulty.

One type of student who poses special problems in a PSI course is the procrastinator. While these students are not unheard of in lecture and discussion courses, they are able to take tests in a more or less unprepared state, turn in sloppy work, or actually complete course requirements in the last week or so of class. This is not the case in a PSI course. Students pace themselves and can take quizzes when they feel prepared for them. Procrastination may reach a point where it is impossible to complete course requirements within the term. PSI instructors are familiar with this problem and try to encourage students to meet target dates for course completion. For most students such guidance facilitates the self-pacing.

Instructor. Development of a PSI course requires a strong commitment to the system. The instructor who is uncomfortable with specifying objectives or laying out the content of a course in precise terms is likely to be uncomfortable using PSI. The system is based on clear specification of desired student behaviors. The instructor who feels this is over-manipulation should not use PSI.

Since the formulation of a PSI course requires a great deal of time and is at best a controversial activity for faculty members, instructors who are not secure in their positions or who do not have the support of colleagues should carefully consider their priorities before developing a PSI course. The development time will most certainly cut into time which might otherwise be available for research or service. Once the course has been developed, however, it should take no more time than a normal course.

For the instructor who is accustomed to lecture and discussion, the development of a PSI course constitutes a change in role. Whereas the instructor in other methods is normally the center or near-center of attention, in a PSI course the written materials convey the information. Many lecturers report that they have much greater contact with individual students in a PSI course; however, some miss lecturing regularly. A prospective PSI instructor should be ready to accept the roles of facilitator of learning and manager of the learning environment without controlling the pacing of instruction.

Environment. The development of a PSI course is facilitated by strong administrative support. A PSI course looks very different from traditional courses. Because mastery is required, all students can potentially earn A's, and most will receive them. Students who get too far behind will withdraw or receive incompletes. Thus, compared to a normal course there will be an increase in superior grades, an increase in withdrawals and incompletes, and a decrease in, if not elimination of, failures. Colleagues or administrators who are not familiar with the method will have difficulty understanding these results.

Moreover, successful PSI courses tend to draw higher enrollments, taking students away from traditional sections. Strong support from colleagues and administrators will facilitate devoting the time required to develop the course at the expense of research, and it would cushion the occasional failure that results from PSI.

The required physical environment of a PSI course includes three rooms, or a room divided into three sections. One section would be a study area where students could read, answer study questions, and discuss problems with each other. A second section would be a test area where students take unit quizzes. The third area would be reserved for the proctors, to be used for discussing problems and checking quizzes. The size of such a room (or rooms) would depend on enrollment in roughly the same way a traditional course does.

The social environment in a PSI course is quite different from that of a lecture course. At any given time, students may be taking quizzes, talking to proctors, studying alone, talking to other students, or not present at all. In such a class, the instructor is clearly not the focus of attention.

How to Do It

PSI courses require a great deal of preparation time. Instructors should plan to convert only courses which they have taught previously. Although it is not necessary to have the entire course converted at the beginning of the term, it is necessary to have a sufficient number of units prepared (i.e., five or six) so that the faster students are not slowed by the instructor's conversion process. For this reason it is usually necessary for an instructor to spend three or four weeks on course development prior to initiating the course. Although the instructor's work will subside once a course is completed, it is usually necessary to make revisions in materials from time to time.

There are a number of excellent references to assist an instructor in developing a PSI course. Anyone designing a course should consult this literature (see Resources) and if possible should meet with someone who is familiar with PSI at several points during the course formulation. In general, there are four areas of preparation required by a PSI course conversion.

Course layout. The first step in course conversion is to identify the *critical* course content. Although it is good to have as rich a course content as possible, it is seldom the case in traditional courses that everything that is covered is learned. Since there is a mastery requirement in PSI, it is necessary to identify the material that *must* be learned: the core material and its prerequisite skills. Other content should be labeled optional and left to the more enthusiastic students.

The course content should be divided into units. Koen (1972) has indicated that there are three stages involved in preparing units. First, the content is divided into logical units, which might be based on the parameters of the various aspects of the subject matter; these pieces are put into sequence so that the basic, prerequisite skills are mastered first. Second, the content units are redivided according to size. Small units are desirable, and a good rule of thumb is to have one-third as many units as class meetings. It is advisable to use approximately one review unit for every four or five regular units. This seems to be important as Kulik, Jaksa, and Kulik (1977) found that students in courses using reviews retained more than in courses that did not have review units. Third, the units are adjusted for motivational purposes. The first unit should be short, but most units should be about equal length, requiring three to six hours of student preparation. It is possible that points in the course can be identified which require extra motivation. A shorter unit can help students recapture their momentum. Often it is good to have the last few units shorter, since students will otherwise have difficulty finishing the course.

Course materials. PSI places a heavy emphasis on written materials. In addition to the course text, other materials are the course outline (reflecting the course layout), the course policy statement, the study guides and quizzes for each unit, and the final exam.

A study guide typically follows this outline: introduction, objectives, suggested procedures, and study questions. The introduction should arouse the student's interest in the unit and identify the value of the skill. It might also show how the content fits in with what precedes and follows it. The instructional objectives should clearly specify what the student is expected to be able to do upon completion of the unit. Five to eight objectives are covered in most units. While the objectives tell the students what they will be able to do, the suggested procedures tell the students how to acquire the skills. The suggested procedures assign readings, guide thinking, point out difficulties in the text, and pose sample problems.

There should be several forms of each unit quiz in order to allow students to retake the quiz with unique questions. Each quiz should be brief, taking no more than a half hour to complete. Each quiz item should have an explicit answer. Items can be multiple-choice, completion, or short essay. Long essay items present difficulties for proctors.

It is important to test each objective fully rather than to sample items randomly based on the objectives. The items should not present unfair traps for the students. Successful completion of the unit quiz is the major reinforcer of the system; the quizzes must not be arbitrary. Normally, on a quiz with ten items, students may achieve mastery with a score of nine correct. This allows some flexibility for proctor judgment without sacrificing the mastery component of the system.

Course policies. The instructor must construct policies concerning time limits and grades and convey them to students. In theory, there would be no time limit on a PSI course. As a practical matter, however, this is generally not possible. An instructor must decide what compromises are to be made on whether there will be a time limit on units and whether there will be an end-of-term limit. Some instructors have open class hours; students can come in at their convenience. This practice is not recommended. It is better to meet during normal class hours to maximize the availability of proctors and to give students a sense of joint participation in the course.

Other instructors are very liberal with incompletes. While this is consistent with self-pacing, it is a mistake to encourage incompletes as an alternative to completing work at the end of the term.

Grading in a PSI course can be based on the number of units mastered by the end of the term, the score on a final exam, or both. Technically, it would be consistent with the mastery component not to have a final at all. It is, however, a good practice in that it does require students to pull together elements of the course, it gives some students an opportunity to improve their grades, and it lends credibility to the course since final exam scores for PSI students are easily compared to other students' exam scores. Normally, instructors will settle on a formula in which the final exam counts no more than 25% of the grade and the remainder is based on the number of units completed by the end of the term.

Selection of proctors. Proctors provide a human contact with the system and provide individualized assistance to the students. Their roles depend on the instructor and range from "test checker" to tutor. Because of the nature of these roles, it is desirable to use proctors who know both the course content and the PSI method. The ideal source for proctors is the previous term's students. Normally, it is not advisable to allow students to proctor a course more than once, since they tend to become too familiar with content and give out information too readily. Typically, proctors are given credit for their work. Occasionally they are paid, but this is not recommended, since such funding can easily be lost. Proctors are required to attend class regularly for assisting students and to attend proctor sessions with the instructor to review problems of content, policy, and materials. Proctor training materials (Kozma, Kulik, and Smith, 1977) have been developed to assist instructors in developing proctor skills. While such training is beneficial, the most important factor is a good selection procedure.

If students from a preceding course are not available, it is possible to use "internal proctors." These are students who are enrolled in the course and who are first to master each unit. The instructor certifies their mastery while they, in turn, work with the other students. Some instructors have even required that students proctor a number of units during the term, since students who proctor typically do better than the other PSI students on final exam questions related to the unit proctored.

Resources

Books and Articles

Keller, F. S., and Sherman, J. G. *The Keller Plan handbook*. Menlo Park, California: Benjamin, 1974. A description of the Plan, how it got started, and how it works, by the people who know.

Kozma, R., Kulik, J., and Smith, B. *A guide for PSI proctors*. Washington, D.C.: Center for Personalized Instruction, 1977. A self-instructional manual that instructors can use to train their proctors.

Kulik, J., Kulik, C. L., and Smith, B. Research on the personalized system of instruction. *Programmed Learning and Educational Technology*, 1976, *13*, 21-30. An excellent review of the research on PSI including an examination of each of the features of the system.

Sherman, J. G. *Personalized system of instruction: 41 terminal papers*. Menlo Park, California: Benjamin, 1974. A compilation of previously published papers which document the history, operation, problems, and results of PSI.

Sherman, J.G., and Ruskin, R. *The Personalized System of Instruction*. Volume 13 in The Instructional Design Library. Englewood Cliffs, New Jersey: Educational Technology Publications, 1978. A comprehensive, authoritative, practical guidebook to PSI, including numerous examples of actual PSI materials (such as study guides) employed in various courses and at different levels.

Periodicals

Journal of Personalized Instruction, Center for Personalized Instruction, Washington, D.C. 20057. A quarterly journal which presents the latest research on PSI. Regular features include brief reports and book reviews.

PSI Newsletter, Center for Personalized Instruction, Washington, D.C. 20057. A monthly newsletter with the latest developments, testimonials, editorials, and "inside dope" on PSI.

Places

Center for Personalized Instruction, Georgetown University, Washington, D.C. 20057. A clearinghouse for materials, information, and research on PSI. The center publishes periodicals, conducts workshops, and provides consultation for faculty members interested in starting PSI courses.

PSI in Physics

George Jirgal teaches physics at Park College, a small liberal arts college in Missouri. After using lecture as his main instructional method for six years, Dr. Jirgal decided to use the Personalized System of Instruction (PSI). He has been using PSI in his physics courses for two years.

Dr. Jirgal has four physics courses that are taught by PSI: Calculus Physics I, Calculus Physics II, Advanced Applied Mathematics, and Intermediate Mechanics. Each of these courses is available to students each semester. Because of the small number of students in these courses, one laboratory serves them all. Dr. Jirgal serves as instructor, proctor, and tutor for each of these students and is available in the self-paced physics laboratory at least twelve hours per week. The scheduling of these lab hours is done at the convenience of the students, subject to the restrictions of Dr. Jirgal's other academic duties.

Each course consists of modules which include objectives, text references, supplementary notes, examples of worked problems, study questions, and sample examination questions. The courses do not include motivational lectures, which are often a part of the PSI design. Students work on the modules in the lab, or at some other convenient place. They come to the lab to get help on study questions, to do experiments, or to ask questions about the written materials. When students complete a module, they come to the lab and take a unit quiz. The quiz is checked in the presence of the student, and his mistakes are discussed in this private session. If the student has achieved less than 100 percent on the quiz, he reviews the unit materials and repeats the quiz until mastery is obtained.

Dr. Jirgal explains that student reaction to the courses has been generally positive: "They complain a bit during the course, but by the end of the semester they realize that they have really learned something. One advantage of the PSI method is that students do not compete with each other. They realize that they are responsible for their own mastery of the material. Since there is no penalty for repeating a quiz, students see no reason to cheat on quizzes."

Dr. Jirgal used materials developed at other universities as the core material for his modules. Even so, he had to spend more than a year to set up the four courses. He was willing to invest this amount of time and energy in developing the courses for many reasons. "I felt a need to change my teaching methods in order to get a new perspective on these courses. It has been difficult for me to get bored with the repetition of the PSI courses, as I did with lecture courses. Now I have more contact with individual students, who present fresh problems each semester. I get a better idea about the needs of the students; and I can revise the courses accordingly. This method of instruction is also a help to scheduling, since each self-paced course is taught each semester in a wide variety of times."

Perhaps the most influential factor in Dr. Jirgal's decision to use the Personalized System of Instruction was economics. In Dr. Jirgal's situation it is more cost-effective to offer courses in the self-paced mode than in the more traditional modes, since the only staff time involved in the four courses is the twelve hours that Dr. Jirgal spends in the laboratory. "If we did not use PSI for these courses we would not be able to offer as many courses as frequently in the physics department. By adopting the Personalized System of Instruction for these courses, I created an opportunity to expand the curriculum at the college; and in these uncertain financial times, that is no small accomplishment."

Recently, Dr. Jirgal received an NSF Grant (LOCI program) to develop and adapt existing materials in the self-paced program in order to increase to ten the number of self-paced physics courses at Park College.

Dr. George Jirgal
Physics and Astronomy
Park College
Parkville, Missouri 64152
(816) 741-2000 Ext. 144

Chapter 19

AUDIO-TUTORIAL INSTRUCTION

One of the most challenging problems facing college faculty who teach courses requiring laboratory work is dealing successfully with large numbers of students. The individual attention needed to explain, explore, and demonstrate complex concepts and principles is prohibited by large classes. This is particularly evident in introductory level courses, but the problem is not confined to them. The audio-tutorial system of instruction (A-T) was developed in the 1960's by the nationally recognized botanist S.N. Postlethwait as a response to this dilemma.

Postlethwait found that audiotape lectures were a useful adjunct to his course. He soon supplemented the tapes with pictures and diagrams and recast the tapes as study guides and commentary for the course's textbook. Next he added laboratory experiments and equipment to the package. Ultimately students were learning independently and at their own paces in laboratory stations equipped with audiotapes, visual materials, and selected equipment. In the face of considerable opposition from his department, Postlethwait made these self-instructional materials the basis of his course, adding periodic quiz sessions and occasional general assemblies or "lectures."

All of the principles at the base of most self-instructional systems (emphasis on student performance, modularization, mastery, and self-pacing) are present to some degree in Postlethwait's audio-tutorial system. In A-T there is special emphasis on selecting the most appropriate medium for each part and step of the learning sequence: the written word for general information, audiotapes for instructor commentary and direction; both still and moving pictures for visual information; practice and experimentation for multi-sensory learning; and written and oral quizzes. These elements are all carefully integrated to produce an optimal learning experience.

The classic audio-tutorial course consists of three components: the independent study session, the general assembly, and the integrated quiz session. Short research projects may also be added.

1. The *Independent Study Session* is the most readily identifiable element in A-T. During the session students listen to the tape, which is arranged by the instructor to simulate person-to-person instruction. The instructor integrates a wide variety of media so that as the student listens she is cued to look at slides, photographs, diagrams, graphs, and tables, as well as texts and other written materials. The student participates in the program by carrying out laboratory assignments or other activities as directed by the tape. This independent study period thus combines in one session what is conventionally presented separately in lectures and laboratories.

The tape does not function as a taped lecture. It is a programming device to tutor the student through a variety of integrated learning experiences, presented in logical sequence. The student works by alternating such activities as listening, reading from texts, reprints or program notes, with handling material, observing or setting up experiments, looking at demonstrations, working out problems or, in short, engaging in any activity which the instructor can devise to allow the student to accomplish the objectives set out for the particular study session.

Each student is independent and progresses at his own pace, determining not only the number of repetitions required but the depth to which he wishes to pursue any part of the subject matter. Guided by the tape, the student automatically becomes involved in the learning process and is prodded into critical thinking and deductive reasoning by questions and quizzes interspersed at regular intervals throughout the tape. These self-quizzes require him to seek out much of the information from material which is readily available in the learning center, and also test the factual knowledge which he should have assimilated.

Like PSI modules, the independent study session is based on the premise that learning must be done by the learner herself and that all study activities should involve the learner as actively as possible. Unlike the PSI module, an independent study session in an A-T course is not entirely self-paced, although it does allow for considerable flexibility with the time allotted for a given unit. Another difference is that unlike PSI where, upon completion of a unit, the student can immediately take a quiz and have it corrected and discussed by a tutor, in an A-T course these functions are taken care of in a scheduled integrated quiz section.

2. The *Integrated Quiz Sections*, consisting of eight to ten students, are held at the end of a unit. Here materials and examples from work done in the independent study sessions are used to test and explore each student's understanding of the unit. Students are given short written and/or oral quizzes on the material they are expected to have covered in the learning center. Then students are picked at random to give short lectures on some "specimens" taken from the independent study session.

The most important feature of this short lecture exercise is that any student must be ready to give an account of any part of the work assigned for the independent study session. The exercise is based on the concept that "one really learns a subject when one prepares to teach it." These mini-lectures allow and invite feedback from other students and the instructor and thus serve as a basis for further discussion of the material.

3. *General Assembly Sessions* are a periodic event offered for the entire class in which material is presented that cannot be effectively and efficiently handled either in the independent study or integrated quiz sessions. General assembly sessions might be used by the instructor for presenting guest lecturers, showing long films, providing course orientation, giving final examinations, and similar large group activities.

If well used, the general assembly can serve as a motivational device. It is important to remember that in an A-T course, general assembly sessions are seldom, if ever, used for instructor lectures. The integrated quiz sessions and general assemblies serve to support, evaluate, and motivate the independent learning done in the individual study sessions.

These three components: independent study, integrated quiz, and general assembly sessions—each selected for specific purposes —comprise the basic elements of the classic A-T course. They distinguish A-T from similar but structurally different forms of individualized instruction.

Postlethwait (Postlethwait *et al.,* 1972) has also introduced a mini-course version of the A-T format which carries the implicit modularization of the original A-T design to its logical conclusion. In this form the various units that comprise a course are divided into self-contained modules. The student, depending on his needs, can choose and complete the most appropriate packages. Ideally, variable credit is offered for the modules in accordance with the amount of work completed.

Advantages and Disadvantages

The fundamental advantages of A-T are those associated with most individualized and self-instructional methods. The focus is on measurable student learning rather than teaching. Within limits determined by the scheduling of integrated quiz sessions, the student can pace himself or repeat the independent study session as necessary. Taped instructions, commentary, and other aids provided at each station in the learning center offer specific information at exactly the time it is needed in the learning process.

One of A-T's advantages is especially worth noting. The student can simultaneously hear, see, touch, and/or use the material she is working with while listening to the instructor. Activating several senses in a coordinated manner is likely to shorten the time required for learning and to make the learning more durable. Finally, A-T instruction need not be the only instructional format used in a course; it can easily be combined with other instructional methods, ranging from lectures to simulations.

It is apparent that considerable time and effort are required to develop an A-T course. Are the results worth the effort? "Student achievement on written examinations with audio-tutorial (A-T) instruction nearly always equals, and usually exceeds, that obtained with the conventional method." This is the conclusion

Fisher and MacWhinney (1976) reached after reviewing 89 studies found in educational journals, science journals, abstracts, conference reports, and dissertations appearing between 1962-75. Such a result is striking. Most comprehensive reviews of alternative instructional strategies, for example, the well-known Dubin and Taveggia (1968) study, conclude that courses taught with unconventional methods are as likely to produce inferior as superior class performance on end-of-course examinations. The Fisher and MacWhinney review of the A-T literature found only one (Russell, 1968) out of 44 comparisons that showed better results with lecture instruction, while more than two-thirds attributed superiority to the audio-tutorial approach. Eighteen out of this group established a statistically significant difference in A-T's favor. Among instructional strategies only PSI has shown similarly positive results across studies.

Student response to A-T is equally impressive. In virtually all cases reviewed, students reported that they liked A-T instruction at least as well as lecture instruction, and in many studies they are reported to favor A-T. Students do not typically embrace innovative forms of instruction, especially during first exposure. They are often more resistant to change than faculty members. With A-T, however, student response is consistently positive.

In general, the research data supports the contention that A-T is at least as effective as, and often superior to, conventional instruction, when student achievement is the only consideration. If, in addition, factors such as the efficient and productive use of instructor and student time, and student attitudes are considered, then A-T is better.

Virtually all of the recently introduced instructional innovations allege cost-effectiveness in addition to learning outcomes as good or better than those produced by conventional means. While claims for instructional effectiveness have in a number of cases been subjected to controlled studies, those for cost-effectiveness have been examined far less frequently, if at all.

Richard Brightman (1973), Director of Research and Planning for the Coast Community College District in California, analyzed the relative costs of several instructional strategies. Among them was an audio-tutorial laboratory course in introductory biology, which was compared to conventional laboratory instruction. An analysis based on 503 students revealed that the cost with A-T was $30,603 (salaries, equipment, and supplies). The estimated cost for conventional instruction, with two laboratories optimally scheduled for 17 sections of 30 students each, was $41,506. A-T cost approximately 25 percent less, and the major cost differential was in salaries. Considerably less faculty time was required in the A-T program than was required for 30 conventional sections.

In Brightman's comparison, further savings occurred with the centralization of facilities and efficient use of equipment and supplies in a learning center. For example, a refrigerator and an incubator to serve the audio-tutorial laboratory cost eight hundred dollars and all 503 students made use of them. This figure would be doubled if the two separate laboratories required for thirty stations each were employed instead. The A-T learning center laboratory required one compound microscope, whereas the conventional laboratories would require at least thirty, and so on.

In another study, John Nance (1971) determined the cost-effectiveness of teaching introductory psychology with A-T. He found that over a five-year period A-T would prove about 35 percent less expensive than a standard format course and yield more effective instruction. Cost studies generally show economic advantages to the A-T method; however, the authors point out that set-up costs (faculty time and learning center equipment and supplies) may be relatively high and several years might be necessary to realize cost-effectiveness. (It is worth noting that elaborate visual materials frequently favored by A-V people and some faculty turn out to be less useful for learning in an A-T program than short, crisp, simple visuals.)

Appropriate Uses

Content. The use of A-T has been most widely accepted and validated for introductory courses in the life and physical sciences. Fisher and MacWhinney (1976) cite examples of successful implementation in history, business, veterinary, accounting, and law courses. The National Council of Geographic Education (Benjamin, 1969) has published a study on the use of A-T for teaching geography. Audio-tutorial instruction is particularly appropriate for content that has substantial visual or manipulative components and which can be presented in an orderly sequence of units and joined to practice and/or experimental work.

Students. The general advantages of the A-T system for students are easily seen. The independent study session, the heart of the A-T system, allows for considerable temporal flexibility. A wide variety of media and instructional modalities make learning more probable for a variety of students with diverse learning styles. Independent study session material can be repeated by the student until mastery is achieved. Among the specific features most often noted by students are the freedom provided by the self-paced independent study sessions, the sense of having learned more with A-T instruction, and greater motivation to learn than with conventional instruction.

Some work has been done on possible correlations between specific student characteristics and A-T instruction. In an A-T physics course, Dederich and Macklin (1973) found that students with high SAT math scores and high pretest scores did better with conventional instruction than those with low SAT and pretest scores. Students in the latter group were more successful with A-T instruction. It appears that in this case the greater individualization benefited students with less math ability and preparation. Similar findings are reported for another A-T physics course (Knopp, 1969), and two A-T biology courses (Nordland and Kahle, 1973; and Meleca, 1968). Kulik, Kulik, and Hertzler (1977) found that required remediation for students who did poorly on unit quizzes resulted in better performance on the final exam. This was particularly true for students with low grade point averages.

Mintzes (1975) summarizes six studies on the interaction between A-T and selected student characteristics in biology courses. Although the evidence is limited, some characteristics do stand out across studies. While introductory biology courses do not typically require much mathematical skill, students scoring high on general mathematical ability do well in the A-T format, whereas scientific aptitude seems more important for success in conventionally taught courses. This may indicate that the intellectual orderliness and ability to apprehend structure that characterizes mathematical aptitude supports A-T learning. On personality tests students who scored higher than average on achievement and "restraint-sobrie-ty" (the tendency to be serious-minded and responsible) did better in A-T courses.

Work by Roland Pare and John Butzow (1975) suggests that "independence" may be related to achievement in A-T courses. This is supported by Postlethwait, *et al.* (1972), who have observed, "Some students having been conditioned over the years to taking little or no responsibility for their own education, find this new relationship (A-T) to their progress rather frightening and overwhelming." (p. 95)

Instructor. As with so many instructional methods, traditional or alternative, there is virtually no research suggesting which type of teacher will profit most and feel most comfortable with audio-tutorial instruction. Among the findings summarized by Fisher and MacWhinney (1976), one study showed the A-T format leads the instructor to better course organization and improves her interest and enthusiasm. Others reported increased coverage of content (usually considered desirable by faculty members); and one study mentioned increased faculty time for direct interaction with students.

John C. Lindenlaub (1974), like Postlethwait, a member of the Purdue faculty, has worked extensively in adapting A-T to engineering education. He has noted some of A-T's most attractive features from the instructor's point of view:

> Audio-tutorial instruction has several features which make it attractive for use in making classroom-oriented instructors more aware of their own teaching methods. The primary instructional mode is the spoken word, just as in a lecture. The transition to this new teaching technique, therefore, should not be abrupt. In preparing an audio tape, the instructor will not have direct feedback from his students, and so must pay strict attention to the organization of his ideas and the objectives for the tape on which he is working, as well as to the interaction of charts, drawings, formulas and other visual material which will accompany the tape. He must consider the likely responses of his students and try to anticipate them. (p. 106)

Environment. Independent study sessions often take place at stations located in a learning center. The learning center is a laboratory which is open to students at a wide variety of times and contains the equipment, supplies, and instructor-made tapes with which the student can perform or practice laboratory or experimental procedures. These stations are in effect free-standing independent study units which the student uses for as long as is required for accomplishing specified learning objectives. The instructor or teaching assistants are frequently present in the learning center to answer student questions. This plus the integrated quiz section allows for more personal contact that is usually available in the typical introductory lecture-lab course. Sullivan's (1974) comprehensive report on learning center environments is very favorable: "The evidence ... supported the hypothesis that learning centers are effective and efficient approaches to instruction. The data further indicated that on a relative basis, learning centers are a more effective and more efficient approach than the conventional group-paced forms of instruction they have replaced." (p. 5)

The characteristics which Sullivan identified as related to the most successful learning centers are: all components are designed to meet a clearly-defined instructional purpose which required student performance as an outcome; the materials (texts, audio-tapes, experiments, films, etc.) are carefully selected, organized, and maintained; learning materials are closely tied to the specific instructional objectives which the course is intended to promote.

How to Do It

In Chapter V, "Operational Aspects," of *The Audio-Tutorial Approach to Learning,* Postlethwait supplies detailed, step-by-step instructions on how to go about preparing an A-T course. This resource is invaluable for those considering A-T. The following outline gives an idea of what is involved and some specific help in getting started.

For the beginner it is best to think big and start small. While ultimately a whole course may be converted to audio-tutorial, better results are usually obtained if one starts on a smaller scale. The instructor begins by selecting a segment of the course which he knows well. He develops an independent study session for this segment of the course and tests it with a few students.

Development of an independent study session. First, the instructor sets the instructional outcomes she wants her students to achieve—the objectives. Next, the specific information, concepts, and skills that will be taught in order to achieve these objectives are placed in logical order. Following this, each is studied to determine the best method for teaching it. For instance, is the instruction best accomplished by referring the student to a piece of equipment, a diagram, or a slide, or by asking the student to read certain paragraphs or to do a small experiment or exercise? This is an important step. The most appropriate methods and necessary materials should be selected before the audiotape that will guide the students is recorded. The materials should be labeled or numbered so that they can be referred to conveniently during the recording.

Making a tape. One technique is to make an initial tape from a written outline. Another method, which can give an air of naturalness, is to make a tape while actually talking to a student. This will provide immediate feedback and allow the instructor to know whether elaboration is required. A third technique is to prepare a complete written script. While this appears to offer a certain security, especially for the beginner, it tempts the instructor to lecture rather than talk to the student. In addition, script preparation is very time consuming.

It is helpful to establish a standard set of cues or phrases to alert the student to refer to notes, stop the recorder, or work with equipment, etc. A short interlude of recorded music is an attractive way to signal the student to stop the tape and carry out instructor directions. The phrase "pick up your pencil" may be used to cue the student for written work. A natural tone is probably the most important thing when recording. The instructor can achieve this by imagining that she is talking to an individual student.

Since the A-T audiotape does not stand alone, a set of notes should accompany the tape. They should begin with an overview of the material, the estimated time required to complete the module, a statement on required preparation and/or prerequisites, and a list of the instructional objectives. The notes themselves should complement, not duplicate, the material on the tape so that the student will have to work through the tape the first time. However, the notes should be complete enough that the student may review without having to replay the tape. Critical sketches, formulas, maps, diagrams, illustrations, etc., should be included in the notes. A self-quiz can be appended as well.

The integrated quiz session. After having created and tested a few independent study sessions the instructor can develop an integrated quiz session to review, discuss, and evaluate the students' learning. Postlethwait found that the integrated quiz session works best when the quiz (oral or written) precedes the discussion; otherwise, the discussion turns into a cram session instead of an exchange and exploration of ideas.

By developing independent study and quiz sessions for various segments of a course over a one- or two-year period, the instructor can design the basic components of an A-T course without the frustration of attempting to apply a new method to an entire course all at once.

Courses relying solely on the basic A-T components, devoid of demonstrations, field trips, and special projects, can become as routine as lectures. Perhaps the most important consideration is the proper sequencing of independent study sessions with objectives and orchestrating the appropriate activities and materials with each of the three basic modes: independent study, integrated quiz, and general assembly sessions.

The faculty member considering A-T must undertake the burdens of careful planning, organization, formative testing, and evaluation if the positive results in student achievement and attitude are to be realized.

Resources

Books and Articles

Creager, J. G., and Murry, D. L. *The use of modules in college biology teaching.* Washington, D.C.: Commission on Undergraduate Education in the Biological Sciences, 1971. A number of articles on what A-T modules are and how they work. Useful for instructors in other disciplines as well.

Postlethwait, S.N., and Lohman, T. *The audio-tutorial system: An independent study approach.* A film available from: Purdue Film Library, Purdue University, Lafayette, Indiana, 1968.

Documents the A-T system as it is used in freshman botany courses at Purdue.

Postlethwait, S.N., Novak, J., and Murray, H.T. *The audio-tutorial approach to learning* (3rd ed.). Minneapolis: Burgess Publishing Co., 1972. A comprehensive guide to Audio-Tutorial, including full explanation of the conceptual foundations of the method and directions on designing and implementing an Audio-Tutorial program. The mini-course format is also included in this edition.

Russell, J.D. *The Audio-Tutorial System.* Volume 3 in The Instructional Design Library. Englewood Cliffs, New Jersey: Educational Technology Publications, 1978. A practical description of A-T instruction, including examples of some lessons and a step-by-step developmental guide.

Sullivan, D. *A study of the present state-of-the-art in learning center operation.* Lowry AFB, Colorado: Air Force Human Resources Lab, 1974. (ERIC Document Reproduction Service No. ED 088-526.) Reports research on the relative effectiveness of learning centers, offers design information, and reports on the use of learning centers for a variety of instructional purposes.

Organization
International Congress for Individualized Instruction (Formerly International Audio-Tutorial Congress), c/o Dr. George Brown, Department of Geology and Geophysics, Boston College, Boston, Massachusetts 02167. This organization hosts a yearly conference on individualized instruction.

An Audio-Tutorial Art History Course

Kathleen Cohen, chairman of the art department at California State University at San Jose, has been using the audio-tutorial method for teaching a course in art history. She developed the audio-tutorial course in spite of some reservations: "I felt there was a good chance it wouldn't work. I thought that a number of students would be turned off by the machines. It was a great surprise to me that the audio-tutorial system worked so well. Seventy-five to eighty percent of my students prefer this method to the traditional lecture method. I have been using it now for three years."

The art history class meets as a large group once a week. This time is used for film presentations and occasionally for tests and exams. Students spend time during the week working in the laboratory, using audiotapes, filmstrips, and study guides. There is also a textbook for the class. Once a week the students meet in small discussion groups with a teaching fellow. The course objectives are clearly designated at the beginning of the course. Students are free to emphasize the instructional method(s) that best suit their individual approach to learning. The individual student takes responsibility for mastery of the course content. All students are required to take the final exam and occasional tests during the course, which are graded on the basis of percentages, rather than class curve.

Dr. Cohen cites many advantages offered by the audio-tutorial method: "The discussion sessions are very popular. Some students want to attend two per week. This opportunity for small group discussion is one feature offered by audio-tutorial that is difficult to attain in the traditional lecture setting. Students can also work at their own pace. They can look at the reproductions of art works as many times as they wish, and they can condense the course into a shorter time period or extend the time needed for mastery. Students have commented that they retain more material when it is taught by the audio-tutorial method."

Perhaps the reason that students retain more information is that they must put more effort into the class taught by audio-tutorial methods. Dr. Cohen explains that some students drop out at the beginning of the course when they realize how much work will be involved. For those who stay in the class, however, the rewards are great. One student commented that he couldn't help but learn in this course. The audio-tutorial materials are all mutually reinforcing. If the student has missed a point in the text, he will be able to pick it up in the study guide, or on the tape, or in discussion.

Dr. Cohen's audio-tutorial art history course has been successfully taught by other faculty at California State University, and is also being tried at a few other colleges. Perhaps the best indication of the success of the program is that Dr. Cohen is now developing materials to convert another one of her art history courses to the audio-tutorial method, and students who have taken the first course keep inquiring about when it will be ready.

Dr. Kathleen Cohen
Chairman, Art Department
California State University
San Jose, California 95192
(408) 277-2543

Chapter 20

PROGRAMMED INSTRUCTION

Programmed instruction is a prime example of an instructional technique for which the claims far exceeded the realizations. The excitement and anticipation generated in the mid-fifties by B.F. Skinner, the intellectual father of PI, was followed by literally thousands of programs that flooded the educational market. Both major publishers and small companies invested in what was heralded as a "guaranteed method of teaching," and programmed books rivaled traditional texts for classroom use in practically every subject matter area.

By the mid-sixties, educational researchers had examined the phenomenon, and of the hundreds of studies involving programmed instruction, most showed little or no difference between programmed instruction and conventional instruction. Research results corresponded to common experience as commercially produced programs, many of them poorly written, sat on classroom shelves unused by students and instructors, who found them to be ineffective and uninteresting.

Now, some twenty years after its introduction and after the furor has subsided, programmed instruction can be reconsidered, not as a panacea, but as one resource in a repertoire of methods which can be effectively used for instruction. To use it appropriately, however, it is important to be familiar with the characteristic features of the method.

The characteristics of early programmed instruction are closely wedded to B.F. Skinner's understanding of learning in the 1950's.

It was Skinner who introduced PI through an article in the *Harvard Educational Review* (1954). Complex learning, according to Skinner, occurs through a series of attempts or trials at a task by the learner. Trials which are successful and which are immediately followed by some positive consequence, or reinforcement, are repeated in the future. Attempts which are not reinforced are extinguished. Because the chances of success on the initial trial of a complex behavior are quite small, Skinner suggests that learning start with rather simple behaviors which in some way approximate the more complex behavior. As successful trials on the simple task occur and are reinforced, slightly more complex behaviors can be successively introduced until the final behavior is achieved.

Skinner constructed a mechanical device, christened the teaching machine, which arranged many of the conditions he felt were necessary for learning. The machine presents a small amount of information, called a frame, to the learner. The learner is expected to make some kind of response by answering a question or filling in a blank in a sentence. Upon completion of the response, the machine exposes the correct answer, thereby reinforcing the student. The assumption here is that the instructional step is so small that the chance of the student's answer matching the machine's is very great, and he will feel good about the accomplishment. The machine subsequently advances the student to the next frame in the sequence. A complex set of behaviors, such as those composing a course, may require between 25,000 and 50,000 such trials.

An early adaptation of this mode of instruction was the programmed text. Matching the machine in format, it hid and subsequently exposed the right answers with the turn of a page or through the student's use of a cardboard mask or a special pen with disclosing ink. Because it matched the features of the teaching machine but was less expensive and easier to use, the programmed text was much more commonly used of the two.

The essential characteristics shared by teaching machines and programmed texts are:

1. A logical sequence of small steps. Students are led through a presentation of small amounts of information sequentially arranged to progressively approximate the final complex behavior. For example, to learn how to compute

an index of light refraction for materials, the student would first learn to compute sine functions.

2. Active response. The student is asked to operate on the information in an appropriate way. Typically the student must complete a sentence with the appropriate word, or answer a question.

3. Immediate feedback. The student is reinforced by being given the correct answer as soon as the response is completed.

4. Individual rate. Each learner is allowed to progress through the sequence at her own rate. Thus, programmed instruction accommodates individual differences in ability, not by teaching less but by varying pace.

If these features sound similar to those of the Personalized System of Instruction (Chapter 18), it is not by coincidence. Fred Keller, the founder of PSI, and Skinner were graduate students and close friends at Harvard, and have both worked on behavioral research. The principal differences between the two are basically matters of degree and operation. In PSI the chunks of information are larger; the responding is not as frequent and is done via a unit quiz rather than through questions embedded in the text; and the reinforcement comes from the peer proctor who checks the quizzes.

The above description of programmed instruction is frequently referred to as the "product definition" of PI. This is to distinguish it from what has come to be called the "process definition." The emergence of the process definition of programmed instruction came as research on the technique began to appear, and was due mainly to the work of Arthur Lumsdaine (1964) and Susan Markle (1967). It became clear from early research that there were "good" programs and "bad" ones, and that only the ones that *worked* should be considered programmed instruction. The definition of PI thus became more pragmatic, being described as "validated instruction" or any set of reproducible instructional events which produces a measurable and consistent effect on student behavior.

A process subsequently evolved by which programmers could design validated instruction. The process begins with the selection of a topic and the specification of the program objectives, or intended student performance. The objectives are analyzed to determine the sequence of prerequisite subskills. The program is written, tested with a small group of students, and revised. The revision process continues until the criterion for effectiveness is met. Only then is the program published.

However, beneficial this "process definition" is, it obscures any understanding of the meaning of programmed instruction. As its proponents contend, this definition can be applied to practically any medium; but a film, even though validated, is not what one thinks of when using the term programmed instruction. In this chapter the examination of programmed instruction will apply the product definition, although recommendations for its development and use will stress empirical validation.

The product definition has also changed over time, probably for the better. Although there are still traditional programs in use, the "frames" of the many recent programs are larger. Thus, a student may read anywhere from a page of text to a whole chapter before making a response. The number of response requests may be only a dozen items presented ten to twenty times in a semester; a far cry from the 50,000 proposed by Skinner. The responses may also be more complex. Instead of filling in a missing word, the student may write a brief essay, conduct a project, or perform a simulated task. The sequences are more complex as well. Instead of moving through the information in a linear fashion, students may be branched into remedial lessons, or around material to more advanced units depending on their responses. In general, modern programmed instruction has retained its basic characteristics such as active responding and individual pacing, but they have been modified to correspond to the complex nature of adult learning.

Advantages and Disadvantages

Because programmed instruction was designed specifically for learning, it has several features which give it advantages over other techniques. The self-pacing allows for differences in rate of learning between students. The immediate feedback verifies student learning, avoids mislearning, and allows for quick and penalty-free adjustment to error.

The active responding engages students in learning. These responses are limited, however. PI is not as interactive as a discussion or as computer-assisted instruction; the student, for the most part, is not able to alter the scope or sequence of the learning. Nor are the responses usually as complex as in more interactive modes. Programs which are limited to requesting students to fill in missing words usually appear uninteresting.

The fact that PI is a stable and enduring form of instruction (as opposed to the transient nature of a lecture) allows the instructor to modify and revise the program until it is effective and efficient.

With regard to effectiveness and efficiency, several reviewers have examined research comparing PI to "traditional" instruction. Jamison, Suppes, and Wells (1974) found PI to be as effective as traditional instruction, while taking less time. Nash *et al.* (1971) confirm this finding, stating that PI takes on the average one-third less time than traditional instruction. Costin (1972) concluded that programmed instruction is probably better than lecture for the amount of information learned. And Kulik and Jaksa (1977) found that in studies where students used PI, they scored on the average five percent higher on the criterion measure than students using alternative methods. (PSI students scored thirteen percent higher.)

In summary, programmed instruction is an effective and efficient mode of instruction (at least for information learning), which actively involves students in learning and accommodates differences in their learning rates.

Appropriate Uses

Content. Judging by the subject matter for which instructional programs have been produced, PI is appropriate for any discipline or level. Carl Hendershot's (1973) comprehensive bibliography of programs in print lists approximately 3500 programs in subjects ranging from Latin to chemistry, and for levels from kindergarten to graduate and professional school.

At the college level, studies have supported the *effectiveness* of programs in a variety of areas, including accounting (Hong, 1972), algebra (Bartz and Darby, 1966), chemistry (Moriber, 1969), enzymology (Portnoy and Glasser, 1974), foreign languages (Blyth,

1962; and Carroll and Leonard, 1963), logic (Elder and Elder, 1973), mathematics (Collagan, 1968), psychology (Himmel, 1972), and the analysis of expository writing (Harris, 1972). However, several reviewers (Beard and Bligh, 1972; and Costin, 1972) suggest that the effectiveness of programmed instruction may be limited to the simple acquisition of information. The systematic progression of students through content, characteristic of PI, would seem to lend itself to the instruction of more complex cognitive tasks, but this assumption has not yet been established through research.

The rather asocial nature of PI would seem to inhibit learning in the affective domain. Nor do other features of PI, such as small steps and self-pacing, seem to contribute to this type of learning.

The inherent limitations of any print medium makes programmed instruction inappropriate for developing psychomotor skills, without being accompanied with some visual demonstration. The procedural steps and decision matrices implicit in such tasks could be taught through PI.

Students. The initial proponents of PI felt that it was a way for teachers to accommodate student differences. They felt that the self-pacing feature of PI would allow less able students to take the time they needed to learn, thus eliminating differences in amount learned due to ability. This assumption has not been borne out. Of the studies that looked at the association of ability and achievement for college students using PI, two have shown some advantages for lower ability students (Owen *et al.*, 1965; and Knight, 1964), one has shown that higher ability students learn better (Doty and Doty, 1964), and three show no difference (Carroll and Leonard, 1963; Smith, 1962; and Unwin, 1966). It would seem that although programmed instruction can be effective for students of all ability levels, the independence which it allows might have to be compensated for by instructor monitoring of students with poor study habits.

A review by Nash *et al.* (1971) concludes that programmed instruction does save student time. This seems to be the effect of branching that would allow the more able students to finish more quickly (Hartley, 1974).

There is some indication (Tobias and Abramson, 1971; Knight

and Sassenrath, 1966) that certain personality characteristics are associated with achievement via PI. A student's need to achieve and her level of anxiety may be associated with achievement using programmed instruction. Positive attitudes toward programmed instruction are also associated with achievement (Doty and Doty, 1964). Apparently PI does not compensate for a student's lack of motivation.

As for other personality characteristics, Arthur Chickering (1976) suggests that the structure provided by PI is probably suited to field-dependent students; however, the lack of interpersonal communications would not appeal to these students. Some support for this position is provided by Doty and Doty (1964) who found a negative correlation between social need and achievement via programmed instruction.

In summary, generalizations cannot be made at this point about the differential effect of programmed instruction with students, other than to say it seems individual differences are not eliminated by this approach. An instructor can feel free to use PI with any student until or unless experience indicates otherwise.

Instructor. There was much concern when programmed instruction first appeared that it would, or at least was intended to, eliminate teachers. Skinner (1958) refutes this but does concede that the teacher's role would probably change. In general, Skinner contends PI would save time and money. The instructor would not have to be concerned with the more mundane aspects of teaching, such as checking weekly assignments. Frequent feedback would be handled by the program; indeed, it is likely to be even more frequent with PI. The program would also do some things that most teachers find infeasible, such as providing personalized pacing of instruction.

The instructor would be left with time to counsel students and provide assistance on a one-to-one basis for those who need it. The instructor would also need to monitor the materials, testing their effectiveness and modifying those portions which do not prove to be adequate.

If instruction is principally or exclusively provided via PI, the instructor should be prepared for and comfortable with an independent, individualized class. The instructional focus will be on the students and the materials rather than the teacher, for the class may never meet as a whole. It may be beneficial, however, to use PI as an adjunct to a lecture; supplementing the self-instructional materials with discussions, films, and other presentations will make the class more traditional. This combination of methods is becoming a common way to use programmed instruction; whereas an instructor formerly had to accept the behavioral philosophy that accompanied PI, it can now be used as unphilosophically as an overhead projector.

Environment. As alluded to above, a course for which programmed instruction is used predominately or exclusively looks very different from the traditional classroom. Students can work independently in the library or at home. They may see each other (and the teacher) only occasionally to clear up a question or to take an exam. Because of these aspects of PI, it is frequently used for extension or correspondence courses, or in other settings where students may not be able to meet regularly.

The environmental changes are not necessary if programmed instruction merely replaces the text, or is used for only an occasional unit. Lectures and class discussion can be scheduled as in a more traditional class. Used in this way, PI can supplement or complement the regular instruction.

How to Do It

An instructor who has decided that programmed instruction is appropriate for her instructional setting is likely to be confronted by one of two situations: (1) programs are commercially available for consideration, or (2) the instructor must write a program. Guidelines are provided here for each of these situations.

Selecting a program. Jacobs, Maier, and Stolurow (1966) offer a checklist to evaluate commercial programmed instruction. Four questions are asked:

1. *Is it really programmed instruction?* If the teacher is to rely on the materials for substantial assistance in instruction, it is important that they qualify as programmed material. Specifically, the materials should require periodic responses, provide feedback, be self-paced, and, most importantly, be validated. Field test data should be provided to verify the effectiveness of the materials.

2. *How does the program fit into the curriculum?* As with a textbook (see Chapter 10), it is important that a program match the instructor's course objectives. When considering a program, the instructor can examine the listed objectives, the quizzes, and a sampling of the frames. Also to be considered is the level of difficulty. This would include the reading vocabulary, as well as the necessary skills prerequisite to learning from the program. All of these features should match the instructor's situation within acceptable limits.

3. *How well would the program teach?* A properly developed and documented program should be accompanied by a manual with information needed for an instructor to make an adoption decision. Information included would be field test data on student scores for the final exam, completion time, error rate on the response requests, and student attitude. Also included should be a rather detailed description of the situation and the students tested. Information regarding age, experience, preparation, ability, motivation, and preferences would allow the instructor to make comparisons between the test group and the students who will be using the program. The test environment may also be critical. Whether the program was given in class or as homework, the amount of guidance provided, and the use of additional materials and techniques are all important factors. The extent to which test conditions match the instructor's situation and results match instructor's expectations are central selection questions.

4. *Is it affordable?* The price of the program is only one of its costs. Whether it requires a machine, whether it is reuseable, and whether it will release instructor time for other activities, are also cost factors.

Even if the program is adequate by these tests and adopted, it is recommended that the instructor do so tentatively. Subsequent tests conducted by the instructor on the user population are advised. Details on how this can be done are in the following section.

Writing a program. Writing a program is no simple matter and should be approached with some caution. Several good books exist on writing programs (see Resources) and these should be studied or a workshop should be taken (such as the Programmed Learning Workshop offered by the Division of Management Education,

University of Michigan) before programming is attempted. The following guidelines are not intended as a substitute for these preparations but are meant to give the reader an idea of what is involved. The procedure and ideas are synthesized from a number of sources (Lysaught and Williams, 1963; Markle, 1967, 1969, 1970; Mechner, 1967; and Green, 1967).

1. *Specify the outcome.* The instructor/programmer should begin the process by specifying the final outcome desired. Frequently in higher education this is a rather complex set of skills and abilities, sometimes difficult to state explicitly. A good way to start is to write the final exam first. This is typically the way an instructor operationalizes his expectations. It is important, however, that this exam be an accurate representation of the skill in the real world. If the students are to apply some knowledge, the instructor should not just ask them to talk about it. Situational questions which are simulations of real life problems should be used.

2. *Analyze the task.* Once the final outcome is operationalized, this complex task should be broken down into its components. These are the processes, decision rules, exceptions, and conditions embedded in the final task. A list of these component skills will serve as an outline for the "curriculum" of the program. Frequently, these procedures have been articulated by the discipline, especially when symbolized in a mathematical equation. However, there may be cases when the process is not so apparent. In such cases the observation of a "master performer" (such as the course instructor) while she performs the task will result in the identification of the component tasks.

3. *Analysis of learners and determination of program content.* The steps so far have not involved the writing of a frame. That is because the precise determination of exactly what needs to be programmed is at least in part the reason why programmed instruction is so efficient. Once the instructor has determined what the final performance is and what its components are, the determination of program content depends on the characteristics of the intended learners. If the instructor/programmer can find out, for example, that 90 percent of the students already know the first four component steps in the final task, this material can be eliminated from the program or covered only briefly.

4. *Write criterion items*. After having determined which components will need to be taught, the instructor can devise a set of items which test each component. As with test items these items must also approximate the way this skill is applied in the intended setting.

5. *Write learning exercises*. This is the process that is typically identified with programming: the construction of program frames. This advanced skill requires much knowledge and practice; the reader should refer to the resources listed. For each component the programmer would convert a number of the criterion items into learning exercises. This is done by giving the learner some information critical to figuring out the answer. This could be a prompt, an example, or a rule. Thus, for each learning exercise there should be some information, a response request, and an answer, with instructions as to how the learner should proceed. The last is particularly important if the learner is to be branched to different frames depending on his answer.

6. *Developmental tryout*. Upon completion of the first draft of the program, the instructor should conduct a developmental tryout. This is done with a small sample (one to four) of learners from the target population. The instructor should sit with each learner as he goes through the program, thinking outloud. No intervention or prompting should be made by the author, but any errors made should be noted.

7. *Revision*. Patterns and types of errors should be identified and modifications made. Unclear passages should be reworded, examples added, or distractions eliminated. These changes would be based on data obtained from the students. For example, an item missed on a criterion test which was properly answered in the learning exercise may need more practice rather than a new learning exercise.

8. *Field test*. When developmental testing results in a satisfactory program (which may take several trials) the programmer would then try it out with the larger group. Information on achievement, time, response errors, and attitude can be used either to refine the program further or to justify its use to administrators and colleagues.

Because of the amount of time involved in the programming effort it is recommended that this be reserved for a small subset of skills within the course for which commercial material is not available. These could include remedial or advanced topics which the instructor does not care to cover in class, or some other sub-section appropriate for programmed instruction, such as basic concepts or terms.

Resources

Books and Articles

Brethower, D. M., Markle, D. G., Rummler, G. A., Schrader, A. W., and Smith, D. E. *Programmed learning: A practicum.* Ann Arbor, Michigan: Ann Arbor Publishers, 1965. A programmed workbook on how to write programmed instruction.

Bullock, D.H. *Programmed instruction.* Volume 14 in The Instructional Design Library. Englewood Cliffs, New Jersey: Educational Technology Publications, 1978. A highly useful handbook on the process and the product of programmed instruction.

Hendershot, C. H. *Programmed learning and individually paced instruction* (5th ed.). Bay City, Michigan: Carl Hendershot, 1973. A comprehensive directory of off-the-shelf programs and devices.

Lange, P.C. (Ed.). *Programmed instruction.* Chicago: University of Chicago Press, 1967. A valuable examination of the issues and research in programmed instruction.

Lysaught, J. P., and Williams, C. M. *A guide to programmed instruction.* New York: John Wiley, 1963. A step-by-step review of the programming process for those who want to do their own materials.

Markle, S. *Good frames and bad.* New York: John Wiley, 1969. The best how-to-do-it book on the market.

Periodicals

Educational Technology. Educational Technology Publications, 140 Sylvan Avenue, Englewood Cliffs, New Jersey 07632. A monthly magazine which has been covering PI, as well as other technologies, since 1961.

Improving Human Performance, National Society for Performance and Instruction, Washington, D.C. 20017. A quarterly research journal for both researchers and practitioners.

NSPI Journal, National Society for Performance and Instruction, Washington, D.C. 20017. A monthly newsletter for Society members. Regular features include editorial, local chapter news, and research abstracts.

Programmed Learning and Educational Technology, Association for Programmed Learning and Educational Technology, London. A quarterly research journal.

Organization

National Society for Performance and Instruction, Washington, D.C. 20017. Formerly the National Society for Programmed Instruction, this organization facilitates the communication of information on programmed instruction and promotes its use in education and training.

Programmed Instruction: Effective and Efficient

Jim Henkel is using programmed instruction to teach a course in Medical Terminology at the University of Minnesota. "The material in this course lends itself well to programmed instruction. We are dealing with a well-defined domain: medical terms and how they are put together. This type of material is easily presented by frames."

Although Mr. Henkel has only been involved with this course for one year, it has been taught by the programmed instruction method for at least five years. "One advantage of using this technique is economic. Our course handles three hundred students in each quarter and it is administered by one professor and two teaching assistants."

Students coming into the course sign up for five bi-weekly testing sessions. A syllabus explains which frames students will be responsible for on each test. A programmed text, *Medical Terminology* by Smith and Davis, provides the main material covered in the course. A supplementary dictionary of medical terms is also used. Students study the course material two to three hours per week on the average. A set of audiocassettes is also available in two learning resource centers on campus for students to use if they wish to concentrate on pronunciation. These cassettes provide additional reinforcement of the terminology learned through the text.

High expectations are placed on students in the course. They are expected to achieve a ninety-five percent (95%) average for the five tests. If this is accomplished, they are not required to take the final exam. Apparently these expectations do not discourage students: "Students seem to love the course. There are three courses in medical terminology offered on our campus. The enrollment in the programmed instruction course has been steadily increasing."

Mr. Henkel has taken an interest in further improving this course. "One problem that we have had in the past is that students save and share tests from year to year so that it becomes impractical to use tests over again. This year we are using computer generated tests, developed through a domain-referencing technique, based on a test item bank of about 5,000 items, all keyed to Smith and Davis. Terminology covered in the course was divided into domains, and terms are drawn from domains by the computer in stratified but random fashion. Each student takes a different but equivalent test." Another change that Mr. Henkel plans to incorporate is a flexible scheduling option so that students can work at a faster pace if they wish, and take tests whenever they complete a new section of material.

Mr. Henkel explains that using the programmed instruction technique for this course material has been a successful experience. "It is an exciting program. I'm very enthusiastic about it. I believe that given the proper attitude it can be an effective and efficient method."

Prof. Jim Henkel
College of Pharmacy
University of Minnesota
Minneapolis, Minnesota 55455
(612) 376-4892

Chapter 21

COMPUTERS

Computers are as controversial as they are pervasive in contemporary society. To some they carry connotations of dehumanization, centralization, and standardization. To others, they can relieve society of routine, repetitive tasks and free people to enjoy their leisure.

Just as in the society at large, there is controversy over the role of computers in higher education. Some applications have paralleled those in industry and business. Computers have been used to facilitate registration, to maintain student records, to store information for catalogs, to schedule rooms for classes, and for normal business routines such as accounting, payroll, and personnel records. Computers have also been used extensively in research and for data processing.

There are, in addition, many instructional applications of computing in higher education. Formal course work is offered in computer science. Students in engineering, science, education, and other disciplines use the computer as a tool to solve complex problems and for data analysis in much the same manner that calculators are used for less complex computations. Students may use computer graphic capability to plot relationships which might otherwise take hours to do by hand or might be impossible to visualize in other ways. Architecture students may simulate designs and models and experiment with them or analyze them on the computer. Engineering students may process experimental data or use the computer for problem-solving. It is possible to view computing proficiency as a technological literacy, and students should be given opportunities to develop competencies in this area.

As pervasive as they are in higher education it is not surprising to find there is no *one* definition for computer use in education. Presented here are five general types of applications.

Testing and Scoring. Computers can be of value in the management of certain instructional tasks. Some schools have scoring services for multiple-choice tests. Students are asked to respond on machine scored answer sheets. The scoring service provides the instructor with individual test scores, routine test statistics, and item difficulty and item discrimination indices. The scoring is normally fast and accurate, and the traditional "grading party" is eliminated (at least for this reason).

Faculty members can build a computerized item pool for multiple-choice tests by retaining items in the computer data base. This system facilitates the development of a pool of reliable, validated test items.

Distinct from scoring applications, the computer can be used to manage the testing of students in competency-based courses. One can assume that individual students are at various points in the curriculum at any given time. Therefore, the normal pattern of giving the same test items to all students is not the most efficient testing pattern. A computer managed testing program can individualize the items which are presented to students, giving each student those items for which he is ready.

Students could be presented comprehensive items which require mastery of a number of course objectives. Those who answer correctly go on to other items. Those who are in error can be given individual items which test all of the objectives which were included in the original item. In this manner, the computer collects data to diagnose the general topic which is a problem and can then pin-point the objective on which the student needs to work. Multiple item pools can be maintained and the computer can be programmed to provide parallel test forms. Statistics on student performance can be retained for instructor review.

Drills and Practice. The computer can be programmed to present the student with problems and exercises, to evaluate responses, and to present the student with additional practice items based on prior responses. This basic instructional function is usually relegated to workbooks, but if the problems involved are complex enough to warrant the use of the computer in their solution, the method can be justified.

Tutorial Programs. The computer can be used to deliver specific instruction. Tutorial programs often resemble programmed texts but utilize the computer's capability to control the sequence of information presentation and to introduce additional or remedial materials depending on the responses of students. A typical tutorial program might present printed or graphic information in a frame or series of frames. This presentation would be followed by a multiple-choice or short answer test item. If the student responds correctly, new information is presented. If the response is incorrect, remedial frames are introduced which the author believes will explain the specific error the student made. Additional material may be presented to clarify items. The student may be given choices to go on, to review material, or to stop at any time. The student has control over the pacing of information and often has some control over the sequence of information. The author's capability to prescribe branching and remedial loops controls certain aspects of the student's access to program information.

An alternative tutorial approach is to allow the student more control of the instruction and to cast the computer in the role of an interactive library. If the student is unclear about a point, she may ask for an example, a definition, or an elaboration of the material.

Tutorial programs need not be dull or repetitious. They can exploit the full graphic capability of the computer, the problem-solving and data processing capability, feedback, and provision for remedial instruction. Tutorial programs, as with other individualized study formats, may be thought of as an opportunity for an instructor to extend his contact with students.

Two highly sophisticated tutorial systems have been developed. PLATO and TICCIT (see Resources) greatly extend the instructor's ability to prepare interesting visual material for presentation by computer.

Simulations, Games, Problems. The computer can be used to

present complex models, games, simulations, and creative problems which require the computer's capacity to process and manipulate data for solution. EXPER SIM is a simulation which represents this basic capability. It is a system for teaching research design through computer simulation. The goal of the course is to instruct students in the proper design of experiments. Although originally designed for introductory psychology students, modules have been developed for use in sociology, statistics, chemistry, fluid mechanics, and demographic studies.

Since running actual experiments requires a great deal of time for data collection, EXPER SIM was developed to permit students to design experiments and then to receive data immediately for analysis. Thus, the students can test out a series of designs in one term, which would be impossible to do through real experiments because of financial and time constraints. It is important to note that the program is not conceived as a replacement for actual experimentation but as an extension of the student's experience in experimental design. Students are still expected to design and completely execute an experiment.

Games and simulations are available in economics, wildlife management, political science, and other fields which give students the opportunity to test out hypotheses in controlled situations, without incurring "real world" consequences or wasting resources in experimentation. Such applications of computer technology are often very creative, involving experiences which could not be obtained using conventional instruction.

Computer Conferencing. It is possible with appropriate programming for a group of students or faculty to use a computer terminal system as a communications network. To do this a group member would go to the terminal and call up the conferencing program. He or she could then type a message on the terminal to be stored in the computer memory. This message might be a question, an idea that he or she wants to present, a comment on someone else's idea, or simply a reminder about a commitment. It may be directed to an individual or left open for access by anyone.

To receive messages, the group member only requests a printout of whatever has been stored in memory by other group members. What emerges from this simple exchange of messages is a computer-based communications system which is an alternative to placing a conference telephone call or having a face-to-face discussion.

When one examines the logistics and dynamics of in-person discussions or telephone discussions, they have many limitations. One is that they require each participant to be available at the same time. Often a major effort is required to stage a meeting or even a teleconference. Another problem is that much time is wasted in meetings going over familiar material, bringing people up to date, and dealing with countless interruptions. A computer-based system has the potential to overcome many of those limitations. An idea can be placed on the computer much like an idea could be thrown open for discussion in a meeting. The difference is that the idea is entered into a computer file, and consequently should avoid many of the redundancies of normal speech; reactions can be made literally at any time rather than immediately as in face-to-face discussions. Individuals can react openly or anonymously without the threat of being overpowered by more verbal group members. Anyone in the network, whether local or in remote locations, can react and have the message instantaneously available. At the same time, however, all non-verbal communication is lost. Withdrawn members cannot be brought into the discussion by an effective group leader, and deep-seated emotional reactions may never surface. Nonetheless, computer conferencing can be a mechanism for exchanging verbal information with some unique potentials for interactions that are not fixed in time or place.

In summary, whether the computer is testing, drilling, tutoring, or simulating, its principal characteristic is its ability to manage the instructional situation. If properly programmed, it can diagnose a student's ability or prior achievement, provide appropriate instruction which accommodates individual differences, and assess the student's learning. Its ability to interface with graphic screens or other media is ancillary.

Advantages and Disadvantages

Computer-assisted instruction (CAI) has been compared to normal patterns of instruction without computers in health education (Lawler, 1971), accounting (Allen, 1974; Solomon, 1974), education (Lorber, 1970), calculus (Lang, 1973; Ibrahim, 1970), chemistry (Culp, 1969), engineering (Bass, 1971), and French (Andrews, 1973). The evidence suggests that computer-assisted instruction can improve student performance in a wide variety of disciplines, although these improvements are not as dramatic as with PSI (Kulik and Jaksa, 1977).

When compared to traditional laboratory instruction in geology, instruction using computers has maximized learning for males, science related majors, and students with prior computer experience (Lee, 1973). Compared to programmed instruction, computer-assisted instruction was better for aggressive students and poorer for deferent, orderly, nurturant, and endurant students (Blitz, 1972). Faculty members should not assume, therefore, that CAI will improve performance for all students. The current evidence would indicate that while CAI can improve traditional teaching practices, there is a complex interaction involving student traits which will dictate how individuals benefit from the instruction. The best utilization pattern for CAI would then be to use it in combination with a variety of other instructional techniques rather than to replace existing instruction totally with computers.

Computers have remarkable data processing and graphic capabilities. Whereas print and audiovisual media have the capacity to present data and graphics they are limited in that they cannot interact with students. The computer can summarize data, simulate complex interactions, and generate elaborate graphic displays in response to student and/or faculty input. Wherever an interactive visual approach is required, computer graphics are preferred over regular graphic techniques. In addition, in some cases computer-generated graphics are less expensive than regular artwork.

When complex feedback and/or branching is required in programmed learning formats, the computer is preferred to text for presentation; it can handle more complex responses and prescribe more complex branches than texts, which tend to present frames in a linear sequence. Small step linear programs, on the other hand, are better presented in text, since they can then be used at student convenience and do not take advantage of the extensive response capability of the computer.

When information is to be presented to students and no interaction is required, texts and audiovisual media are normally cheaper alternatives. They are more convenient for student use and can incorporate color and pictorial materials. Where highly visual material involving motion is presented, television or motion pictures would be preferred to computer presentations.

At present, the graphic capabilities of the computer are limited and do not compare to the visual presentations of audio-visual media. However, it is reasonable to assume that computers may eventually be able to interface with and control a variety of media so as to be responsive to student data input, inquiries, traits, and a complex of other variables. The present limitations of the computer are no indicator of its potential for educational presentations.

One of the biggest disadvantages of computers has been the difficulty of transferring programs from one system to another, thus necessitating the time and expense of rewriting or modifying each program to be used. Most computer systems have been developed as autonomous units which support the needs of a single campus. Often computer programming is produced specifically for one campus and relies extensively on the availability of local software. Consequently, one cannot transport computer-assisted instruction programs—particularly graphics programs—conveniently between campuses. One way of coping with this problem is by the interconnection of computer systems through networks. Networks can provide the central back-up which is not possible on local systems. Moreover, they can greatly extend the range of contact for programs which are dependent on local software for operation. A network might connect all the systems in a regional area. To connect with the computing facilities on another campus, the user simply dials a special phone number to connect his terminal to the network. Such sharing of resources can help to overcome the limitations of local computer systems, while still maintaining the flexibility and advantages of local control.

A final comment on the advantages and disadvantages of computers. Computer technology has changed drastically in the last ten years, thus making even "new" systems outdated. The trend toward miniaturization, however, seems to have long-range advantages for instructional applications. First, the minicomputer made departmental administration of computers possible. Next, the micro-processor should result in the widespread individual use of computers. Particularly where data analysis, problem-solving, or drills are such that large memory capacity is not required, micro-processors can be used extensively and reduce the load on large central processing units. The micro-processor can extend the range of student interface with computers by making small systems available for individual use at student discretion. These small, very low-cost systems have enormous potential, which we can barely glimpse today.

Appropriate Uses

Content. Computer-assisted instruction has been used in many disciplines. Hickey (1968) identified applications in social science, psychology, economics, languages, physics, chemistry, biology, mathematics, health professions, business and accounting, engineering, and in teaching problem-solving and nursing skills. The proceedings of the 1977 Conference on Computers in the Undergraduate Curricula (Christensen, 1977) presented papers on current CAI projects in all of these same areas, and more. Computer applications are not limited to mathematics and physical sciences. They extend into the humanities, social sciences, education, and business.

Computer-assisted instruction is particularly effective in presenting content which requires practice for mastery or comprehension. The identification of principles through repeated experience with raw data, the teaching of problem-solving through the use of varied examples, and the teaching of skills which require drill or extensive practice can be facilitated by computer tutorial programs which evaluate student performance, give immediate feedback, and progressively move the student from introductory to advanced levels of performance. Higher order objectives involving synthesis and evaluation can be accomplished with computer simulations in which students control and use the computer in various problem-solving areas.

Thus, the potential of computer-assisted instruction ranges from programs which stand in place of the teacher and control the rate and direction of student progress, to software which encourages students to explore creatively and define the learning content. In general, computers can make a unique contribution in those highly interactive areas of problem-solving, synthesis, and evaluation while they contribute to goals of knowledge, transmission, and comprehension through practice and drill.

The computer is not normally selected to influence attitudes, but its impact on student attitudes is often quite clear. Computer testing can lead to high states of anxiety and negative attitudes (Hedl *et al.*, 1973); computer-assisted instruction can improve student attitude toward statistics (Byers, 1973); and CAI can contribute to more realistic attitudes toward self-concept, feelings of internal control, and level of aspiration (Smith, 1971). Faculty should carefully evaluate the affective impact of any computer use which is anticipated. Cognitive areas of performance do not exist in isolation, and it is the general goal of instruction to produce favorable student responses to the instructional process.

Students. Individual student traits are important factors to consider in the evaluation of the effectiveness of computer-assisted instruction. Hickey (1968) cites literature which suggests that independence, mathematics ability, reading ability, and anxiety are traits which can influence performance under CAI treatments. Students with strengths in mathematics fundamentals tended to learn better from laboratory-like situations. Students high in reading skills were superior in highly verbal modes. High anxiety can interfere with performance on CAI materials.

Subsequent research on anxiety has indicated that this is an important trait to consider in using CAI. Students who evidence high curiosity tend to evidence low anxiety (Judd *et al.*, 1973). High state curious individuals tend to perform better on CAI (Leherissey, 1971). High state anxiety combined with low math ability resulted in poorer performance with CAI, whereas high anxiety combined with high ability did not (Rappaport, 1971). Memory support and curiosity stimulation may help high anxiety students (Leherissey, 1971; Leherissey *et al.*, 1971). In summary, instructors should provide support for anxious students by trying to stimulate their curiosity in the subject matter and by providing outlines, or guides which help students identify significant points to be remembered in a CAI program.

Proponents of CAI indicate that self-paced interactive programs would benefit low aptitude students. Cronbach and Snow (1977) cite studies which are inconsistent on this point. One cannot conclude that CAI will necessarily be better for low aptitude students. Instructors should be ready to provide these students with support through guides or personal contacts to insure that instructional objectives are met.

Students who are active learners and positively inclined to this mode of instruction perform better than others (Gallagher, 1970). Dental students who favored CAI tended to show higher intellect and independent learning traits than students who did not prefer CAI (Gaston, 1972). In general, then, the students who stand to profit most from CAI are independent learners, who are high in curiosity and low in anxiety.

Instructor. One difficulty instructors have with accepting and developing computer-assisted instruction is that the traditional view of teaching depends on talking to students, giving students reading assignments, and communicating the instructor's concept of the field. This contrasts sharply with the assumptions underlying CAI (Starks *et al.,* 1969). While all computer use does not require rigid adherence to tutorial features like specifying objectives in performance terms, engaging students at their level of proficiency, allowing students to proceed at their own pace, and operating on the basis of mastery, there is a need for specificity in developing computer-assisted instruction which is not typical of lecturing or using audiovisual presentations. The instructor who is already comfortable with specifying objectives will not have difficulty working with computer-assisted instruction. Faculty members who have not already experienced this pattern of teaching will often have to reassess their traditional teaching methods systematically.

Unlike interpersonal methods, in which the instructor can react spontaneously to students, computers require elaborate programming of responses to give the appearance of spontaneous interaction with students. Anticipating student responses, programming alternatives, and specifying outcomes requires a very disciplined and systematic approach to instruction. Some instructors will find this tedious and may object to specificity on philosophical and educational grounds. They may have difficulty developing programs due to the current limitations of computing technology.

Person-centered instructors will probably have the most difficulty accepting computer-assisted instruction, since the computer intervenes between them and their students. If the computer is viewed as an extension of their contact with students rather than as a substitute for it, these instructors will probably find computing to be capable of contributing to the accomplishment of their instructional goals.

One reason that it is difficult to specify the type of instructor who potentially can most effectively utilize instructional computing is that the present state of the art, for all its technical complexity, is really quite primitive. For the most part, it requires skills to produce programs that only experts possess. It requires access to terminals and central support to deliver the programs. But this is in theory not so different from television or motion pictures. Computing is just not as widely accepted. One of the great needs of the field is for faculty members of varying backgrounds, interests, and philosophies to define and extend the parameters of the contribution which computers can make to instruction. Here a faculty member can make a significant contribution to a field which is literally in a state of infancy. Instructors who demonstrate enthusiasm for the medium and who are challenged by its potential will probably be the most successful in its utilization.

Environment. Effective utilization of computers in instruction requires convenient student access to terminals. For sophisticated visual programs, graphics terminals may be required. Since such equipment is expensive and may not be readily available for student use, students are often forced to use terminals at odd hours and in inconvenient locations.

Moreover, the instructor generally has no control over the reliability of the computer system. Computers and terminals inevitably break down, and back-up equipment for such highly centralized systems is generally not available. When computer-assisted instruction is based on a system which is also used for research and administrative purposes, or where many terminals are in use simultaneously, the system can become overloaded to the point where response time is very slow. In programs where rapid feedback is essential, such delays are irritating to the user at best and at worst may seriously interfere with learning.

Thus, a supportive environment is one which provides terminals for convenient student access, and which has committed a sufficient resource to instructional computing to maintain high reliability and rapid response time. On most campuses, the integrated use of the computer system for administration, research, and instruction is economically advantageous and does not significantly interfere with user requirements. Moreover, the rapid drop in the cost of terminals and the increase in the need for them on a departmental basis should naturally result in the additional availability of terminals for student use.

Ultimately, terminals should be as conveniently available as telephones for student access, and microprocessors as readily available as cassette recorders or simple calculators. In a truly supportive environment, faculty members require departmental and central administrative support. The development of CAI programming can take an extensive commitment of a faculty member's time. This needs to be viewed as legitimate and productive faculty effort on a par with original research. Colleagueal and departmental support and recognition is important for any faculty member who undertakes an innovative instructional pattern. In addition, access to technical staff will greatly facilitate the development of CAI materials, for few faculty members have the skills necessary to program graphic simulations or complex interactive programs.

How to Do It

Since most faculty members have not had any experience with instructional computing, the first step in using computers is to learn about the applications of computer technology which might be appropriate for a specific field. This can be done by reviewing standard references (see Resources), but there is no substitute for a personal introduction to several computer-assisted instruction programs. Unlike motion pictures, television, books, and slides— which most faculty members have seen or used enough to have a "feel" for their application—CAI offers such new potential for instruction that it must be experimented with to be fully appreciated.

It will be important for an instructor to connect with the formal and informal groups involved in instructional computing. Hopefully, the institution will have some formal agency or consultant to assist in developing computer-assisted instructional programming. Just as important as this formal resource, however, will be the informal group of computer users on campus. They may or may not have meetings, but like gamesters they will comprise a small group of computer enthusiasts who have overcome or are involved in overcoming many of the logistical problems of CAI.

Once an instructor has formulated an idea for a computer unit, she will need to discuss it at length with colleagues and support staff. So much effort goes into developing a program that it is important to have a focused idea of the instructional goals of the program and to be sure that they cannot be accomplished more easily with another medium.

The next step will be to specify an instructional strategy to accomplish the objective. If the goal is to engage students in solving problems or to formulate concepts based on verbal or graphic examples, the instructor may select a tutorial format for a program. In this case there may be a formal system available to assist him in writing the program and entering it into the system.

Many systems are designed for input by novice faculty. The "programming" will not involve a computer language, but will require the instructor to write text, specify graphics, write quiz items, formulate problems, and specify remedial loops.

If a tutorial system is not available, all of the manipulations which the computer is to perform on the content in reaction to student responses will have to be programmed. This is a difficult task and one which should be assigned to a professional programmer. Only if a faculty member has considerable experience programming should she undertake this work alone.

If the students are to synthesize models based on data or to evaluate and critique computer simulations, the instructor may have to arrange to have an entire program designed for this purpose. In other cases, it may be possible to use an existing simulation which has been developed for a specific purpose. Such a model is EXPER SIM, a system for teaching research design which has been used in various disciplines, and for which a system has been developed to facilitate instructor utilization. In any case, it is very important to have the assistance of someone who is familiar with computers at the time the program is entered into the computer.

Once the program is on line, it must be thoroughly tested to "debug" it. Then it should be tested by students to see if it actually works. Computer programs are often in a constant state of revision prior to actual use. After the program is finished, instructions for student utilization will have to be written, and its documentation will need to be formalized for future use.

If an instructor wishes to use programming which has been done at another institution, he should obtain a formal documentation of the programming prior to use. Computer programs are not necessarily compatible between systems, and some require special terminals for proper display. Since adapting a program to a new system can be a very expensive and time-consuming operation, it is important to have the documentation examined by an expert to determine whether or not the program is usable.

Normally, the students will use a program when the instructor is not present. Nonetheless, his enthusiasm for the experience should be communicated to them. He should make sure that the students understand the purpose for the unit and what they are expected to learn.

The students will learn more if they pace themselves consistently rather than massing their work in extended sessions (Dunn, 1971). If the instructor provides pacing assistance for those students who are having problems, their performance will likely improve (Dienes, 1972). A simple technique useful for monitoring students is a feedback sheet for reporting contact time with the computer.

When computer programs are used in addition to normal classroom teaching, time should be allotted to discuss the experiences and to receive feedback on the programs. Since anxiety can interfere with learning in CAI, the instructor should use class time to try to overcome any problems students are having at the terminals. He should give very explicit instructions on how to sign on and off and what to do if error messages occur. A detailed guide for students to follow will avoid many problems. This support, combined with regular monitoring of the system, should help make computer use a positive learning experience for students.

Resources
Books and Articles

Bailey, D.E. (Ed.). *Computer science in social and behavioral science education.* Englewood Cliffs, New Jersey: Educational Technology Publications, 1978. Three dozen chapters provide comprehensive coverage of the uses of computers in teaching undergraduate and graduate courses in the social and behavioral sciences. A valuable source book.

Bunderson, C.V., and Faust, G.W. Programmed and computer-assisted instruction. In N.L. Gage (Ed.), *The psychology of teaching methods.* The seventy-fifth yearbook of the national society for the study of education, part I. Chicago, Illinois: University of Chicago Press, 1976, 44-90. Descriptive introduction, state of the art, discussion of PLATO and TICCIT projects, and instructional implications.

Christensen, D.A. *Proceedings of 1977 conference on computers in the undergraduate curricula.* Iowa City, Iowa: CCUS Proceedings, University of Iowa Computer Center, 1977. Collection of articles on instructional computing. Survey of innovative contemporary uses in many curricular areas. Proceedings of this annual conference are available from 1970 to the present.

Dyer, C. H. *Preparing for computer-assisted instruction.* Englewood Cliffs, New Jersey: Educational Technology Publications, 1972. For educators with no prior computing experience. Includes how a computer works. Flow charting, planning a program, and a glossary.

Hunter, B. *et al. Learning alternatives in U.S. education: Where student and computer meet.* Englewood Cliffs, New Jersey: Educational Technology Publications, 1975. An extensive survey of computer utilization for instruction, featuring a number of interesting higher education applications.

Levien, R.E. *The emerging technology: Instructional uses of the computer in higher education.* New York, New York:

McGraw-Hill, 1972. Comprehensive report of the Rand Corporation study for the Carnegie Commission on Higher Education. Includes historical introduction to instructional computing, survey of current uses, and projection of future uses of computing in higher education.

Lippey, G. (Ed.). *Computer-assisted test construction.* Englewood Cliffs, New Jersey: Educational Technology Publications, 1974. The standard book on the topic of how to use computers to assemble test items for either traditional or individualized teaching techniques.

Periodicals

ACM SIGCUE Bulletin, SIGCUE, Association for Computing Machinery, P.O. Box 12105, Church Street Station, New York, New York 10249. Bulletin of the Special Interest Group on Computer Uses in Education (SIGCUE) published four times a year. Includes brief reports, book reviews, and news.

Creative Computing, Box 789-M, Morristown, New Jersey 07060. Six issues per year. Computing applications in elementary, secondary, and higher education. Light, enjoyable style.

Educational Technology, Educational Technology Publications, Inc., 140 Sylvan Avenue, Englewood Cliffs, New Jersey 07632. Published monthly, the periodical contains articles on instructional computing and, occasionally, issues are devoted to the topic. Also articles on instructional systems, programmed instruction, audiovisual media, and educational change. The April, 1978 number is a special issue devoted to "Trends in Computer-Assisted Instruction."

EDUCOM Bulletin, EDUCOM, Box 364, Rosedale Road, Princeton, New Jersey 08540. News on computer and information systems and activities of EDUCOM (Interuniversity Communications Council) published four times a year, general information and references to sources of information.

Places

Project Extend, Center for Research on Learning and Teaching, The University of Michigan, 109 E. Madison, Ann Arbor,

Michigan 48109. Source of information and publications on the Midwest region, plus national and international applications of instructional computing.

Organization

Special Interest Group on Computer Uses in Education (SIGCUE) of the Association for Computing Machinery (ACM), P.O. Box 12105, Church Street Station, New York, New York 10249.

Computer-Assisted Instruction: A Success Story

Sally Wallace at Parkland Community College in Champaign, Illinois is the author of eighteen PLATO lessons used in teaching English grammar. "The computer lessons are a supplement to the classroom lecture and text. All of the materials present a developmental sequence of English skills. We start with grammar and show how this will help in composition."

Based on performance on a battery of tests, students at Parkland Community College are placed in either Remedial English, Composition, or Accelerated Composition classes. The remedial course makes the greatest use of the PLATO lessons. Remedial classes meet three hours per week. One hour per week is spent in computer-assisted instruction. Students in the composition courses may also be assigned computer lessons if they need instruction in specific grammar skills.

The computer-assisted instruction approach to teaching basic English skills has been very successful for Sally Wallace at Parkland. "Most of the students really love it. Though they are only required to use the computer for one hour per week, most of the students come back in the evenings and on weekends to work at the computer. I have seen some fascinating student responses to the computer lessons. Many of our students who have been turned off by English all of their lives become very interested in it, and have a successful experience with this program. Some students who have great difficulty reading a book can sit all day and read the computer terminal screen."

Of course, successful use of computer-assisted instruction is not simply a matter of good luck. CAI has a great deal of faculty support at Parkland Community College. In the English Department, ten of the twenty full-time faculty use CAI in some phase of their instruction. Another factor in the success of CAI is the quality of the lessons. "I have tried to make the lessons very personal. The snappy positive responses seem to motivate the student to continue working." Perhaps the computer itself can also take some of the credit for the success of the program. The computer is a sophisticated, modern machine. Students feel pride in their ability to operate the computer, and this feeling of success is transferred to the subject matter.

Ms. Wallace points out some definite advantages that computer-assisted instruction offers over traditional teaching methods: "Students get individual attention during the lesson. They receive immediate feedback when they answer questions. If they give the wrong answer, the computer tells them why it is wrong. The student is also given responsibility for his own learning. Some students seem to like the privacy offered by CAI. They don't need to worry about making mistakes in front of classmates, and they can work at their own pace."

CAI presents some advantages for the teacher, too. "The computer lessons have allowed me to plan a flexible program for each student. I also have more time to help students with their individual problems. Instead of de-personalizing the learning process, the computer has helped me to take a more personal approach to each student."

Prof. Sally Wallace
Department of English
Parkland Community College
Champaign, Illinois 61820
(217) 351-2307

Chapter 22

THE LABORATORY FORMAT

The laboratory format is typically associated with the hard sciences and engineering. It is, however, being used with increasing frequency in a variety of other content areas where the practice of a skill and/or some direct experiences are considered necessary for learning. Labs have been used in language courses and with training in interpersonal relations. They have also been employed to teach writing skills and mathematics. With the growing appreciation for experiential forms of learning, laboratory exercises are likely to be used more frequently and more widely in college instruction.

Laboratory instruction is a type of structured experiential learning. It is used when some form of "hands-on" experience is desirable or essential for learning a specific skill, gaining a special understanding, or both. The comparatively high focus and structure of the typical laboratory experience distinguish it from other forms of experiential learning such as studio and field experience. Although it is a protected environment, it differs from a simulation in that students work with "real experiences."

The furnishings of the lab—the benches and equipment—are not the essential characteristics of laboratory instruction. What is essential is the active participation of individual students in structured experiences. Thus, at Dickinson College (Steiner, 1972) when students in beginning German are given a text and asked to deduce grammar and design their own linguistic experiments, they are engaged in laboratory work.

Expensive, time-consuming, and widely used in sciences, engineering and elsewhere, the laboratory as a generic instructional form has received comparatively little attention in teaching-learning research. It is indicative that in a standard work such as McKeachie's *Teaching Tips* (1969), laboratory instruction is treated in three pages. Gagne (1970) merely says, "The design of laboratory exercises ... is indeed a challenging task." Publications dealing in *general* with how laboratory work as a form of learning might best be designed and conducted are not easily found. Perhaps the fullest discussion of the theory and practice of laboratory instruction is *The Laboratory, A Place to Investigate*, edited by John Thornton (1972) and published by the American Institute of Biological Sciences.

Advantages and Disadvantages

When learning requires practice and experience—learning that will not take place through reading, hearing a lecture, seeing a film or demonstration—the laboratory offers clear advantages. It simultaneously offers an opportunity for the student to work independently and yet receive personal and individualized attention. Moreover, the laboratory is student-centered, providing a high level of student participation and involvement. The student's level of progress, achievement, and skill can be fostered and monitored.

While there is frequently no substitute for lab work in learning skills, and perhaps higher order objectives of inquiry and appreciation, its advantages are not without cost. Laboratory work is time-consuming for both instructor and student. More often than not, it requires special rooms and equipment; because of the special purpose of laboratory space, it is frequently useless for other kinds of instruction. Equipment maintenance and replacement are expensive, as are consumable supplies. Typically, the student-instructor ratio must be lower in laboratory work than in other forms of instruction if the special advantages of structured practice with feedback are to be realized. In some cases, economies can be realized by using audio-tutorial (Chapter 19) methods and computer-assisted instruction (Chaper 21) in conjunction with the lab. Unless it is well organized, laboratory work can become wasted time and effort for everyone concerned.

Appropriate Uses

Content. There is no research on what is best taught in a laboratory setting. The National Training Laboratories achieved considerable recognition in using laboratory methods in human development and interpersonal relations. A laboratory format has been involved in improvement in mathematical skills, especially where remedial work is required (Fitzgerald, 1974). Experience supports the use of the laboratory for learning *skills* that require the manipulation of equipment and/or material in such courses as electronics, anatomy, and mechanics.

Laboratory work is considered to be appropriate for illustrating material and concepts introduced in other, usually verbal, ways. It can be argued that illustration through experience enhances learning through repetition, by increasing the number of senses employed and by helping the learner relate verbal abstractions to real objects and events. However, illustrations through laboratory exercises are necessarily limited to a few ideas because of the time and expense involved. It is likely that similar effects can be achieved with less time, trouble, and expense using well-planned demonstrations and high quality audio-visual materials.

Many instructors in science, engineering, and other disciplines believe that laboratory exercises can substantially enhance a student's understanding of a discipline and the methods of inquiry used by professionals in the field. Further, they are convinced that through "hands-on" experience, students may develop a more positive attitude toward the subject. Science educators working with NSF support to develop major new curricula in chemistry, biology, and physics assumed that laboratory work was an important, even essential, element for promoting a real understanding of the methods of scientific inquiry.

Despite these claims of higher order learning for laboratory instruction, it may be that what students master is merely technique. Robert Yager and his colleagues (1969) compared the relative effectiveness of laboratory, demonstration, and lecture. The study was done in a high school biology course, but the results are not without implications for other courses with laboratory components. Using a variety of standard instruments to test critical thinking, understanding of science, and attitudes toward science,

Yager found that those students who had laboratory experiences scored no higher than their classmates in the lecture and demonstration sections on the higher order thinking that learning laboratories are alleged to promote. Only in handling and using the relevant equipment did they achieve more. Other studies show similar findings, whether the laboratory is "content-centered," with activities following explicit directions from a manual or instructor, or "process-centered," with students solving relatively open-ended problems.

Yager himself has suggested, and commentators (Shulman and Tamir, 1973) agree, that the lack of measurably significant differences in understanding, method, and appreciation may result from deficiencies in present measures of higher order learning. Proponents of laboratory work as an instructional strategy for developing a deeper understanding are in much the same position as advocates of games, simulations, or experiential learning. They are convinced that the experience adds something significant but cannot demonstrate it through controlled research studies.

Students. When the object of instruction is learning a skill, virtually any student will profit from laboratory experience appropriately organized for student ability level, with feedback and knowledge of results available, and with the necessary resources provided.

With respect to understanding, inquiry, and appreciation, some research suggests that for certain students, laboratory is a necessity. Renner and Stafford (1972) did some testing of high school students to determine their ability to understand and manipulate formal concepts typically presented in biology, chemistry, and physics. The majority of high school seniors were *unable* to understand formal scientific concepts presented solely by verbal means. They were still in what the Swiss psychologist Piaget (1970) calls the concrete operational stage of development; they needed to think in concrete rather than abstract terms. While it is likely that many students who are markedly deficient in formal conceptual thinking abilities do not go on to college, it is also fair to assume that a significant number of students in introductory courses still learn largely in concrete operational terms. Renner and Stafford strongly maintain that such students must interact with concrete objects, events, and situations to profit intellectually. For these students, learning needs to be grounded in experience, not textbooks.

For others, non-laboratory forms of instruction may be sufficient for understanding and appreciation. Advanced students especially may find laboratory work to be a waste of time, merely a means of slowing their pursuit of new theories and concepts. The effectiveness of the laboratory may be a function of when it is introduced during the learning sequence and of the student's cognitive development. It is not known for what students and at what point laboratory learning fosters higher order objectives.

When planning a laboratory course, instructors often wonder whether it should be taught inductively or deductively. That is, should the lab be a way for students to generalize principles from their experiences, or apply principles to solve problems? The tentative but cautious response to this issue is that less able students benefit from a deductive approach, and more able students by an inductive approach (Cronbach and Snow, 1977). Furthermore, it may be that the lack of structure in the inductive approach would be appropriate for more independent, less anxious students.

Instructor. The basic assumption underlying laboratory instruction is that in certain instances "doing" is more powerful than being shown or told. It seems reasonable, therefore, that the instructor should be prepared to provide the student with experience rather than information in a laboratory setting. He should foster activity and interaction rather than listening. The success of a laboratory exercise is largely dependent on the instructor's skill and ease as a facilitator of student-centered activity.

The laboratory setting can establish a different relationship between the student and teacher than is common in the lecture-classroom. Unfortunately, some instructors have failed to realize the teaching and learning potentials in the situation by relying excessively on teaching assistants. Many "cook book" laboratory exercises serve as much to keep students busy, and/or at bay, as to acquaint them with the discipline and the experiences of investigation.

Environment. The environmental considerations of laboratory learning are similar whether the goal is skill mastery or complex understanding. Appropriate resources in sufficient quantities must be available: space, equipment, supplies, assistance, and time. Too often, shortages in these resources make laboratory learning frustrating and ineffective. In those disciplines where lab work entails some physical hazard, safety is a primary consideration.

How to Do It

Skill teaching. When objectives, students, the environment, and the instructor's disposition make laboratory work a suitable way of teaching a skill, attention to some simple guidelines will help bring about the desired learning. They concern information and sequencing.

How much and what kind of information should be provided to the learner before, during, and after the laboratory work? The student should have a clear idea of what is to be learned and what level of proficiency is expected. Depending on the nature of the laboratory exercise, the objectives can be relatively open or closed. In the case of an elementary biological dissection, for instance, the student will be told precisely what incisions to make and how to make them as well as what organs to identify. In a laboratory where the student is to learn how to use a piece of equipment or technique, for example, paragraphing in a writing lab, the procedures and the level of mastery will be clearly specified. The content itself is left to the student's imagination.

In addition to the objectives of the exercise, the student needs an overview of the task as it is to be performed. The instructor can supply this in a number of ways, including a demonstration, film, or videotape. It is very important that the overview be kept short. Nothing undermines a student's motivation in learning how to *do* something more than over-explaining.

As the student begins the exercise, guidance can minimize the possibility of errors that will have to be unlearned. Yet too much guidance will inhibit the direct discovery which is the foundation of learning in a laboratory situation.

During the laboratory session, the instructor should direct the student's attention to critical cues amidst all the information she is experiencing. For example, in a human relations training lab, students can be cued to attend to the distance and posture of the participants rather than what they are saying. In a chemistry lab the student's attention might be directed to subtle color changes signaling that a reaction is about to take place. Cueing should be used at the minimum level required to accomplish the stated learning objectives.

Feedback and knowledge of results are probably the most important kinds of information to be given in the laboratory; their usefulness to the student is directly related to the speed with which they are given. If a student does not know whether results are incorrect until a week later, there is little likelihood she will be able to relate the information to the specifics of her actual performance.

Negative feedback provides the learner with very little information. It does not give guidelines about how to perform the task correctly. It is often redundant, because the learner often already knows he is doing something wrong. By adding to this anxiety, negative comments generally cause a further deterioration of performance.

Debriefing is increasingly regarded as an important element in laboratory learning. Whereas feedback and knowledge of results are directed to the individual student, debriefing is a review of the whole class' laboratory experience. Using this method, generally experienced successes and results can be fully elaborated and explained.

How should the instructor sequence what the student will do in a skills laboratory? Kempa and Palmer (1974) directed a controlled study comparing the relative effectiveness of written instruction to a television presentation on chemistry techniques. They concluded that success in performing a manipulative skill results from the correct sequential linking of requisite sub-skills.

The kinds of skills appropriately learned in a laboratory setting vary from the simple (cutting glassware) to the complex (spectroanalysis). In addition to mastering a number of sub-skills, the student engaged in a complex procedure must decide among alternative behaviors at certain critical points. Whether the procedure or task should be taught as a whole or in parts is an important instructional decision in designing and conducting a laboratory exercise. The choice depends to a large extent on the very nature of the skill(s) to be learned and the student's level of preparation and experience.

As a general rule, the more complex the skill to be learned, the more profitable it will be to divide the learning into parts. However, "baby steps," like too much instructor talk, undermine interest and motivation. While many skills need to be taught "by the numbers," the instructor is well advised to salt the exercise with some surprises and deviations.

Teaching principles. The procedures for designing laboratory work intended to foster understanding, a sense for the methods of inquiry, and appreciation are in many respects different than those for a laboratory in which teaching or increasing skills is the primary purpose. They are also more difficult objectives to determine and specify.

Common sense strongly suggests that when the primary purpose of laboratory work is to foster understanding, a sense of inquiry, and appreciation, the session should encourage genuine involvement and investigation. Prefabricated experiments seem poorly suited to these purposes. They are usually intended to serve as demonstrations or illustrations and to "prove" to the student that the concepts which have been introduced elsewhere in the course are "true." In general, lab work that emphasizes investigation and process rather than following directions is likely to be more effective.

John Fowler, Director of the Commission on College Physics, has formulated a set of guidelines (1968) for an investigative laboratory in introductory physics. Paraphrased, they can prove useful to instructors in a variety of fields who believe that laboratory experience may yield a deeper understanding and appreciation of content and method.

Axioms:

1. It is in the lab and only in the lab that the student can experience the discipline as it actually is.
2. For learning to take place most effectively, the student must be motivated through interest.

Objectives:

1. The student should have the opportunity to make personal

investigative decisions.

- At some stage in the work the student must choose an experimental path and the choice must be based on work already completed.
- The student should be allowed to carry through incorrect decisions occasionally without being immediately corrected by the instructor.

2. The laboratory should broaden a student's exposure to the behavior of phenomena and to the professional's description and prediction of that behavior.

- An opportunity should be provided for the student to experience a broad range of phenomena.
- Whenever possible, some theoretical analysis should be demanded as part of the lab experience. This should consist of application of broadly-based principles.
- The student should have the opportunity to test some simple model of a phenomenon in the lab and to construct and test a more complex model.
- Reality is a complex interaction of many processes. In the lab, a student should learn by experiment the importance of these various processes and evaluate their magnitude.

3. The lab instruction should provide an environment in which discovery by the student is both possible and encouraged.

- As many experiences as possible should lead to results that are not likely to be known to the student in advance.
- Student questions which appear as appropriate for exploration in the lab are allowed to take precedence over preconceived routines.
- The lab should be the source of experiences which are unexpected and difficult to explain, for such experiences facilitate learning.

Resources
Books and Articles

Fitzgerald, W. (Ed.). *Mathematics laboratories: Implementation research and evaluation.* Columbus, Ohio: Environmental Education, 1974. A thorough discussion of the laboratory approach to mathematics.

Thornton, J.W. (Ed.). *The laboratory: A place to investigate.* Washington, D.C.: American Institute of Biological Sciences, 1972. One of the few publications dealing with the laboratory format conceptually. Although the discussion is directed to the use of investigative laboratories in the biological sciences, the ideas are applicable to virtually any learning situation involving directed experience.

Periodicals

The Journal for Research in Mathematics Education, National Council of Teachers of Mathematics, 1906 Association Drive, Reston, Virginia 20091.

Journal of Research in Science Teaching, John Wiley and Sons, Inc., One Wiley Drive, Somerset, New Jersey 08873.

Science Education, John Wiley and Sons, Inc., 605 Third Avenue, New York, New York 10016.

These are the best and most easily accessible sources for what little controlled research is done in the area of instructional effectiveness of specific laboratory formats.

Several periodicals offer ideas for specific laboratory exercises. For example:

American Biology Teacher
College Composition and Communications
Engineering Education
Foreign Language Annals
Journal of Chemical Education
Journal of Chemical Engineering
Journal of College Science Teaching
Journal of Geography
The Mathematics Teacher
The Physics Teacher
School Science and Mathematics
Teaching of Psychology

A Social Work Laboratory

Richard Goldman and Shlomo Sharlin have designed a social work laboratory now in operation at the University of Haifa, Israel. "We had identified several elements that we felt should be essential parts of a program for any helping profession: a conceptual basis that reflects the professional role rather than a collection of courses; well-defined objectives; experiences which link theory to practice; and a continuous process of program evaluation. We developed the laboratory as a training tool that could provide some of these essential parts."

Students who are in the second year of the three-year social work program spend four and one half months in the laboratory and four and one half months in a field experience. There are three laboratories that students attend each week: interviewing skills, community organization skills, and group work skills. There is one faculty member in charge of each laboratory.

The faculty member helps the student choose a specific topic to work on within the skill area of the laboratory. For example, a student in the interviewing lab may want to study the use of various types of questioning. The student then chooses from a list of objectives the specific one on which he needs help. The student works through a module which may include listening to an audiotape, watching a videotape, reading suggested literature, taking part in a role play and/or being videotaped himself. The modules provide students with the opportunity to practice skills until they are mastered. When mastery has been attained, the student looks at the list of objectives for that topic and selects the next one that he will work on.

Students have had a positive response to the laboratory. "They have been unanimously positive in their reactions. Students who have gone through the lab have said that they are not as concerned about going into the field as they had been before the lab experience. They feel that they have some concrete skills to rely on when interacting with clients."

Dr. Goldman explains that a new challenge has presented itself as an outgrowth of the laboratory. "We are now finding that we must have more contact with people in the field who supervise social work field placements. These people need to have a better idea of what skills our students have developed in the lab. The laboratory will not replace field experience; rather, it will provide a set of experiences which will link theory to practice."

Dr. Richard Goldman
Nova University
Ft. Lauderdale, Florida 33314
(305) 587-6660

Chapter 23

INDEPENDENT STUDY, EXPERIENTIAL LEARNING, AND LEARNING CONTRACTS

"Independent study is a student's self-directed pursuit of academic competence in as autonomous a manner as he (or she) is able to exercise at any particular time" (Dressel and Thompson, 1973). Independent study projects vary, but most have three common elements. First, the student (sometimes a group of students) selects a problem, theme, area, or issue to investigate. In conjunction with the selection, relevant materials and resources are sought. In the course of the search the topic is more closely defined. Second, having selected a problem, the student then sets about solving it with further investigation, research, or experimentation. Finally, third, a suitable presentation of results is organized and presented. The instructor's role is indirect and consultative.

Individualization is not synonymous with independence. PSI, computer-assisted instruction, instructor-assigned projects, etc., are individualized but not independent. Rather, independent forms of study give the *student* the opportunity to adapt goals, resources, and activities to her own needs. The student actively participates in *what* is to be learned as well as *how* it is to be learned.

The absence of classes, other students, or faculty is not the essential mark of independent study; these are incidental characteristics. *What distinguishes independent study is the growth of the student's skills and abilities to pursue learning on his own.*

Advantages and Disadvantages

In an important book, Adderly and associates (1976) make the fullest case for independent study. With independent study, students clearly have a large responsibility for their own learning. The method obliges students to look deeply into a subject and often to combine knowledge from different disciplines. Students are likely to gain satisfaction from doing their own work. They gain experience in research techniques by selecting, collecting, and presenting information. When independent study is undertaken by a team, students can learn cooperation, leadership, and decision-making. Most importantly, the use of independent study fosters the ultimate aim of formal education: to enable the student to become her own teacher.

For all its potential benefits, the instructor and student considering independent study sometimes encounter certain difficulties. Worthwhile projects must sometimes be modified, indeed abandoned, for lack of suitable materials or because the student or the teacher lacks the necessary research skills. Because of their unique character, independent study projects are difficult to evaluate. These possible difficulties should be considered at the very outset of project planning.

By virtue of its design and purpose, the effectiveness of true independent study cannot easily be measured by controlled studies. These require that large numbers of students learn the same material, and the learning is in turn measured on standardized examinations. Accordingly, controlled studies from Seashore (1928) through Novak (1958) and the Antioch study (Churchill and Baskin, 1958) have not shown that the independent study of teacher-assigned objectives and materials is significantly more effective than classroom coverage. These results tell us little about the amount and kind of learning that take place in projects for which the student has the major responsibility for initiating, designing, and carrying out the work.

Research conducted by Hoffman (1973) on independent study by high school students of high, medium, and low ability yields statistically significant results. Analysis of the data showed that there were gains in self-acceptance, sociability, and intellectual efficiency. Participating students and faculty claimed that the independent study students developed increased self-confidence, responsibility, tolerance, and independent thinking.

Appropriate Uses

Content. Independent study has been used for a variety of subjects in many circumstances. Arthur Chickering (1975) cites examples in which independent study, via contract learning, was used for each of Bloom's cognitive categories, from knowledge to synthesis and evaluation. The overall goal of independent study remains the development of intellectual competence. Independent study can help a student become a problem-solver, a manager of his own time, and a learner who is learning how to learn.

Some courses are especially designed for independent study. Courses such as "Special Problems," "Special Topics," tutorials, and seminars are frequently offered as opportunities for independent learning in a group setting. When properly managed, such formats present the dual advantages of permitting a student to pursue independently a topic of personal interest and, at the same time, enjoy the benefits of collaboration. The potential for independent learning can be thwarted when special courses such as these are controlled by instructor-designated topics and specified assignments.

Over the last decade there has been an increasing use of independent study courses offered under titles like "individual research" and "supervised readings." Special intensive independent study periods may be set aside under the 4-1-4 calendar. In courses of this kind, individual students pursue interests as wide-ranging as developing a video color image processor to geodesic architecture. They may explore topics for which there are no equivalent academic courses.

Proponents of independent, student-centered forms of study typically claim that if properly conceived and executed, such forms of learning should give students increased capability for generalization and transfer, a sense of the relevance of learning, and the ability to analyze, synthesize, and apply what is learned. They offer the prospect of greater personal satisfaction, continuing interest, and self-reliance than students can obtain from conventional forms of instruction.

Students. Frequently, students have been admitted to independent study on the basis of intellectual and academic criteria, or this option has been reserved for advanced or senior students. A number of studies suggest that intellectual attainment or years in school are not the distinguishing characteristics of students who select and perform successfully in independent study situations. Social, emotional, and attitudinal factors are more important. Chickering (1964) identified the independent study student as one who is well-controlled, highly motivated, self-assured, and liberally oriented. McCullough and Van Atta (1958) found that students who are less rigid and less in need of social support are likely to profit more from independent study. Thus, students who show the characteristics of independence tend to like and do well in independent study. Nonetheless, they need instructor guidance and support.

At the risk of overgeneralizing from studies cited earlier (Domino, 1971; Dowaliby and Schumer, 1973), students scoring high on scales of Achievement-via-Conformance or Anxiety will probably not do well with independent study.

Instructor. Dressel and Thompson (1973) found latent and overt resistance to student-centered independent study from some instructors. Objections stem from an insufficient regard for the integrity and/or ability of students, a feeling of insecurity at the prospect of dealing with knowledge beyond the classroom domain, and reservations about the time and energy required. Any instructor undertaking an independent learning venture with a student should frankly consider these issues.

The role of the instructor in student-centered independent study is a sensitive and important one. The instructor should work at sympathetically understanding and interpreting the student's objectives. Without twisting these goals into personal preconceptions, she should help the student refine and implement them. Definition of objectives, resources, evaluation, and similar matters should be jointly resolved. The needs and expectations of both student and instructor should be honored. The instructor should also be available at regular and, if possible, specified times to discuss and review the course of the student's independent learning.

Environment. Openness to risk, flexibility, and interdisciplinary, non-traditional directions characterize the environment in which independent study is likely to yield good results. If the instructor restricts independent learning with rules prescribing time, circumstances, amount of work, topic, and elaborate review and approval procedures, its potential for encouraging self-directed learning is diminished.

When placed in competition with the demands of conventional course requirements, independent study frequently gets slighted. Sufficient time is needed to accommodate false starts, reduce the distraction of other activities, and allow for the cumulative effect of independent work to take place. Faculty members must be provided with sufficient time and rewards for conscientiously fostering independent learning.

How to Do It

The development of an effective independent study experience requires more than an agreement on topic, objectives, credit, and completion date, although these are crucial concerns and will be discussed in the following section on "Learning Contracts." Perhaps the most significant issue regarding objectives of independent study is whether the aim of the learning experience is the attainment of specific knowledge and skills or the development of habits and capacities for self-directed learning.

A related issue concerns the criteria appropriate for evaluating learning. Evaluation should emphasize whether the student has demonstrated the behaviors of self-directed learning, including being able to frame objectives, gather resources, overcome obstacles, and apply, integrate, and report on accomplishments. The instructor should be prepared to discuss these issues frankly with students wishing to undertake independent study.

Experiential Learning

Experiential learning is in some respects a natural extension of independent study. Like independent study, it recognizes the power and importance of the student's interests and motivations; through these, experiential learning seeks to enhance the student's responsibility for and ability to create his own learning. It differs markedly from independent study and other instructional formats in formally recognizing the worth and utility of knowledge gained outside the academic setting. While experiential forms of learning are only now coming to be widely accepted in higher education, Sexton and Ungerer's (1975) review of the literature shows that from Dewey to John Gardner, experiential education is supported by a very substantial body of educational theory. Sexton and Ungerer argue persuasively that experiential learning is not only justified but necessary to further the goals of general education and to promote the skills necessary for work, citizenship, and service.

John Duley (1974), a leading spokesman for experiential learning, defines it as a "type of education, the primary focus [of which] is actively undertaken in a particular off-campus setting under the sponsorship, but not direct supervision, of a faculty member." (p. i) The definition encompasses cross-cultural experiences, pre-professional training, career exploration, cooperative education, internship, and field research.

Advantages and Disadvantages

In an important essay, the sociologist James Coleman (1976) distinguishes between *information assimilation*, the usual mode of classroom instruction, and *experiential learning*. Each method has its own advantages and disadvantages. Information assimilation is very time-efficient because it uses symbols, usually verbal. It provides generalizations and structures that tie generalizations to examples, and it fosters intellectual analysis. But its efficiency and effectiveness are very much dependent on the student's ability to understand and associate the symbols used. Perhaps the weakest factor in symbolic information assimilation is its links with concrete experience and action. The typical test of information assimilation is the paper-and-pencil examination.

The characteristics of experiential learning are quite different. It is relatively time-consuming. It relates action and concrete events in direct ways and does not necessarily develop symbolic general knowledge—the stock and trade of academics. It appears that experiential learning is less easily forgotten than symbolic learning. The typical test of experiential learning is the ability to take appropriate action. The motivation for experiential learning is immediate and concrete, whereas that for information assimilation is successful test-taking.

Traditional educational practice has confined experiential learning to the young and the educationally disadvantaged. Coleman (1976) argues that experiential learning offers potential benefits for learning "any knowledge of skill, throughout the whole period of education." (p. 59)

Harrison and Hopkins (1969) make a similar distinction between classroom instruction and experiential learning. They place special emphasis on the power of experiential learning in mediating and extending academic information through interpersonal and social experiences.

Appropriate Uses

Content. Experiential education is uniquely appropriate for certain kinds of learning. It offers an opportunity for the *application* of knowledge in "real world settings" that is seldom, if ever, possible in classroom learning. The ability to link knowledge to action in the world is the announced intent of many college and university programs, notable in the helping professions (teaching, nursing, social work, etc.) but also in the applied disciplines (business, engineering, etc.). Informational and conceptual learning in these domains is both completed and extended by the experience of practical application. The immediate concern of many students and their parents, if not necessarily college faculty members, is with satisfactory employment after graduation. The prospect of significant career changes in the course of a working life emphasizes the value of experiential education as preparation for the world of work.

School is a certain kind of environment—individualistic, oriented toward cognitive achievement, imposing dependency, and withholding authority and responsibility from students. Insofar as education is envisioned as a preparation for life, however, it has a responsibility to train students in the skills of collaboration, interpersonal communication, decision-making, leadership, cultural understanding, and environmental awareness. For these purposes experiential education is especially suitable. When the content to be learned has a practical application, career, and/or interpersonal dimensions, experiential learning can be an effective teaching-learning strategy.

Students. Studies specifically designed to determine what type of student is likely to benefit most from field experience are yet to be done. Given the resemblance of field experience learning to independent study, the traditional indices of academic aptitude may not bear a significant relationship to successful learning in a field setting. The basic assumptions and objectives of field experience education obviously place the student in a different role than the one he normally plays in the classroom.

In field experience the student has a large part to play in initiating, identifying, and planning the experience. Once in the field he will have to function as a problem-solver and decision-maker in a non-school environment; this will typically require interpersonal and observational skills not normally demanded in the conventional classroom. The student will have to work and learn in a setting of unforeseen problems without predetermined correct answers and without the classroom support systems of assignments, syllabi, and tests.

A number of factors may be useful in determining whether a student is ready to benefit from a field experience. Does the proposed experience make sense in terms of the student's program and personal objectives? Does the student possess the prerequisite knowledge and specific skills that are judged necessary? Does the student demonstrate motivation and realistic expectations for the experience and can he develop well-defined objectives? A well-planned field experience program helps the student develop necessary prerequisites and objectives where they are lacking.

As Dudley and Gordon (1977) have aptly remarked, "Students are systematically educated for further schooling; they are rarely educated for learning through their own experience outside the classroom." (p. 6) Thus, a special effort must be made to prepare students for field experience. Typical academic courses designed to give the student necessary background information and skills can contribute. Beyond these, however, the student will often need training in observation, reporting, research, and interviewing skills. In order to develop goals and get the most out of the field experience, the student should be given an opportunity to explore systematically her strengths and weaknesses, accomplishments, life plans, and similar matters. Further, the student will need guidance in developing a learning plan for the field experience. Finally, it is essential that the student have a full and complete understanding of her program, the setting, the faculty member's expectations, reporting and evaluating procedures, time limits, and acceptable ways of changing her plans. Preparations for the field such as these are best done outside the standard course format. Simulations, role playing, and one-day "immersions," combined with extensive individual discussions between the student and the faculty member, are the most appropriate means for preparing the student.

Instructor. The instructor arranging a student's field experience is responsible for insuring that the experience provides a genuine opportunity for learning. The instructor abandons his traditional role of offering a general opportunity to learn (the course) in order to provide each student with a specific opportunity to learn. In addition, the instructor must plan, coordinate, and develop placements.

As is more fully outlined below, the instructor should aid the student in defining goals and objectives, monitor the field experience while it is taking place, and develop appropriate forms of evaluation. Related to the design of objectives, plans of study, and evaluation instruments is the instructor's special responsibility for securing institutional recognition, i.e., credit, for the field experience.

In addition, the instructor has a responsibility for selecting and preparing students for the field placement. This entails making initial contacts and maintaining appropriate placement possibilities. The relationship between the instructor and the supervisor or manager in the field is especially critical.

It is clear that the faculty member's role in experiential learning is substantially different from that which he assumes in either the conventional classroom or in various forms of individualized instruction such as PSI or the Audio-Tutorial system. In experiential learning, the teacher's role is that of a careful and active advisor rather than an instructor.

Environment. Experiential learning takes place in two environments: the academic environment where the experience is planned and approved and to which the student returns, and the field placement itself.

Placements can be as varied as the intended learning and the needs of the individual student require. Nonetheless, there are several general questions that bear on the suitability of virtually any placement. Will the placement actually afford the student opportunities to fulfill his objectives and plan of study? Does the placement afford the appropriate degree of structure and/or supervision to cover the intended learning in the student's style? Is there a reasonable match between the field placement's time frame, the student's needs, and the academic calendar? Precisely what is expected of the supervisor and other support personnel in the field setting? What do they expect from the student and from her instructor and institution? Legitimate conflicting expectations can arise between the supervisor's desire for routine production and service and the student's hoped-for learning experience.

The attitude toward experiential learning at the student's and instructor's institution is also a significant environmental factor. Obviously, at those institutions with explicit provisions for experiential learning, both student and teacher are more likely to find approval and support for a field project. By and large, the crucial factor governing the degree of acceptability of field experience is the faculty's attitude. The more they are oriented toward contemporary problems and issues, the more readily they will recognize and encourage the relationship of practical experience to theoretical study. The most important task for the instructor seeking acceptance and academic credit for field study is to emphasize the conditions that will make the field work more than the experience alone. The more clearly the intended learning outcomes are stated along with evaluation criteria, the better the prospects for acceptance.

How to Do It

For the instructor interested in supporting and supervising students in experiential learning, the publications of Cooperative Assessment of Experiential Learning (CAEL) are invaluable. The points made here briefly summarize the pertinent CAEL materials. One is well advised to read them before beginning. *College-Spon-*

sored Experiential Learning (Duley and Gordon, 1977) is particularly useful.

In good teaching, a primary condition of success is clarity. From the start, the instructor should determine with the student what goals and purposes he intends for the proposed field experience. Among goals particularly appropriate to experiential learning are:

- Specific Job Competency
- Career Exploration
- Broadening Horizons
- Interpersonal Skills
- Learning from the Local Environment
- Taking Responsibility
- Research Skills

In the case of broadening horizons, for example, appropriate objectives might include such things as understanding how city government is practiced, or gaining familiarity with social welfare programs, with the processes of marketing, or with the culture of Italian families.

Guidelines for framing objectives for experiential learning are much the same as for classroom learning. As a result of experiential learning: What is the student to accomplish and at what level of proficiency? How will the instructor be able to recognize these outcomes when they occur? In the process of developing answers to these key questions, institutional goals and standards of acceptability should be considered along with instructor preferences and student needs.

The placement of the student in an appropriate setting is a *sine qua non* for experiential learning. Possibilities need to be investigated, connections made, expectations clarified, responsibilities and time periods determined, and so forth. Otherwise well-conceived plans of experiential learning go awry for lack of clarity. Matching student and faculty expectations for a placement with the expectations of the supervisor in the placement setting is of particular importance.

While the student is doing her placement, it can be important for the instructor to stay in touch. This monitoring responsibility might include telephone calls or letters, field reports, seminars, and site visits, as well as contact with the student's supervisors. Assessment and evaluation of the student's learning need not wait until the experience is completed but can be done periodically while the student is at his placement. A placement, despite the instructor's best efforts, is not always everything the student had hoped for; the best made objectives and plans are frequently altered by experience. Maintaining regular contact with the student in the field may allow the instructor to make positive adjustments. For additional guidance the reader should see the section on "Learning Contracts" below.

Another very useful CAEL publication is *A Compendium of Assessment Techniques* (Knapp and Sharon, 1975). It begins:

> Because experiential learning ... often differs from traditional classroom learning, its assessment and evaluation require the consideration of measurement techniques that have not been widely employed in higher education. (p. 5)

There are a number of assessment techniques the instructor (or an assessment team) may want to consider, depending on the objectives of the experiential learning to be evaluated. An actual sampling of the student's work or on-the-job observations are useful where experiential learning is intended to result in a skill. If the student performance is likely to be affected by an evaluator's presence, some form of unobtrusive observation is advisable. This is an especially important consideration where affective learning is involved. Simulations, role playing, and case studies are also appropriate techniques for assessing experiential learning. They are an economical, if somewhat synthetic, way to observe the student perform the skills he has learned. For more general learning, various well-structured interview techniques by the instructor or a panel can be employed. And, of course, for certain outcomes, written objective and/or essay tests have a place in an evaluation. In the process of assessment, a student's self-evaluation of the experience should have a primary role.

Learning Contracts

In the typical college or university course, there is an implicit contract between the teacher and student. In registering for the course the student usually assumes obligations for attendance, assignments, quizzes, and tests. In offering the course, the instructor is presumed to promise information, instruction, evaluation, and grading. Recently, for certain purposes, these obligations have been made more explicit in the form of a learning contract.

Arthur Chickering (1977), the former Vice President of New York's individualized Empire State University, contends that a good learning contract must clearly state both the long-range and short-range goals of the student, take into account the student's prior preparation, describe the student's learning activities, and specify the methods and criteria used for evaluation. Figure 23.1 shows an example of such a contract.

In negotiating the objectives, activities, resources, products, and results, the teacher and student are engaged in fashioning an individualized program of instruction. In specifying the criteria and the manner by which learning will be judged (tests, papers, logs, portfolios, etc.), the contract serves as an evaluation tool. Usually, the grade awarded on completion of the contract reflects not how well the student did in competition with other students (norm-referenced) but how well the student has executed the learning to which he has explicitly made a commitment (criterion-referenced).

The use of learning contracts can be justified on several counts. It makes provisions for individual characteristics of the learner; needs, preparation, and motivation have been shown to affect learning significantly. This consideration gains special force with the increasing heterogeneity of the student community. As knowledge grows exponentially, the primary responsibility of education is considered by some to be the development of the skills and techniques required for lifelong learning. In addition, the perceived impersonal and prescriptive quality of mass higher education is considered increasingly inadequate by both individual students and society. Contract learning offers one viable alternative for responding to these issues and concerns.

A learning contract can be readily adaptable to a wide variety of teaching/learning situations. It can be used for a segment of a course, and contract arrangements have been devised for the entirety of an otherwise conventional course. In courses with large enrollments, a menu of instructor-determined options can be dis-

Figure 23.1. Sample Learning Contract.

Title of Learning Experience: Family Aid Bureau.

Date: September to December, 1978

Goals: Mr. Smith has only recently begun work on his master's in Social Work, and has not had previous experience in a social service agency. His intent upon graduation is to work in a family service agency, and he would like to gain skills that would enable him to do this. He would also like to acquire experiences needed to refine his intentions for future employment.

Specific Objectives: Specifically, Mr. Smith would like demonstrated the techniques of interviewing and screening clients to determine the nature of the problem and whether or not a client is eligible for family aid services. He would also like to be able to describe the procedures and functions of the Family Aid Bureau.

Learning Activities: Mr. Smith will read the regulations governing family aid in Cleveland, read the textbook (*Family Services* by Milton Gavin), and attend family court hearings. He will also sit in on counseling sessions conducted by family service personnel.

Evaluation and Criteria: Within three months, Mr. Smith will make a presentation (oral or written) to the instructor which will take the form of a critical analysis of the procedures and functions of the Family Aid Bureau. An acceptable presentation would demonstrate a knowledge of the family aid regulations of Cleveland and how they are implemented at the Family Aid Bureau, as well as include suggestions as to how client services might be improved. Mr. Smith will also conduct several counseling sessions with clients, to be observed by the Family Aid Supervisor. The sessions will be judged to be acceptable by the Supervisor if they follow regulations and Bureau procedures, and if Mr. Smith's advice seems to be in the best interest of the client.

Student . . . .

Instructor . . . .

---

tributed from which students can select those they wish to pursue in order to achieve a desired grade. Such a menu might offer minimum test scores, papers, presentations, projects, and other activities from which the students can choose those content options and learning modes which most suit their purposes, interests, and abilities (Figure 23.2). At the other extreme, institutions like New York's Empire State College and Minnesota Metropolitan State College employ contractual arrangements in developing a student's complete degree program.

Contract learning is particularly applicable to independent study and experiential learning. The potential that learning contracts afford for organizing formal study, experience, research, and creative production makes them particularly suitable for independent study and experiential learning. Among other advantages for learning of this kind, the contract reduces the ambiguity and anxiety that can arise in non-classroom learning. By specifying the objectives, means, evaluation, and time frame for a given experience, student and instructor alike can have a sense of shape, progress, and completion.

Research on the effectiveness of learning contracts is as yet quite limited. Most reports on contract learning are case studies of its successful use (see Berte, 1975). A study done at Boston State College (1975) has shown that the contract instructional methods used there facilitated reading, writing, and research skills of students. Poppen and Thompson (1971), in a controlled study using four sections of a standard course, Educational Psychology, attempted to determine whether learning contracts, as contrasted to regular course procedures, resulted in a difference in learning. The criteria included performance on mid-term and final examinations; the quality of case study reports, reaction papers, independent study projects; and student responses to the contract and conventional formats. While differences in scores ran in favor of the contract learning sections, such differences were not statistically significant. Nonetheless, Poppen and Thompson observed that learning contracts improve performance of students who have faired poorly in conventional courses. Students who opted for contracted projects over standard examinations became more involved in "relevant" learning. While research studies have yet to

Figure 23.2.
Learning Contract Form for Use in a Conventional Course.

General Objectives
   The purpose of this learning contract is to enable me to investigate . . . . .
. . ., to provide me with an understanding of . . . . . so that I can . . . . . .
Specific Objectives
At the completion of this contract I will be able to:
   1. Attach a meaning to . . . .
   2. Answer factual questions pertaining to . . . .
   3. Trace the . . . .
   4. Identify the type of . . . .
   5. Etc. . . . .
Evaluation Procedure
   To earn a grade, I must complete all of the items in the category for that
grade. If I choose a grade and fail to complete the criteria, it will result in a
lower grade.
   1. Answer prepared questions about . . . .
   2. Record observations.
   3. Satisfactorily complete items listed on the "menu" of activities
      a) . . . . b) . . . . c) . . . .
   4. Synthesize data and draw conclusions . . . .
   5. Write a . . . .
   6. Etc. . . . .

For a grade of . . . . .

Approximate Time to Complete
The duration of this contract will be . . . . weeks, which means the final
date for completion is . . . .

Contract Terms
I, ..., am contracting for the grade of . . . . . I understand
that the contracting is a privilege and that if I do not fulfill the terms of the
grade for which I have contracted, my contract will be re-evaluated.

Date . . . . Instructor's Signature . . . .

                       Student's Signature . . . .

---

confirm the effectiveness of contract learning, anecdotal reports from both students and faculty tend to be positive. The instructor's role as a facilitator or mentor in independent and experiential learning has been discussed above. Specifically, with respect to negotiating a contract, the instructor must be keenly aware of her role as a clarifier and resource person. Being overly directive will seriously blunt the independence, intrinsic motivation, and responsibility such instructional formats are intended to enhance. This is not to say the instructor should withhold his own ideas and suggestions from the student during the negotiations or in the course of their work together. The instructor should frequently summarize the discussion of "terms" during the contract negotiation to make sure a clear understanding is being developed. From time to time, while the contract is being carried out, the instructor should assist the student in summarizing and reviewing his progress.

Finally, sometimes special care is required to insure the quality of the contract and the learning that results. It has been suggested by Ericksen (1976) that the instructor who chooses to have his contracts and the student work accomplished under them reviewed by colleagues will benefit from their expert and professional opinions.

Developing a good learning contract is not an easy task. Making and maintaining a contract can require more and certainly different kinds of time, energy, and thoughtfulness from teacher and student than the standard procedures of conventionally-taught courses. Like many alternative forms of instruction and evaluation, the role of the student is changed from recipient to participant and that of the instructor from authority to mentor and facilitator.

From the foregoing it is evident that contracts can facilitate learning in a variety of important ways. They offer a flexible vehicle for arranging and evaluating a host of learning experiences. By their very nature they are individualized and responsive. Learning contracts offer both instructor and student a formal method for jointly defining the nature, purpose, and resources bearing on their educational enterprise. The act of negotiating a contract necessarily raises questions about the student's educational objectives, appropriate activities and resources for learning, and ways of evaluating learning. This process stimulates serious thought and discussion about the purposes and means of education.

Elements in a Contract
The conversations that precede contracting and the contract itself typically include the following elements:
- *General Purposes*
    How does the proposed project fit into the larger pattern of the student's learning? What long-term as well as immediate interactions between the general learning pattern and this particular experience are expected and hoped for?
- *Specific Purposes*
    1. Realistically, what specific outcomes are expected— skills, information, products?
    2. Realistically, what elements in the student's and in the instructor's backgrounds and experience will facilitate these outcomes?
    3. Realistically, within the circumstances that the student and instructor will operate (time and location), what are the opportunities for accomplishing the specific outcomes or objectives?
    4. Who (in addition to the instructor making the contract) are other knowledgeable people with whom the student might consult?
- *Learning Plan and Activities*
    1. Specifically, what is the plan for accomplishing the stated objectives and outcomes?
    2. What learning modes will be used: reading, classes, workshops, experiments, visits, etc.? Are these activities clearly related to the desired outcomes?
    3. What is the schedule for progress and completion?
    4. Is the contract sufficiently specific and sufficiently flexible?
    5. Are the activities and outcomes reasonable, given the student's background and time, the instructor's back-

ground and time, and the available opportunities and resources?

Resources

Books and Articles

Berte, N. R. (Ed.). *Individualizing education through contract learning.* University, Alabama: University of Alabama Press, 1975. Provides procedures for student goal development, assessment of educational resources, and evaluation of contract learning programs. The bulk of the book presents case studies of several institutions which have implemented a wide variety of contracting plans. Most of the content of this book is also published in *New Directions for Higher Education,* San Francisco: Jossey-Bass, Inc., 1975.

Dressel, P.L., and Thompson, M.M. *Independent study.* San Francisco: Jossey-Bass Publishers, 1973. Presents an overview of the status of independent study in higher education, based on a survey conducted by the authors in the early 1970's. Common problems encountered by independent study programs are discussed. Guidelines for building and evaluating an effective program are presented.

New Directions in Higher Education. San Francisco: Jossey Bass, Inc., No. 6, 1974. This issue of *New Directions*, entitled "Implementing Field Experience Education," presents several case studies of programs using experiential learning. Various methods for implementing experiential learning in several disciplines are discussed.

Organizations

The Center for Individualized Education, Empire State College, Saratoga Springs, N.Y. 12866. The Center holds conferences and workshops which promote various approaches to independent and individualized instruction.

Council for Advancement of Experiential Learning, American City Building, Suite 403, Columbia, Maryland 21044. CAEL publishes a number of faculty handbooks, student guides, and project reports dealing with experiential learning. Two publications of particular interest to faculty are *A Compendium of Assessment Techniques* by Knapp and Sharon, and *College-Sponsored Experiential Learning* by Duley and Gordon. Both publications provide "how-to" information. A complete listing of available publications is available from CAEL: Educational Testing Service, Princeton, New Jersey 08540.

The Society for Field Experience Education, Justin Morrill College, Michigan State University, E. Lansing, Michigan 48824. The society publishes a newsletter, available to interested faculty at all universities. For more information, contact Dr. Harold Johnson at Justin Morrill College: (517) 353-5082.

Centennial Education Program

The Centennial Education Program at the University of Nebraska is a program that emphasizes the needs and interests of students. Students may enroll in the program for as many as six credit hours per semester. Courses from all disciplines are taught—ranging from art to biology to history. Although many methods of teaching are used by faculty, two commonly chosen techniques are experiential learning and independent study. Gene Harding, Senior Fellow in the program, explains that "the typical course consists of a small group of students studying a specialized subject matter. Within the subject area the students pursue independent projects. Sometimes students come to the program with a project already in mind. A special effort is made to find a method that will fit the student's own goals."

The students have a strong voice in determining the direction a course will take. Students and teachers enter into informal contract agreements. The general goals of the course are usually defined by the teacher. Based on the goals, individual students design projects which they feel will meet the course requirements and their own interests. "For example, we usually have one or two dozen students working in social agencies. This experiential learning is combined with readings and written work to fill the course requirements. The student and faculty member decide together whether or not the requirements have been fulfilled."

Students also engage in independent research projects. "During my course on Nebraska history last year, students engaged in a variety of projects. One student researched the role of Sioux Indian women in the 1800's. Another student researched a defunct Nebraska railroad after discovering the remains of a railroad yard on his grandfather's farm."

Teachers are assigned to the Centennial Education

Program on a two-year basis. They are chosen from the regular University faculty by students and staff. "We try to find faculty who are excited about teaching and who are really interested in the student part of the teaching equation." Teaching in this setting often requires an adjustment for faculty. "Even the most dedicated faculty members may find it difficult at first to adjust to this teaching setting. Once the adjustment is made, however, it changes the way you look at students. The role of the teacher in this situation is to guide the student through the learning experience. I find this kind of interaction with students to be refreshing and exciting. Our chief goal is to help people take charge of their own learning. Methods like experiential learning and independent study help to make this goal a reality."

Prof. Gene Harding
Centennial Education Program
University of Nebraska
Lincoln, Nebraska
(402) 472-7211

BIBLIOGRAPHY

Adderley, K. W., and Ashwin, C. *The use of project methods in higher education*. London: Society for Research into Higher Education, 1976.

Adelson, J. The teacher as a model. In N. Sanford (Ed.), *The American college*. New York: John Wiley and Sons, Inc., 1962.

Allen, D., and Ryan, K. *Microteaching*. Reading, Massachusetts: Addison-Wesley, 1969.

Allen, W. G. *Computer-aided instruction for business administration programs in the community college*. Dissertation, University of Florida, 1974.

Allen, W. H. Intellectual ability and media design. *AV Communication Review*, 1975, *23*(2), 139-170.

American Council on Education. The American freshman: National norms for fall 1971. *ACE Research Reports #6*. Washington, D.C.: ACE, 1971.

Andrews, C. S. *An investigation of the use of computer-assisted instruction in French as an adjunct to classroom instruction*. Dissertation, Florida State University, 1973.

Association for Educational Communications and Technology. *Copyright and educational media: A guide to fair use and permissive procedures*. Washington, D.C.: AECT, 1977.

Astin, A. W. *Who goes where to college*. Chicago: Science Research Associates, 1965.

Ausubel, D. P. *Educational psychology: A cognitive view*. New York: Holt, Rinehart, and Winston, 1968.

Axelrod, J. *The university teacher as artist*. San Francisco: Jossey-Bass, 1973.

375

Bailey, D. E. (Ed.). *Computer Science in Social and Behavioral Science Education.* Englewood Cliffs, New Jersey: Educational Technology Publications, 1978.

Banathy, B. H. *Instructional systems.* Belmont, California: Fearon, 1968.

Bartz, W. H., and Darby, C. L. The effects of a programmed textbook on achievement under three techniques of instruction. *Journal of Experimental Education,* 1966, *34,* 65-66.

Baskin, S. Experiment in independent study. *Journal of Experimental Education,* 1962, *10,* 209-210.

Bass, R. A. *A comparison of two teaching strategies for orthographic projection in engineering graphics: Computer-prescribed self-paced instruction versus the traditional approach.* Dissertation, East Texas State University, 1971.

Bayer, A. E. *Teaching faculty in academe: 1972-73.* Washington, D.C.: American Council on Education Research, 1973, *8*(2).

Bazen, E., and Bowles, W. *Evaluation of a simulation game designed to sensitize players to problems of the elderly.* Paper presented at the North American Gaming and Simulation Association Meeting, Los Angeles, 1975.

Beach, L. R. Sociability and academic achievement in various types of learning situations. *Journal of Educational Psychology,* 1960, *51,* 208-212.

Beard, R. M., and Bligh, D. A *Research into teaching methods in higher education* (3rd ed.). Research into Higher Education Monographs. London: Society for Research into Higher Education, 1972.

Benjamin, R. (Ed.). *Geography via the audio-tutorial method.* Chicago: National Council on Geographic Education, 1969.

Bergquist, W.H., and Phillips, S.R. *A handbook for faculty development.* (Council for the Advancement of Small Colleges, Wash. D.C.). Dansville, New York: Dansville Press, Inc., 1975.

Berliner, D. C., and Cahen, L. S. Trait-treatment interaction and learning. In F. N. Kerlinger (Ed.), *Review of Research in Education* (Vol. 1). itasca, Illinois: F. E. Peacock, 1973.

Berliner, D. C., and Gage, N. L. The psychology of teaching methods. In N. L. Gage (Ed.), *The psychology of teaching methods.* Chicago: University of Chicago Press, 1976.

Berlo, D. K. *The process of communication.* New York: Holt, Rinehart, and Winston, 1960.

Bertcher, H., and Gordon, J. *Techniques of group leadership.* Ann Arbor, Michigan: Manpower Science Services, 1972.

Bertcher, H., Gordon, J., Hayes, M., and Mial, H. *Role modeling, role playing: A manual of vocational development and employment agencies.* Ann Arbor, Michigan: Manpower Science Services, 1970.

Berte, N. R. (Ed.). *Individualizing education through contract learning.* Tuskaloosa, Alabama: University of Alabama Press, 1975.

Bigelow, G., and Egbert, R. Personality factors and independent study. *Journal of Educational Research,* 1968, *62,* 37-39.

Blackburn, R. T. *The professor's role in a changing society.* Washington, D.C.: ERIC Clearinghouse on Higher Education, 1971.

Blackburn, R. T. The meaning of work in academia. *New Directions for Institutional Research,* 1974, *2,* 75-99.

Bligh, D. A. *What's the use of lectures?* (2nd ed.). Harmondsworth, Middlesex: Penguin Books, 1972.

Blitz, A. N. *An investigation of the ways in which personality characteristics affect performance on computer-assisted instruction and programmed text.* Dissertation, University of Kentucky, 1972.

Block, J. H. Introduction to mastery learning: Theory and practice. In J. H. Block (Ed.), *Mastery learning: Theory and practice.* New York: Holt, Rinehart, and Winston, 1971.

Bloom, B. S. (Ed.). *Taxonomy of educational objectives.* New York: David McKay, 1956.

Bloom, B.S. Mastery learning. In J.H. Block (Ed.), *Mastery learning: Theory and practice.* New York: Holt, Rinehart, and Winston, 1971.

Bloom, B.S., Hastings, J.T., and Madaus, G.F. *Handbook on formative and summative evaluation of student learning.* New York: McGraw-Hill, 1971.

Blyth, J.W. *The Hamilton College experiment in programmed learning.* Clinton, New York: Hamilton College, 1962.

Boags, W. *A comparison of affective reaction and cognitive learn-*

ing of participants in a simulation-game experience. Dissertation, Syracuse University, 1970.

Bonds, M. *A quasi-experimental study using games and simulations
at the college level.* Paper presented at the National Gaming
Council 13th Annual Symposium, Pittsburgh, 1974.

Boocock, S. An experimental study of the learning effects of two
games with simulated environments. In S. Boocock and E.
Schild (Eds.), *Simulation games in learning.* Beverly Hills, California: Sage Publications, 1968.

Boston State College. *Learning contract (1975) unified students
report No. 1:7,* Boston, 1975.

Bowra, M. The idea of a liberal arts college. *Liberal Education,*
1964, *50*(2), 185-197.

Bragg, L. The art of talking about science. *Science,* 1966, *154,*
1614.

Braskamp, L.A., and Hodgetts, R.M. The role of an objective
evaluation model in simulation gaming. *Simulation and Games,*
1971, *2,* 197-212.

Brethower, D.M., Markle, D.G., Rummler, G.A., Schrader, A.W.,
and Smith, D.E. *Programmed learning: A practicum.*
Ann Arbor, Michigan: Ann Arbor Publishers, 1965.

Bretz, R. *Handbook for producing educational and public-access
programs for cable television.* Englewood Cliffs, New Jersey:
Educational Technology Publications, 1976.

Briggs, L.J. *Sequencing of instruction in relation to hierarchies of
competence.* Pittsburgh: American Institutes for Research,
1968.

Briggs, L.J. *et al. Instructional design: Principles and applications.* Englewood Cliffs, New Jersey: Educational Technology
Publications, 1977.

Brightman, R. Comparing instructional costs. *New Directions in
Community Colleges,* 1973, *2,* 39-55.

Bruner, J. *The process of education.* New York: Vintage Books,
Random House, 1960.

Bullock, D. H. *Programmed Instruction.* Volume 14, The Instructional Design Library. Englewood Cliffs, New Jersey:
Educational Technology Publications, 1978.

Bunderson, C.V., and Faust, G.W. Programmed and computer-assisted instruction. In N. L. Gage (Ed.), *The psychology of teaching methods.* Chicago: University of Chicago Press, 1976.

Burford, T. *A study of student reactions towards audio instructional systems that provide or deny means of individual control of the presentation.* Dissertation, Syracuse University, 1971.

Byers, G. R. *An experimental comparison of three modes of computer-supported instruction.* Dissertation, University of Minnesota, 1973.

Carmody, J. F., Fenske, R. H., and Scott, D. *Changes in goals, plans, and background characteristics of college-bound high school students.* ACT Research Report No. 52. Iowa City: American College Testing Program, 1974.

Carnegie Commission on Higher Education. *Reform on campus: Changing students, changing academic programs.* New York: McGraw-Hill, 1972.

Carnegie Commission on Higher Education. *Priorities for Action.* The final report of the Commission. New York: McGraw-Hill, 1973.

Carroll, J.B. The potentials and limitations of print as a medium of instruction. In D.E. Olson (Ed.), *Media and symbols.* National Society for the Study of Education. Chicago: University of Chicago Press, 1974.

Carroll, J. B., and Leonard, G. *The effectiveness of programmed "Grafdrills" in teaching the Arabic writing system.* Unpublished report, Graduate School of Education, Harvard University, 1963.

Centra, J. A. *Faculty development practices in U.S. colleges and universities.* Princeton: Educational Testing Service, 1976.

Centra, J.A., and Rock, D. College environments and student academic achievement. *American Educational Research Journal,* 1971, *8*(4), 623-634.

Chapman, T.H. *Simulation game effects on attitudes regarding racism and sexism.* Dissertation, University of Maryland, 1974.

Chartier, M.R. An experimental study of a simulation game and instrumented discussion. *Simulation and Games,* 1972, *3,* 203-218.

Chesler, M., and Fox, R. *Role-playing methods in the classroom.* Chicago: Science Research Associates, 1966.

Chickering, A. W. Dimension of independence. *Journal of Higher Education*, 1964, *34*, 38-41.

Chickering, A. W. *Education and identity*. San Francisco: Jossey-Bass, 1969.

Chickering, A.W. Developing intellectual competence at Empire State. *New Directions in Higher Education*, 1975, *10*, 31-40.

Chickering, A.W. Developmental change as a major outcome. In M. T. Keeton and Associates (Eds.), *Experiential learning: Rationale, characteristics, and assessment*. San Francisco: Jossey-Bass, 1976.

Chickering, A. W. Evaluation in the context of contract learning. *Journal of Personalized Instruction*, 1977, *2*(2), 96-100.

Chickering, A.W., and Blackburn, R. *The undergraduate*. Unpublished manuscript, undated.

Christensen, D.A. (Ed.). *Proceedings of 1977 conference on computers in the undergraduate curricula*. East Lansing: Michigan State University, 1977.

Chu, G., and Schramm, W. *Learning from television: What the research says* (Rev. ed.). Washington, D.C.: National Association of Educational Broadcasters, 1974.

Churchill, R., and Baskin, S. *Experiment on independent study*. Yellow Springs, Ohio: Antioch College, 1958.

Clark, B. R., and Trow, M. The organizational context. In T. M. Newcomb and E. K. Wilson (Eds.), *College peer groups: Problems and prospects for research*. Chicago: Aldine Publishing Company, 1966.

Coleman, J. S. Differences between experiential and classroom learning. In M.T. Keeton and Associates (Eds.), *Experiential learning: Rationale, characteristics, and assessment*. San Francisco: Jossey-Bass, 1976.

Collagan, R. B. *The construction and evaluation of a programmed course in mathematics necessary for success in collegiate physical science*. Doctoral dissertation, Catholic University of America, 1968.

Cooley, W. W., and Lohnes, P. R. *Evaluation research in education: Theory, principles, and practice*. New York: Irvington Publishers, Inc., 1976.

Costin, F. Lecturing versus other methods of teaching: A review of research. *British Journal of Educational Technology*, 1972, *1*, 4-30.

Creager, J.G., and Murray, D.L. (Eds.). *The use of modules in college biology teaching.* Washington, D.C.: The Commission on Undergraduate Education in the Biological Sciences, 1971.

Cronbach, L., and Snow, R. *Aptitudes and instructional methods.* New York: Irvington Publishers, 1977.

Cross, K. P. Not can, but will college teaching be improved? *New Directions in Higher Education*, 1977, *17*, 1-16.

Cross, P. *Beyond the open door.* San Francisco: Jossey-Bass, Inc., 1971.

Crowley, R.J., and Rudy, D.J. *Student aptitude and the instructional function of videotape.* Unpublished report. Colgate University, 1969.

Culp, G.H. *An approach to the use of computer-assisted instruction in organic chemistry.* Dissertation, The University of Texas at Austin, 1969.

Dederick, M.E., and Macklin, D.B. *A trait-treatment interaction in a college physics course.* Unpublished manuscript, Cornell University, 1973.

DeVries, D., and Edwards, K. Learning games and student teams: Their effects on classroom process. *American Educational Research Journal,* 1973, *10,* 307-318.

Diamond, R.M. (Ed.). *A guide to instructional television.* New York: McGraw-Hill, 1964.

Diamond, R.M. *et al. Instructional development for individualized learning in higher education.* Englewood Cliffs, New Jersey: Educational Technology Publications, 1975.

Dienes, Z. B. *The time factor in computer-assisted instruction.* Dissertation, University of Toronto (Canada), 1972.

Domino, G. Interactive effects of achievement orientation and teaching styles on academic achievement. *Journal of Educational Psychology*, 1971, *62*, 427-431.

Domino, G. Aptitude by treatment interaction effects in college instruction. Paper presented to the annual meeting of the American Psychological Association, 1974.

Doty, B. A., and Doty, I. A. Programmed instructional effectiveness in relation to certain student characteristics. *Journal of Educational Psychology*, 1964, *55*, 334-338.

Dowaliby, F., and Schumer, H. Teacher-centered versus student-centered mode of college classroom: Instruction as related to manifest anxiety. *Journal of Educational Psychology*, 1973, *64*, 125-132.

Dressel, P. I., and Thompson, M. M. *Independent study*. San Francisco: Jossey-Bass, 1973.

Drew, C. J. Research on the psychological-behavioral effects of the physical environment. *Review of Educational Research*, 1971, *41*, 447-465.

Duberman, M. *Black mountain.* New York: Dutton, 1972.

Dubin, R., and Hedley, R.A. *The medium may be related to the message.* Eugene: Center for the Advanced Study of Educational Administration, 1969.

Dubin, R., and Taveggia, T. *The teaching-learning paradox.* Eugene: Center for the Advanced Study of Educational Administration, University of Oregon, 1968.

Dudley, J. Implementing field experience education. *New Directions,* 1974, *6,* 1-5.

Dudley, J., and Gordon, S. *College-sponsored experiential learning— ACAEI handbook.* Princeton: CAEI, 1977.

Dunn, T.G. *The effects of various review paradigms on performance in an individualized computer managed undergraduate course.* Dissertation, Florida State University, 1971.

Dyer, C. H. *Preparing for computer-assisted instruction.* Englewood Cliffs, New Jersey: Educational Technology Publications, 1972.

Eble, K. E. *Professors as teachers.* San Francisco: Jossey-Bass Publishers, 1972.

Eble, K. E. *The craft of teaching.* San Francisco: Jossey-Bass Publishers, 1976.

Eckert, R., and Williams, H. *College faculty view themselves and their jobs.* Unpublished manuscript, College of Education, The University of Michigan, Ann Arbor, 1972.

Edwards, K. *The effect of ability, achievement, and number of plays on learning from simulation games.* Baltimore: Center for Social Organization of Schools, The Johns Hopkins University, Report No. 128, 1971.

Elder, S.T., and Elder, E.S. Final field test results of traditional logic and the Venn Diagram: A programmed introduction. *Journal of Experimental Education*, 1973, *41*, 12-16.

Ericksen, S. C. *Motivation for learning: A guide for the teacher of the young adult.* Ann Arbor: University of Michigan Press, 1974.

Ericksen, S. C. Institutional support for teachers. *Criteria: For the Evaluation, Support, and Recognition of College Teachers.* Ann Arbor: University of Michigan, Center for Research on Learning and Teaching, 1976, 3.

Ericksen, S. C. Grading by contract. *Memo to the Faculty No. 57*, Center for Research on Learning and Teaching, University of Michigan, Ann Arbor, 1976.

Evans, R. I. *Resistance to innovation in higher education.* San Francisco: Jossey-Bass, 1967.

Fay, F. A. *Effects of a film, a discussion group, and a role-playing experience on architecture students' attitudes, behavioral intentions and actual behavior toward barrier-free design.* Dissertation, University of Illinois, 1973.

Feldbaum, E. G., Buckley, J. J., and Levitt, M. J. Students and simulation. *Simulation and Games*, 1976, *7*, 153-176.

Feldman, K. A., and Newcomb, T. M. *The impact of college on students, Vol. 1.* San Francisco: Jossey-Bass, 1969.

Fisher, K.M., and MacWhinney, B. AV autotutorial instruction: A review of evaluative research. *Audio-Visual Communication Review*, 1976, *24*, 229-261.

Fitzgerald, W. (Ed.). *Mathematics laboratories: Implementation, research, and evaluation.* Columbus, Ohio: Environmental Education, 1974.

Flesch, R. *The art of readable writing.* New York: Harper & Brothers, 1949.

Forsythe, R.D. *Instructional radios: A position paper.* Stanford: Stanford University, 1970.

Fowler, J.M., and Caplan, R. Toward a new lab style. *Commission on College Physics Newsletter*, 1968, *17*, 1-12.

Freedman, M., and Sanford, N. The faculty member yesterday

and tomorrow. *New directions in higher education*, 1973, *1*, 1-16.

Frey, P. W., Lenard, D. W., and Beatty, W. W. Student ratings of instruction: Validation research. *American Educational Research Journal*, 1975, *12*, 435-447.

Gaff, J. G. *Toward faculty renewal*. San Francisco: Jossey-Bass, Inc., 1975.

Gaff, J. G., and Wilson, R. C. Faculty values and improving teaching. In G. K. Smith (Ed.), *New teaching, new learning*. San Francisco: Jossey-Bass, Inc., 1971.

Gage, N. L., and Berliner, D. C. *Educational psychology*. Chicago: Rand McNally, 1975.

Gagne, R.M. Learning and communication. In R.V. Wiman and W.C. Meierhenery (Eds.), *Educational media: Theory into practice.* Columbus, Ohio: Charles E. Merrill Publishing Co., 1969.

Gagne, R. M. *The conditions of learning* (2nd ed.). New York: Holt, Rinehart, and Winston, 1970.

Gagne, R. M., and Briggs, L. J. *Principles of instructional design*. New York: Holt, Rinehart, and Winston, 1974.

Gall, M.D., and Gall, J.P. The discussion method. In N.L. Gage (Ed.), *The psychology of teaching methods*. National Society for the Study of Education. Chicago: University of Chicago Press, 1976.

Gallagher, P. D. *An investigation of instructional treatments and learner characteristics in a computer-managed instruction course*. Dissertation, Florida State University, 1970.

Gaston, G. W. *Dental students' attitudes towards computer assisted instruction*. Dissertation, Ohio State University, 1972.

Gerlach, V.S., and Ely, D.P. *Teaching and media: A systematic approach*. Englewood Cliffs, New Jersey: Prentice-Hall, 1971.

Gessner, P. K. Evaluation of instruction. *Science*, 1973, *180*, 566-670.

Gillen, B., Kendall, P., and Finch, A. Reading ease and human interest scores: A comparison of Flesch scores with subjective ratings. *Teaching of Psychology,* 1977, *4,* 39-41.

Goldberg, L. R. Student personality characteristics and optimal college learning conditions. *Instructional Science*, 1972, *1*, 153-210.

Goldstein, E. The perception of multiple images. *A V Communication Review*, 1975, *23*, 34-68.

Goodman, F. L. Gaming and simulation. In R. M. Travers (Ed.), *Second handbook of research on teaching*. Chicago: Rand McNally, 1973.

Gordon, G. N. Instructional television: Yesterday's magic? *Educational Technology*, 1976, *16*(5), 39-44.

Gould, R. L. The phases of adult life: A study in developmental psychology. *The American Journal of Psychiatry*, 1972, *29*, 521-553.

Grasha, A. Observations on relating teaching goals to student response styles and classroom methods. *American Psychologist*, 1972, *27*(2), 144-147.

Grasha, A. *Workshop handout on learning styles*. Cincinnati, Ohio: Faculty Resource Center, University of Cincinnati, 1975.

Green, E. J. The process of instructional programming. In P. C. Lange (Ed.), *Programmed instruction*. Chicago: University of Chicago Press, 1967.

Greenwood, G. E., Hazelton, A., Smith, A. B., and Ware, W. B. A study of the validity of four types of student ratings of college teaching assessed on a criterion of student achievement gains. *Research in Higher Education*, 1976, *5*, 171-178.

Gronlund, N. E. *Constructing achievement tests*. Englewood Cliffs, New Jersey: Prentice-Hall, 1968.

Hansen, J. E. *A study of the comparative effectiveness of three methods of using motion pictures in teaching*. Dissertation, University of Wisconsin, Madison, 1939.

Harris, M.M. *The effectiveness of programmed instruction for teaching expository writing to college freshmen and high school juniors*. Dissertation, University of Texas, Austin, 1972.

Harrison, R., and Hopkins, R. L. The design of cross-cultural training: An alternative to the University model. *Journal of Applied Behavioral Science*, 1969, *3*, 431-459.

Harrison, S.A., and Stolurow, L.M. *et al. Improving instructional productivity in higher education*. Englewood Cliffs, New Jersey: Educational Technology Publications, 1975.

Hart, W. K. *An analysis of the usefulness of simulation games in affecting attitudinal changes and skill type learning: Final report.* Washington, D.C.: United States Office of Education, Bureau of Research, 1970.

Hartley, J. Programmed instruction 1954-1974: A review. *Programmed Learning and Educational Technology*, 1974, *11*(6), 278-291.

Havelock, R. G. *Planning for innovation through dissemination and utilization of knowledge.* Ann Arbor, Michigan: Institute for Social Research, 1969.

Havelock, R.G. *The change agent's guide to innovation in education.* Englewood Cliffs, New Jersey: Educational Technology Publications, 1973.

Heath, D.H. *Growing up in college.* San Francisco: Jossey-Bass, 1968.

Hedl, J. J., O'Neil, H. F., and Hansen, D. N. Affective reaction toward computer-based intelligence testing. *Journal of Consulting and Clinical Psychology*, 1973, *40*, 217-222.

Heinkel, O. A. Evaluation of simulation as a training device. *Journal of Experimental Education*, 1970, *38*, 32-36.

Hendershot, C. H. *Programmed learning and individually paced instruction* (5th ed.). Bay City, Michigan: Carl Hendershot, 1973.

Hess, J. H. *Selected bibliography on educational innovation: With emphasis on the Keller plan.* Occasional paper #2, Psychology Department, Eastern Memmonite College, Harrisonburg, Virginia, 1972.

Hickey, A. E. (Ed.). *Computer-assisted instruction: A survey of the literature* (3rd ed.). Newburyport, Massachusetts: Entelek, Inc., 1968.

Highet, G. *The art of teaching.* New York: Knopf, 1950.

Highet, G. *The immortal profession.* New York: Weybright Pub., 1976.

Hildebrand, M. The character and skills of the effective professor. *Journal of Higher Education*, 1973, *44*(1), 41-50.

Hildebrand, M., Wilson, R., and Dienst, E. *Evaluating university teaching.* Berkeley: Center for Research and Development in Higher Education, University of California, 1971.

Hill, W. F. *Learning thru discussion.* Beverly Hills, California: Sage Publications, 1969.

Himmel, C. E. College learning with and without formal classroom instruction—a comparison. *Psychology in the Schools*, 1972, *9*, 272-277.

Hoban, C., and van Ormer, E. *Instructional film research 1918-1950*. New York: Arno Press and The New York Times, 1951.

Hodgkinson, H. L. Adult development: Implications for faculty and administrators. *Educational Record*, 1974, *55*, 263-274.

Hoffman, T. F. *An evaluation of selected personality changes arising from participation in independent study programs*. Dissertation, Boston University School of Education, 1973.

Hong, S.T. *An empirical study of the effectiveness of programmed instruction and computer-assisted instruction in elementary accounting*. Doctoral dissertation, New York University, 1972.

Horn, R. E. How students can make their own simulations/games. In R. E. Horn (Ed.), *The guide to simulations/games for education and training* (3rd ed.). Cranford, New Jersey: Didactic Systems, Inc., 1977.

Horn, R. E. (Ed.). *The guide to simulations/games for education and training* (3rd ed.). Cranford, New Jersey: Didactic Systems, Inc., 1977.

Hovland, C., Lumsdaine, A., and Sheffield, F. *Experiments on mass communication*. Princeton: Princeton University Press, 1949.

Hoyt, D. P. College grades and adult accomplishment. *Educational Record*, 1966, *47*, 70-75.

Hoyt, D. P. Interrelationships among instructional effectiveness, publication record, and monetary reward. *Research in Higher Education*, 1974, *2*(1), 81-88.

Hunter, B. *et al. Learning alternatives in U.S. education: Where student and computer meet.* Englewood Cliffs, New Jersey: Educational Technology Publications, 1975.

Ibrahim, A. T. *A computer-assisted instruction program for teaching the concepts of limits in freshman calculus (A comparative study)*. Dissertation, State University of New York at Buffalo, 1970.

Ide, T. R. The potentials and limitations of television as an educational medium. In D. R. Olson (Ed.), *Media and symbols: The forms of expression, communication, and education.* Chicago: University of Chicago Press, 1974.

Inbar, M. Individual and group effects on enjoyment and learning in a game simulating a community disaster. In S. Boocock and E. Schild (Eds.), *Simulation games in learning.* Beverly Hills, California: Sage Publications, 1968.

Ingersoll, V. Role playing, attitude change, and behavior. *Organizational Behavior and Human Performance*, 1973, *10*, 157-174.

Jacobs, P., Maier, M., and Stolurow, L. *A guide to evaluating self-instructional programs.* New York: Holt, Rinehart, and Winston, 1966.

Jamison, D., Suppes, P., and Wells, S. The effectiveness of alternative instructional media: A survey. *Review of Educational Research*, 1974, *44*(1), 1-67.

Jester, R., and Travers, R. The effect of various presentation patterns on the comprehension of speeded speech. *American Educational Research Journal*, 1967, *4*, 353-359.

Judd, W. A., McCombs, B. L., and O'Neil, H. F. *Further validation of a state epistemic curiosity measure in computer-managed instruction.* Proceedings of the 81st Annual Convention of the American Psychological Association, Montreal, Canada, 1973, *8*, 621-622.

Katz, J. and Associates. *No time for youth.* San Francisco: Jossey-Bass, 1968.

Keller, F. S. Good-bye teacher ... . *Journal of Applied Behavior Analysis*, 1968, *1*, 79-89.

Keller, F. S. An international venture in behavior modification. In F. S. Keller and E. Ribes-Inesta (Eds.), *Behavior modification: Applications to education.* New York: Academic Press, 1974.

Keller, F. S. and Sherman, J. G. *The Keller plan handbook.* Menlo Park, California: Benjamin, 1974.

Kemp, J. E. *Planning and producing audiovisual materials* (3rd ed.). New York: Crowell, 1975.

Kempa, R. R., and Palmer, C. R. The effectiveness of video-tape recorded demonstrations. *British Journal of Educational Technology*, 1974, *11*, 62-71.

Kidder, S. J., and Guthrie, J. T. Training effects of a behavior modification game. *Simulation and Games*, 1972, *3*, 17-28.

King, A., and Brownell, J. *The curriculum and the disciplines of knowledge*. New York: John Wiley, 1966.

Knapp, J., and Sharon, A. *A compendium of assessment techniques*. CAEL, Princeton, 1975.

Knight, H. The Autotutor and classroom instruction. *Programmed Instruction*, 1964, *1*, 89-96.

Knight, H., and Sassenrath, J. M. Relation of achievement motivation and test anxiety to performance in programmed instruction. *Journal of Educational Psychology*, 1966, *57*, 14-17.

Knopp, L. *Individualization in high school physics through the audio-tutorial mode*. Paper presented at the Audio-Tutorial System Conference, Purdue University, October, 1969.

Koen, B.V. *Determining unit structure in a PSI course*. Paper presented at the American Society of Engineering Education annual meeting, Lubbock, Texas, 1972.

Koenig, K., and McKeachie, W. Personality and independent study. *Journal of Educational Psychology*, 1959, *5*, 132-134.

Kohlberg, L. The concepts of developmental psychology as the central guide to education: Examples from cognitive, moral, and psychological education. In M. C. Reynolds (Ed.), *Proceedings of the conference on psychology and the process of schooling in the next decade: Alternative conceptions*. Washington, D.C.: Bureau for Educational Personnel Development, U.S. Office of Education, 1973.

Koon, J. *Types, traits, and transitions: The lives of four-year college students*. Berkeley: Center for Research and Development in Higher Education, University of California, 1971.

Kozma, R., Kulik, J., and Smith, B. *A guide for PSI proctors*. Washington, D.C.: Center for Personalized Instruction, 1977.

Krathwohl, D., Bloom, B., and Masia, B. *Taxonomy of educational objectives*. New York: David McKay Co., 1964.

Kulik, J.A. Student reactions to instruction. *Memo to the Faculty*, No. 58, Center for Research on Learning and Teaching, University of Michigan, Ann Arbor, 1976.

Kulik, J. A., and Jaksa, P. A review of research on PSI and other educational technologies in college teaching. *Educational Technology*, September, 1977, *18*(9), 12-19.

Kulik, J. A., Jaksa, P., and Kulik, C. L. *Research on Component*

Features of Keller's Personalized System of Instruction. Unpublished manuscript, Center for Research on Learning and Teaching, Ann Arbor, Michigan, 1977.

Kulik, J.A., and Kulik, C.L. *College teaching.* Unpublished manuscript, Center for Research on Learning and Teaching, Ann Arbor, Michigan, 1977.

Kulik, J. A., Kulik, C. L., and Hertzler, E. C. Modular college teaching with and without required remediation. *Journal of Personalized Instruction*, 1977, *2*(2), 70-75.

Kulik, J. A., Kulik, C. L., and Smith, B. B. Research on the personalized system of instruction. *Programmed Learning and Educational Technology*, 1976, *13*, 21-30.

Kulik, J. A., and McKeachie, W. J. The evaluation of teachers in higher education. In F. N. Kerlinger (Ed.), *Review of research in education (Vol. 3).* Itasca, Illinois: F.E. Peacock, 1975.

Lacy, W.B. *College student socialization and value change: Comparative analysis of an experimental residential college and a traditional university environment.* Unpublished doctoral dissertation, University of Michigan, 1975.

Ladd, E., and Lipsett, M.S. *The Divided Academy.* New York: McGraw-Hill, 1975.

Lang, M. T. *Computer extended instruction in introductory calculus.* Dissertation, University of Texas at Austin, 1973.

Lange, P. C. (Ed.). *Programmed instruction.* Chicago: University of Chicago Press, 1967.

Lawler, R. M. *An investigation of selected instructional strategies in an undergraduate computer-managed instruction course.* Dissertation, Florida State University, 1971.

Lee, A. L. M. *A comparison of computer-assisted instruction and traditional laboratory instruction in an undergraduate geology course.* Dissertation, University of Texas at Austin, 1973.

Leherissey, B. L. *The effects of stimulating state epistemic curiosity on state anxiety and performance in a complex computer-assisted learning task.* Dissertation, Florida State University, 1971.

Leherissey, B. L., O'Neil, H. F., and Hansen, D. N. Effects of memory support on state anxiety and performance in computer-assisted learning. *Journal of Educational Psychology*, 1971, *62*(5), 413-420.

Leifer, A. D. Teaching with television and film. In N. L. Gage (Ed.), *The psychology of teaching methods*. Chicago: University of Chicago Press, 1976.

Levie, W., and Dickie, K. The analysis and application of media. In R. M. W. Travers (Ed.), *Second handbook of research on teaching*. Chicago: Rand McNally, 1973.

Levie, W., and Levie, D. Pictorial memory processes. *AV Communication Review*, 1975, *23*, 81-97.

Levien, R. E. *The emerging technology: Instructional uses of the computer in higher education*. New York: McGraw Hill, 1972.

Levinson, D. J. *et al.* In D. Ricks, A. Thomas, and M. Rooff (Eds.), *Life history research in psychopathology*. Minneapolis: University of Minnesota Press, 1974.

Lewin, K. *Field theory in social science*. New York: Harper and Row, 1951.

Lewis, R. Course content in structured knowledge areas. *Improving College and University Teaching*, 1972, *20*(3), 131-133.

Light, D. W. Introduction: The structure of the academic professions. *Sociology of Education*, 1974, *47*(1), 2-28.

Light, D., and Marsden, I. *The impact of the academic revolution on faculty careers*. ERIC/AAHE Research Report No. 10, 1972.

Limbacher, J. I. *Feature films on 8mm and 16mm* (5th ed.). New York: R. R. Bowker, 1977.

Lindenlaub, J. C. Audio-tutorial instruction at Purdue University. In L. P. Grayson and J. M. Biedenbach (Eds.), *Individualized instruction in engineering education*. Washington, D.C.: American Society for Engineering Education, 1974.

Lippey, G. *et al. Computer-assisted test construction*. Englewood Cliffs, New Jersey: Educational Technology Publications, 1974.

Livingston, S.A. *Simulation games and attitudes toward the poor*. Baltimore: Center for Social Organization of Schools, The Johns Hopkins University, Report No. 118, 1971.

Livingston, S.A., and Stoll, C.S. *Simulation games*. New York: Free Press, 1973.

Loevinger, J., and Wessler, R. *Measurement ego development: Construction and use of a sentence completion test.* Vol. 1. San Francisco: Jossey-Bass, 1970.

Lorber, M. A. *The effectiveness of computer-assisted instruction in the teaching of tests and measurements to prospective teachers.* Dissertation, Ohio University, 1970.

Lumsdaine, A. A. Educational technology, programmed learning, and instructional science. In E. R. Hilgard (Ed.), *Theories of learning and instruction.* Chicago: University of Chicago, 1964.

Lysaught, J. P., and Williams, C. W. *A guide to programmed instruction.* New York: John Wiley, 1963.

Magarell, J. The imminent videodisc revolution. *The Chronicle of Higher Education,* April 11, 1977, 4-5.

Mager, R. F. *Preparing instructional objectives.* Palo Alto: Fearon Publishers, 1962.

Maier, N. R. F. *Problem-solving discussions and conferences.* New York: McGraw-Hill, 1963.

Makay, J. J., and Sawyer, T. C. *Speech communication now!* Columbus, Ohio: Charles Merrill, 1973.

Mancuso, L.C. *A comparison of lecture, case study, and lecture-computer simulation teaching methodologies in broadcast economics.* Paper presented at the National Gaming Council 13th Annual Symposium, Pittsburgh, 1974.

Mancuso, L. C. *The effects of the lecture-case study and lecture-computer simulation instructional methodologies in teaching minority students principles of management.* Paper presented at the North American Gaming and Simulation Association Meeting, Los Angeles, 1975.

Mann, R. D., Arnold, S. M., Binder, J., Cytrynbaum, S., Newman, B. M., Ringwald, B., Ringwald, J., and Rosenwein, R. *The college classroom: Conflict, change, and learning.* New York: John Wiley, 1970.

Markle, S. Empirical testing of programs. In P. C. Lange (Ed.), *Programmed instruction.* Chicago: University of Chicago Press, 1967.

Markle, S. *Good frames and bad.* New York: John Wiley, 1969.

Markle, S. Programming and programmed instruction. In S. G. Tickton (Ed.), *To improve learning.* New York: Bowker, 1970.

Mattingly, G., and Smith, E. *Introducing the single-camera VTR system*. New York: Charles Scribners and Sons, 1971.

May, M., and Lumsdaine, A. A. *Learning from films*. New Haven: Yale, 1958.

Mayhew, L.B. Institutional factors and the learning environment. In L.E. Dennis and J.K. Kauffman (Eds.), *The college and the student*. Washington, D.C.: American Council on Education, 1966.

McCullough, C., and Van Atta, E. *Experimental evaluation of teaching programs utilizing a block of independent work*. Paper presented at the meeting of the American Psychological Association, Washington, D.C., September, 1958.

McGraw, J. M., Marcia, J. E., and Wright, C. K. Branching programme, text, and lecture: A comparative investigation of instructional media. *Journal of Applied Psychology*, 1966, *50*, 505-508.

McKeachie, W.J. *Teaching tips*. Lexington, Massachusetts: D.C. Heath and Co., 1969. (Second Edition, 1978.)

McKeachie, W. J. The decline and fall of the laws of learning. *Educational Researcher*, 1974a, *3*(3), 7-11.

McKeachie, W. J. Instructional psychology. *Annual Review of Psychology*, 1974b, *26*, 161-193.

McKeachie, W. J. Textbooks: Problems of publishers and professors. *Teaching of Psychology*, 1976, *3*, 29-30.

McKeachie, W. J., and Kulik, J. A. Effective college teaching. In F.N. Kerlinger (Ed.), *Review of research in education*. Vol. 3. Itasca, Illinois: F.E. Peacock, 1975.

McKeachie, W. J., and Lin, Y. G. *Use of student ratings in evaluation of college teaching*. Final report, grant no. NE-G-00-3-0110, National Institute of Education, March, 1975.

McLeish, J. The lecture method. In N. L. Gage (Ed.), *The psychology of teaching methods*. National Society for the Study of Education. Chicago: University of Chicago Press, 1976.

McLuhan, M. *Understanding media: The extensions of man*. New York: McGraw-Hill, 1964.

Mechner, F. Behavioral analysis and instructional sequencing. In P. C. Lange (Ed.), *Programmed instruction*. Chicago: University of Chicago Press, 1967.

Megargee, E.I. *The California psychological inventory handbook.* San Francisco: Jossey-Bass, 1972.

Meleca, C. B. *An analysis of the relationship of student abilities to level of achievement in an audio-instructional program.* Unpublished doctoral dissertation, Syracuse University, 1968.

Menne, J. W., Hannum, T., Klingensmith, J., and Word, D. Use of taped lectures to replace class attendance. *AV Communication Review*, 1969, *17*, 42-46.

Messick, S. (& Associates). *Individuality in learning.* San Francisco: Jossey-Bass, 1976.

Miller, W.C. Film movement and affective response and the effect of learning and attitude formation. *AV Communication Review*, 1969, *17*, 172-181.

Minnesota Mining and Manufacturing Co., *Bright ideas in overhead projection: A guide to more effective meetings.* St. Paul, Minnesota: Visual Products Division, 3M Co., 1976.

Minor, E., and Frye, H. R. *Techniques for producing visual instructional media.* New York: McGraw-Hill, 1970.

Mintzes, J.J. The A-T approach 14 years later: A review of the research. *Journal of College Science Teaching*, 1975, *4*, 247-252.

Moriber, G. The effects of programmed instruction in a college physical science course for nonscience students. *Journal of Research in Science Teaching*, 1969, *6*, 214-216.

Morris, C. J. Choosing a text for the introductory course. *Teaching of Psychology*, 1977, *4*, 21-24.

Morris, C.J., *et al.* Individual differences and PSI: A reanalysis. *Journal of Personalized Instruction*, 1977, *2*, 47-48.

Nance, J. B. *An operations research study of the Fullerton Junior College audio-tutorial system.* Unpublished dissertation, University of Southern California, 1971.

Nash, A. N., Muczyk, J. P., and Vettori, F. I. The relative practical effectiveness of programmed instruction. *Personnel Psychology*, 1971, *24*, 397-418.

National Information Center for Educational Media. *Index to educational videotapes.* Los Angeles: NICEM, 1971.

Newcomb, T.M. Student peer-group influence. In N. Sanford (Ed.), *The American college.* New York: John Wiley, 1962.

Nordland, F.H., and Kahle, J.B. *Audio-tutorial instruction and learning.* Paper presented at the Fifth Annual International Audio-Tutorial Congress Conference, Ohio State University, 1973.

Novak, J.D. An experimental comparison of a conventional and project-centered method of teaching a college general botany course. *Journal of Experimental Education*, 1958, *26*, 217-230.

Olmstead, J. A. *Small-group instruction.* Alexandria, Virginia: Human Resources Research Organization, 1974.

Olson, D. R., and Bruner, J. S. Learning through experience and learning through media. In D.R. Olson (Ed.), *Media and symbols: The forms of expression, communication, and education.* Chicago: University of Chicago Press, 1974.

Orr, D.B. A perspective on the perception of time-compressed speech. In D. L. Horton and J. J. Jenkins (Eds.), *The perception of language.* Columbus, Ohio: Charles E. Merrill, 1971.

Owen, S.G., Hall, R., Anderson, J., and Smert, G.A. A comparison of programmed instruction and lectures in the teaching of electrocardiography. *Programmed Learning*, 1965, *2*, 2-13.

Pace, C. R. *College and university environment scales* (CUES). (2nd ed., technical manual). Princeton, New Jersey: Educational Testing Service, 1969.

Pare, R., and Butzow, J. W. The relationship among independence of work habits, attitude, and achievement in an audio-tutorial physics course. *Journal of Research in Science Teaching,* 1975, *12,* 1-3.

Parker, L., and Riccomini, B. (Eds.). *The status of the telephone in education: Second annual international communications conference.* Madison: University of Wisconsin-Extension, 1976.

Pascal, C. E. Instructional options, option preference, and course outcomes. *Alberta Journal of Educational Research*, 1971, *17*, 1-11.

Pascal, C. E. Individual differences and preference for instructional methods. *Canadian Journal of Behavioral Science*, 1973, *5*, 272-279.

Pascarella, E. Interaction of motivation, mathematics preparation, and instructional method in PSI and conventionally taught calculus course. *AV Communication Review*, 1977, *25*, 25-42.

Phenix, P. H. *Realms of meaning.* New York: McGraw-Hill, 1964.

Piaget, J. Piaget's theory. In P. H. Mussen (Ed.), *Carmichael's manual of child psychology,* Part 1. New York: John Wiley, 1970.

Popham, W. J. Tape recorded lectures in the college classroom. *AV Communication Review,* 1961, *9,* 109-118.

Popham, W. J. Tape recorded lectures in the college classroom II. *AV Communication Review,* 1962, *10,* 94-101.

Popham, W. J. Probing the validity of arguments against behavioral goals. In M. B. Kapfer (Ed.), *Behavioral objectives in curriculum development: Selected readings and bibliography.* Englewood Cliffs, New Jersey: Educational Technology Publications, 1971, 390-398.

Popham, W. J. Higher education's commitment to instructional improvement programs. *Educational Researcher,* 1974, *3*(11), 11-13.

Poppen, W. A., and Thompson, C. L. The effect of grade contracts on student performance. *Journal of Educational Research,* 1971, *64,* 420-424.

Portnoy, A. L., and Glasser, M. A four-year experience with a programmed text in clinical pathology. *Journal of Medical Education,* 1974, *49,* 457-459.

Postlethwait, S., and Lohman, T. *The audio-tutorial system.* A film produced by Postlethwait, S., and Lohman, T. Available from the Purdue Film Library, West Lafayette, Indiana.

Postlethwait, S., Novak, J., and Murray, H.T. *The audio-tutorial approach to learning* (3rd ed.). Minneapolis: Burgess Publishing, 1972.

Rappaport, E. *The effects of trait anxiety and dogmatism on state anxiety during computer-assisted learning.* CAI Center Technical Memorandum, Florida State University, 1971 (May), 33.

Reichman, S. W., and Grasha, A. F. A rational approach to developing and assessing the construct validity of a student learning style scales instrument. *The Journal of Psychology,* 1974, *87,* 213-223.

Renner, T. W., and Stafford, A. G. *Teaching science in the secondary school.* New York: Harper and Row, 1972.

Ripple, R. E. Comparison of the effectiveness of a programmed text with three other methods of presentation. *Psychological Reports*, 1963, *12*, 237.

Rodin, M., and Rodin, B. Student evaluation of teachers. *Science*, 1972, *177*, 1164-1166.

Rothkopf, E. Z. Variable adjunct questions, schedules, interpersonal interaction, and incidental learning from written material. *Journal of Educational Psychology*, 1972, *63*, 87-92.

Rothkopf, E. Z. Writing to teach and reading to learn: a perspective of the psychology of written instruction. In N. L. Gage (Ed.), *Psychology of teaching methods*. National Society for the Study of Education. Chicago: University of Chicago Press, 1976.

Russell, J. D. *The Audio-Tutorial System*. Volume 3 in The Instructional Design Library. Englewood Cliffs, New Jersey: Educational Technology Publications, 1978.

Russell, W. B. *Some comparisons of the audio-tutorial method with the conventional method in introductory college biology*. Unpublished dissertation, North Texas University, 1968.

Sanford, N. Academic culture and the teacher's development. *Soundings*, Winter, 1971, 357-371.

Schmuck, R.A., Chesler, M., and Lippitt, R. *Problem solving to improve classroom learning.* Chicago: Science Research Associates, Inc., 1966.

Schmuck, R. A., and Schmuck, P. A. *Group processes in the classroom*. Dubuque, Iowa: William C. Brown, 1971.

Schramm, W. (Ed.). *Quality in instructional television*. Honolulu: University of Hawaii, 1972.

Schwab, J. J. Problems, topics, and issues. In S. Elam (Ed.), *Education and the structure of knowledge.* Chicago: Rand McNally, 1964.

Scott Graphics. *A guide to overhead projection and transparency making.* Holyoke, Massachusetts: Scott Graphics, 1974.

Seashore, S. E. Elementary psychology: An outline of a course by the project method. *Aims and Progress Research.* Iowa City: University of Iowa Studies, 1928, 153.

Seidner, C. J. Teaching with simulations and games. In N. L. Gage (Ed.), *The psychology of teaching methods*. Chicago: University of Chicago Press, 1976.

Senour, R. A. *A study of the effects of student control of audio-tape learning experiences.* San Bernadino: California State College, 1971.

Sexton, R.F., and Ungerer, R.A. *Rationales for experiential learning.* Washington, D.C.: American Association for Higher Education, 1975.

Sharan, S., and Sharan, Y. *Small-group teaching.* Englewood Cliffs, New Jersey: Educational Technology Publications, 1976.

Shavelson, R. J. Teacher's decision making. In N. L. Gage (Ed.), *The psychology of teaching methods.* Chicago: University of Chicago Press, 1976.

Sheffield, E. F. (Ed.). *Teaching in the universities: No one way.* Montreal: McGill-Queen's University Press, 1974.

Sherman, J. G. (Ed.). *Personalized system of instruction: 41 germinal papers.* Menlo Park, California: Benjamin, 1974.

Sherman, J.G., and Ruskin, R. *The personalized system of instruction.* Volume 13 in The Instructional Design Library. Englewood Cliffs, New Jersey: Educational Technology Publications, 1978.

Shulman, L., and Tamir, P. Research on teaching natural science. In R. M. W. Travers (Ed.), *Second handbook of research on teaching.* Chicago: Rand McNally, 1973.

Sieber, J.E. How shall anxiety be defined? In J.E. Sieber, H.F. O'Neil, and S. Tobias (Eds.), *Anxiety, learning, and instruction.* Hillsdale, New Jersey: Lawrence Erlbaum Associates, 1977.

Simpson, E. Educational objectives in the psychomotor domain. In M. B. Kapfer (Ed.), *Behavioral objectives in curriculum development: Selected readings and bibliography.* Englewood Cliffs, New Jersey: Educational Technology Publications, 1971, 60-67.

Skinner, B. F. *Walden two.* New York: Macmillan, 1948.

Skinner, B. F. The science of learning and the art of teaching. *Harvard Educational Review*, 1954, *24*, 86-97.

Skinner, B. F. Teaching machines. *Science*, 1958, *128*, 969-977.

Smith, D. G. College classroom interactions and critical thinking. *Journal of Educational Psychology*, 1977, *69*(2), 180-190.

Smith, I. D. *The effects of computer-assisted instruction on student self-concept, locus of control, and level of aspiration.* Dissertation, Stanford University, 1971.

Smith, N. H. The teaching of elementary statistics by conventional classroom methods versus the method of programmed instruction. *Journal of Educational Research*, 1962, *55*, 417-419.

Snow, R.E. The importance of selected audience and film characteristics as determiners of the effectiveness of instructional films. *Journal of Educational Psychology,* 1965, *56,* 315-326.

Snow, R.E. *Research on aptitude for learning: A progress report.* Stanford University, School of Education, 1974.

Snow, R.E. Learning and individual differences. *Review of Research in Education,* 1977, *4,* 50-105.

Solomon, L. M. *Computer-assisted instruction in undergraduate accounting education.* Dissertation, Case Western Reserve University, 1974.

Spencer, R., Conyers, D., Sanchez-Sosa, J., and Semb, G. An experimental comparison of two forms of personalized instruction, a discussion procedure, and an independent study procedure. In R. Ruskin and S. Bono (Eds.), *Personalized instruction in higher education.* Washington, D.C.: Center for Personalized Instruction, 1974.

Stadsklev, R. *Handbook of simulation gaming in social education.* (2 vols.), Tuscaloosa, Alabama: Institute of Higher Education Research and Services, University of Alabama, 1975.

Stanford, G., and Roark, A. *Human interaction in education.* Boston: Allyn and Bacon, 1974.

Stanton, H. E. Teaching methods and student personality. *Instructional Science,* 1974, *2*(4), 477-501.

Starks, D.D., Feldhusen, J.F., and Bell, N.T. Problems of working with university faculty and graduate students in CAI programming. *NSPI Journal,* 1969, *8,* 10-11.

Stasheff, E., and Bretz, R. *The television program: Its direction and production* (5th ed.). New York: Hill and Wang, 1977.

Steiner, P. Using language to learn language. *Foreign Language Annals,* 1972, *1,* 40-49.

Stern, G. *People in context.* New York: John Wiley, 1970.

Sullivan, D. *A study of the present state-of-the-art in learning center operations.* Air Force Human Resources Laboratory, Lowry Air Force Base, Colorado, 1974, (ERIC ED088-526).

Thornton, J. (Ed.). *The laboratory: A place to investigate.* Washington, D.C.: American Institute of Biological Sciences, 1972.

Tobias, S. Achievement treatment interactions. *Review of Educational Research,* 1976, *46,* 61-74.

Tobias, S. Anxiety-treatment interactions: A review of research. In J. E. Sieber, H. F. O'Neil, and S. Tobias (Eds.), *Anxiety, learning, and instruction.* Hillsdale, New Jersey: Lawrence Erlbaum Associates, 1977.

Tobias, S., and Abramson, T. Interaction among anxiety, stress, response mode, and familiarity of subject matter on achievement from programmed instruction. *Journal of Educational Psychology*, 1971, *62*, 357-364.

Tom, F. K. T., and Cushman, H. R. The Cornell diagnostic observation and reporting system for student description of college teaching. *Search*, 1975, *5*(8), 1-25.

Tosti, D. T., and Ball, J. R. A behavioral approach to instructional design and media selection. *AV Communication Review*, 1969, *17*, 5-25.

Turner, R. L., and Thompson, R. P. *Relationships and residual learning.* Paper read at the Annual Meeting of the American Educational Research Association, April 1974 in Chicago.

Tyler, R. W. *Basic principles of curriculum and instruction.* Chicago: University of Chicago Press, 1949.

Ulrich, R. E., and Pray, S. L. Comparison of direct self-study versus lecture in teaching general psychology. *Psychological Reports*, 1965, *16*, 278.

Unwin, D. An "organizational" exploration for certain retention and correlation factors in a comparison between two teaching methods. *Programmed Learning and Educational Technology*, 1966, *3*, 35-39.

Vandermeer, A. W. Relative effectiveness of exclusive film instruction, films plus study guides and typical instructional methods. *Progress Report No. 10*, State College: Pennsylvania State College, Instructional Film Research Program, 1949.

Videofreex, *The spaghetti city video manual: A guide to use, repair, and maintenance.* New York: Praeger, 1972.

Wales, C.E. *The guided design systems approach.* Unpublished manuscript, West Virginia University, Morgantown, West Virginia, 1974.

Wales, C. E., and Stager, R. *The guided design approach.* Volume 9 in The Instructional Design Library. Englewood Cliffs, New Jersey: Educational Technology Publications, 1978.

Warren, J. *Current grading practices. Research report no. 3.* American Association for Higher Education, January, 1971.

Warren, J. Adapting instruction to styles of learnings. *Findings.* Educational Testing Service, 1974, *1*(1), 1-4.

Watson, J. D. *Double helix.* New York: Atheneum, 1968.

Wentworth, D. R. *The effectiveness of a learning game for teaching introductory economics in selected two-year colleges.* Doctoral dissertation, Minneapolis: University of Minnesota, 1972.

Wilkinson, G. Projection variables and performance. *AV Communication Review,* 1976, *24*, 413-436.

Wilson, M. K. *A study of college administrator attitude development through a simulation game.* Dissertation, University of Alabama, 1974.

Witkin, H. A. Cognitive style in academic performance and in teacher-student relations. In S. Messick and Associates, *Individuals in learning.* San Francisco: Jossey-Bass, Inc., 1976.

Witkin, H.A., Morre, C., Goodenough, D., and Cox, P. Field-dependent and field-independent cognitive styles and their educational implications. *Review of Educational Research,* 1977, *47*(1), 1-64.

Wittick, W., and Schullier, C. *Instructional technology: Its nature and use* (5th ed.). New York: Harper and Row, 1973.

Wittrock, M. C., and Lumsdaine, A. A. Instructional psychology. *Annual Review of Psychology,* 1977, *28*, 417-459.

Yager, R. E., Englen, H. B., and Snyder, B. C. Effects of the laboratory and demonstration methods upon the outcomes of instruction in secondary biology. *Journal of Research in Science Teaching,* 1969, *6,* 76-86.

Yinon, Y., Shoham, V., and Lewis, T. Risky-shift in a real versus role-played situation. *Journal of Social Psychology,* 1974, *93*, 137-138.

Young, R. B. Programmed instruction in teaching economics. *Psychological Reports,* 1967, *20*, 1146.

Zimbardo, P., Haney, C., and Banks, W. C. *The psychology of imprisonment: Privation, power, and pathology.* Stanford: Philip G. Zimbardo, Inc., 1971.

GLOSSARY

Ability. Sometimes referred to as general mental ability or scholastic ability; the performance of students on tests intended to measure general skills such as reasoning and verbal comprehension.

Achievement. The student's acquisition of specific knowledge and skills as might be measured on a quiz or course examination.

Achievement motivation. Sometimes referred to as a need to achieve; a student's interest in being good at something—in succeeding. *Achievement-via-Conformance* (Ac) and *Achievement-via-Independence* (Ai) are terms for specific scales on the California Psychological Inventory.

Affective. A domain of instructional objectives which emphasize a feeling tone, an emotion, or a degree of acceptance or rejection (Krathwohl *et al.*, 1964).

Analysis. Cognitive instructional objectives which involve breaking down an idea into its constituent elements and demonstrating the relationship among these parts (Bloom, 1956).

Anxiety. A student's concern about an event in which he perceives that he may be unable to deal easily and satisfactorily (Sieber, 1977). This may be a temporary concern or a more stable personality characteristic.

Application. Cognitive instructional objectives which involve the use of general ideas, rules, or methods in particular and concrete situations (Bloom, 1956).

Aptitude. Used generally to refer to any characteristic of a person that forecasts her probability of success in a given situation (Cronbach and Snow, 1977).

Aptitude-treatment interaction. A moderating relationship between the characteristics (or aptitudes) of people and instructional treatments (or methods), such that people with different characteristics will be affected in consistently different ways by different methods.

Avoidant. Students who are uninterested or overwhelmed by what goes on in class and do not participate with students and teachers (Grasha, 1972).

Cognitive. A domain of instructional objectives which emphasize the remembering or reproducing of something or the solving of some intellective task (Krathwohl *et al.*, 1964).

Cognitive styles. A consistent way a person has of organizing and processing information and experience (Messick, 1976).

Collaborative. Students who feel they can learn the most by sharing ideas and talents with teachers and peers (Grasha, 1972).

Competency. That part of an instructional objective which specifies what the student will be able to do.

Competitive. Students who view the classroom as a win-loose situation, and who feel they must compete with other students in the class for rewards such as grades and teacher attention (Grasha, 1972).

Compliant. Students who are task-oriented, and contented with their classes, their teachers, and themselves (Mann *et al.,* 1970).

Comprehension. A class of cognitive instructional objectives which involves the understanding or apprehension of a statement without necessarily relating it to other material (Bloom, 1956).

Content-centered. A teacher or student for whom the facts and principles of the course content are most important (Axelrod, 1973).

Dependent. Students who show little intellectual curiosity and do only what is required, relying heavily on authority figures to be told what to do.

Elements. (See *System.*)

Evaluation. A process of collecting relevant data for decision-making (Cooley and Lohnes, 1976).

Feedback. The process or product of supplying information or the results of some behavior or program.

Field-dependent. Those people who are strongly influenced by the prevailing field, or context of situations (Witkin *et al.*, 1977).

Field-independent. People who are more independent of their surrounding context, and who operate on a more abstract or analytical level (Witkin *et al.*, 1977).

Independent. Students who like to think for themselves and who prefer to work on their own (Grasha, 1972).

Instructional objective. A statement of the competency or capability which the instructor intends for the student to acquire upon completion of instruction.

Instructional situation. The arrangement of teacher, student, content, media, evaluation, and environment characteristics for a particular class.

Instructor-centered. An instructor who provides herself as an intellectual model which the students are invited to emulate (Axelrod, 1973), or students who prefer a class structured by the teacher, with explicit requirements and assignments (Warren, 1974).

Intellect-centered. An instructor whose primary concern is the intellectual development of students through their use of reason, language, and problem-solving skills (Axelrod, 1973).

Interaction. (See also *Aptitude-treatment interaction.*) The capability of reciprocal exchange of information, ideas, and feelings.

Knowledge. Cognitive instructional objectives which involve the verbal recall of facts and principles (Bloom, 1956).

Management. The capability of an instructional presentation to manipulate or adjust the message to accommodate particular needs or problems as they arise.

Need-for-affiliation. Students who want and need friendly relationships with other people.

Objective. (See *Instructional objective.*)

One-way media. Those media which can present information to the learner but which do not lend themselves to the reciprocal exchange of ideas and feelings.

Participant. Those students who want to learn course content, like to go to class, and take part in class related activity (Grasha, 1972).

Person-centered. An instructor who places importance on the emotional and personal development of students (Axelrod, 1973).

Psychomotor. A domain of instructional objectives which involve some muscular or motor skill, manipulation of materials, or neuromuscular coordination (Krathwohl *et al.,* 1964).

Response. That activity that students perform in reaction to instruction. Responses may be *covert* (i.e., subvocal) or *overt.* Overt responses may be *selective* (requiring a choice between two or more present alternatives) or *constructed* (requiring the composition of a reply). Constructed responses may be vocal, written, or motor (i.e., performed).

Self-instructional. Forms of instruction which minimize direct supervision by the teacher, but which rely on student management of instruction, or on previous structure from the teacher regarding their provisions for student management or choice.

Stimulus. That instructional information which is presented to the students. This information may be *environmental* (as it appears without representation or interpretation) or represented *pictorially, symbolically* (with words, numerals, or other symbolic forms), *verbally,* or *kinesthetically* (through the sense of movement).

Student-centered. Students who prefer loosely organized classes which accommodate students' interests and activities (Warren, 1974).

Synthesis. Cognitive instructional objectives which involve the putting together of parts, elements, or ideas to form a pattern, structure, or whole (Bloom, 1956).

System. A collection of interrelated parts or *elements* which can be conceptually separated from its surroundings (Banathy, 1968). The instructional system is composed of the teacher, the content, the medium, the student, the evaluation, and the environment.

AUTHOR INDEX

SUBJECT INDEX